DANIEL
In God I Trust

A DEVOTIONAL STUDY BY
PRACTICAL CHRISTIANITY FOUNDATION
L.L. SPEER, FOUNDER

GREEN KEY BOOKS

2514 ALOHA PLACE • HOLIDAY, FLORIDA 34691

DANIEL: IN GOD I TRUST
Published by Green Key Books

©2001 by the Practical Christianity Foundation.
All Rights Reserved.
International Standard Book Number: 0-9705996-0-9

Cover Art: Mike Molinet

Printed in the United States of America

For information:
GREEN KEY BOOKS
2514 ALOHA PLACE
HOLIDAY, FLORIDA 34691
www.greenkeybooks.com

Library of Congress Cataloging-in-Publication Data
available on request.

Table of Contents

Preface

From the conception of the Practical Christianity Foundation, it has been the goal of the organization to convey the truth in Scripture through verse-by-verse devotional studies such as this one. As part of that goal, we agree in an attempt neither to prove nor disprove any traditional or alternative interpretations, beliefs, or doctrines, but rather to allow the Holy Spirit to reveal the truth contained within the Scriptures. Any interpretations relating to ambiguous passages that are not directly and specifically verifiable by other scriptural references are simply presented in what we believe to be the most likely intention of the message based upon those things that we are specifically told. In those instances, our conclusions are noted as interpretive, and such analyses should not be understood as doctrinal positions that we are attempting to champion.

This study is divided into sections, usually between six and eight verses, and each section concludes with a "Notes/Applications" passage, which draws practical insight from the related verses that can be applied to contemporary Christian living. The intent is that the reader will complete one section per day, will gain a greater understanding of the verses within that passage, and will daily be challenged toward a deeper commitment to our Lord and Savior Jesus

Christ. Also included at certain points within the text are "Dig Deeper" boxes, which are intended to assist readers who desire to invest additional time to study topics that relate to the section in which these boxes appear. Our prayer is that this study will impact the lives of all believers, regardless of age, ethnicity, or education.

Each of PCF's original projects is a collaborative effort of many writers, content editors, grammatical editors, transcribers, researchers, readers, and other contributors, and as such, we present them only as products of the Practical Christianity Foundation as a whole. These works are not for the recognition or acclamation of any particular individual but are written simply as a means to uphold and fulfill the greater purpose of our Mission Statement, which is "to exalt the Holy Name of God Almighty by declaring the redemptive message of His Son, the Lord Jesus Christ, to the lost global community and equipping the greater Christian community through the communication of the Holy Word of God in its entirety through every appropriate means available."

Practical Christianity Foundation
Value Statements

1. We value the Holy Name of God and will strive to exalt Him through godly living, committed service, and effective communication. *"That you may fear the LORD your God, to keep all His statutes and His commandments which I command you, you and your son and your grandson, all the days of your life, and that your days may be prolonged." (Deuteronomy 6.2)*

2. We value the redemptive work of the Lord Jesus Christ for a lost world and will strive to communicate His redemptive message to the global community. *"And He said to them, 'Go into all the world and preach the gospel to every creature.'" (Mark 16.15)*

3. We value the Holy Word of God and will strive to communicate it in its entirety. *"16All Scripture is given by inspiration of God, and is profitable for doctrine, for reproof, for correction, for instruction in righteousness, 17that the man of God may be complete, thoroughly equipped for every good work." (2 Timothy 3.16–17)*

4. We value spiritual growth in God's people and will strive to enhance that process through the effective communication of God's Holy Word, encouraging them to be lovers of the truth. *"But grow in the grace and knowledge of our Lord and Savior Jesus Christ. To Him be the glory both now and forever." (2 Peter 3.18)*

5. We value the equipping ministry of the church of the Lord Jesus Christ and will strive to provide resources for that ministry by the communication of God's Holy Word through every appropriate means available. *"11And He Himself gave some to be apostles, some prophets, some evangelists, and some pastors and teachers, 12for the equipping of the saints for the work of ministry, for the edifying of the body of Christ." (Ephesians 4.11–12)*

Introduction

The book of Daniel focuses upon many of God's past and future judgments upon His people, the Israelites. The prophet Daniel lived during the same time period as Ezekiel, Ezra, and Jeremiah, and a study of these books reveals several coinciding accounts and prophecies. However, the book of Daniel is also a discourse on world history from the Babylonian Empire to the Second Coming of the Lord Jesus Christ and the beginning of His eternal reign as King of kings.

During its time, Babylon was the greatest city in the world. Ancient historians have calculated that the city's wall was sixty miles in circumference, fifteen miles on each side, three hundred feet high, and eighty feet thick. It also extended thirty-five feet below the ground to prevent enemies from tunneling underground. The massive wall featured over two hundred towers and one hundred brass gates. In addition, the waters of the Euphrates River flowed through the city and provided water for the city's moat. This large moat ran along the city wall and somewhat protected Babylon from invasion.[1]

Nabopolassar, king of Babylon, led a revolt against the Assyrians and established the Babylonian Empire in 625 BC. In 609 BC, Necho II, the pharaoh of Egypt, invaded Palestine to protect his political interests there. Necho then fought King Josiah of Israel at Megiddo in

608 BC. As a result, Josiah was killed, and Necho II returned victoriously to Egypt with a large army and extended his territory to the Euphrates River:

> *29In his days Pharaoh Necho king of Egypt went to the aid of the king of Assyria, to the River Euphrates; and King Josiah went against him. And Pharaoh Necho killed him at Megiddo when he confronted him. 30Then his servants moved his body in a chariot from Megiddo, brought him to Jerusalem, and buried him in his own tomb. And the people of the land took Jehoahaz the son of Josiah, anointed him, and made him king in his father's place. (2 Kings 23.29–30)*

In 605 BC, Nabopolassar sent his son Nebuchadnezzar to fight Necho's Egyptian army. This bloody battle at Carchemish drove the Egyptians back to their own land and subjugated Judah to Babylon. During this time, Nebuchadnezzar received news that his father had died; therefore, Nebuchadnezzar returned to ascend Babylon's throne. After its subjection, Judah rendered tribute to Nebuchadnezzar for three years and then revolted:

> *1In his days Nebuchadnezzar king of Babylon came up, and Jehoiakim became his vassal for three years. Then he turned and rebelled against him. 2And the LORD sent against him raiding bands of Chaldeans, bands of Syrians, bands of Moabites, and bands of the people of Ammon; He sent them against Judah to destroy it, according to the word of the LORD which He had spoken by His servants the prophets. (2 Kings 24.1–2)*

In response, Nebuchadnezzar went to Palestine to suppress this revolt and then returned to Babylon after defeating Jehoiakim, king of Judah and son of Josiah. Nebuchadnezzar dispersed the Jewish captives to different parts of the Babylonian Empire and thereby obtained the slave labor needed to construct his numerous projects, including the Great Wall of Babylon, several majestic temples, and a magnificent palace. In addition, he commissioned the construction of the Hanging Gardens of Babylon, one of the seven wonders of the ancient world, for his wife. He also built a great reservoir for irrigation that records indicate measured 140 miles in circumference and 180 feet deep.[2]

This brings us to the time when Daniel, as a teenager, was transported with the other captive Jews to Babylon. The name *Daniel* means, "my judge is God," and at this time, God's judgment did fall upon Israel.[3] Daniel was a man both tested and exalted. However, regardless of external circumstances, his commitment to the Lord God Almighty never fluctuated. He relied upon God for both life-saving miracles and the smallest of provisions. As we begin to study this intriguing book, we will see this one man's unwavering faith in his God, beginning from the time that he arrived in Babylon as a young Jew and continuing throughout his years of service under the authority of several kings and kingdoms. There is perhaps no better example of godly faith, dependency, trust, and worship than in the character of the prophet Daniel.

Chapter One

Daniel 1.1–7

Verse 1- In the third year of the reign of Jehoiakim king of Judah, Nebuchadnezzar king of Babylon came to Jerusalem and besieged it.

Jehoiakim began his rule of Judah in 609 BC, and this verse dates itself as 606 BC, the third year of his reign. The Hebrew name *Jehoiakim* means, "Jehovah will set up."[1] We know from other scriptures that he became king when he was twenty-five years of age and that he collected heavy taxes for the pharaoh of Egypt. (*2 Kings 23.35–36*) Jeremiah, a prophet of God who lived during Daniel's time, warned Jehoiakim of divine judgment unless retribution was made. God gave this king three years to repent, but Jehoiakim treated the matter with contempt. (*Jeremiah 36.1–3*) Therefore, in the third year of Jehoiakim's reign, God judged Jehoiakim by allowing Nebuchadnezzar to besiege Jerusalem.

Sometimes, people associate the word *besiege* with a swift, violent overthrow. However, in this situation, Nebuchadnezzar came to Jerusalem to conquer the city and to make its inhabitants loyal to him. Up to this point, the confrontation had been relatively nonviolent, though later there would be much bloodshed.

Verse 2- And the Lord gave Jehoiakim king of Judah into his hand, with some of the articles of the house of God, which he carried into the land of Shinar to the house of his god; and he brought the articles into the treasure house of his god.

The Lord God allowed Jehoiakim to be taken captive by Nebuchadnezzar, who also had the holy vessels of King Solomon's temple placed into bags and carried away from the holy city. This temple was magnificent, as were all of its furnishings. There had never been riches like those in the days of Solomon. The stolen vessels were ornaments that King Solomon had made for the temple, so all of these vessels were exceptionally beautiful. (*2 Kings 24.13; 2 Kings 25.15*) Nebuchadnezzar carried these goods into the land of Shinar in which the city of Babylon was located. *"Nebuchadnezzar also carried off some of the articles from the house of the LORD to Babylon, and put them in his temple at Babylon." (2 Chronicles 36.7)*

Verse 3- Then the king instructed Ashpenaz, the master of his eunuchs, to bring some of the children of Israel and some of the king's descendants and some of the nobles,

Eunuchs were the king's loyal servants. As a requirement, they were castrated so that they would not desire women, least of all the king's wives and his daughters.[2]

Nebuchadnezzar spoke to Ashpenaz, who was the master of the eunuchs at the king's courts, and told him to gather many young Israelite people. Some of these were to be children of royal blood or direct descendants from Jerusalem's king, which would make them of the tribe of Judah and of the line of David.

Verse 4- ...young men in whom there was no blemish, but good-looking, gifted in all wisdom, possessing knowledge and quick to understand, who had ability to serve in the king's palace, and whom they might teach the language and literature of the Chaldeans.

The king further directed Ashpenaz to choose young men who were without physical blemish. They were to be physically attractive and mentally "gifted in all wisdom," which indicates that they were to display discernment and sensibility in words and in actions.

In addition, they were to possess the intellectual aptitude to learn the Chaldean language, customs, and culture. In the Babylonian Empire, the Chaldeans were the dominant race and were considered extremely intelligent. These captives, with their ability to learn and to understand the Chaldean language and culture, ranked among the elite of the Jewish captives. These Israelites, then, were to be young people who would be very competent to stand in the king's court as physically, morally, and mentally exceptional individuals of whom the king could be very proud.

Important to note in all of this is the fact that these men were picked because they possessed these qualities as judged by their fellow man, yet they were given these characteristics by Almighty God. They were God's chosen people, singled out and set apart by Him. Because of their Jewish heritage and their special relationship with Jehovah, they could trust His leading in every aspect of their lives, even as they experienced the cruel circumstances of captivity.

Verse 5- And the king appointed for them a daily provision of the king's delicacies and of the wine which he drank, and three years of training for them, so that at the end of that time they might serve before the king.

Once these young people were chosen, they were brought into the king's palace in Babylon and were served the choicest meats and the finest wines, selected by and suitable for the king himself. By worldly standards, this was the best food and drink available since they were the same provisions consumed by the king.

This was to be a daily regimen and not just a special favor that occurred only periodically. The captives were to partake of this food for three years, and at the end of that time, they were to stand before King Nebuchadnezzar as beautiful, seemingly perfect human beings.

Verse 6- Now from among those of the sons of Judah were Daniel, Hananiah, Mishael, and Azariah.

Among the young men who were taken captive, four were singled out: *Daniel,* whose Hebrew name means, "my judge is God"; *Hananiah,* whose Hebrew name means, "the grace of Jehovah"; *Mishael,* whose Hebrew name means, "who is what God is?"; and *Azariah,* whose Hebrew name means, "helped of Jehovah." These Hebrew children were from the tribe of Judah. *Judah* means, "He shall be praised," and these four men certainly would praise God throughout their lifetimes in Babylon. [3]

Verse 7- To them the chief of the eunuchs gave names: he gave Daniel the name Belteshazzar; to Hananiah, Shadrach; to Mishael, Meshach; and to Azariah, Abed-Nego.

These four—and presumably all of the captives—had their names changed from their given Jewish names to Babylonian names. Daniel's name was changed to *Belteshazzar,* which means, "lord of the straitened's treasure." *Hananiah* was given the name of Shadrach, which means, "the breast was tender." *Mishael* was given the name Meshach, which means, "waters of quiet." Azariah's name was changed to *Abednego,* which means, "servant of brightness." [4]

The king delegated the mundane task of renaming the Jewish captives to the head eunuch. This was probably done as an attempt to dissociate the captives from the significance of their Jewish identity.

Notes/Applications

King Nebuchadnezzar seized the Israelites and carried them back to his kingdom in Babylon. As a result, the Israelite captives found themselves in a foreign land that was strange to them. Not only were they forced to leave their homeland, but they were also expected to deny their native culture and religion and to embrace the Babylonian culture and pagan gods. *"And it will be when you say, "Why does the LORD our God do all these things to us?" then you shall answer them, "Just as you have forsaken Me and served foreign gods in your land, so you shall serve aliens in a land that is not yours.""" (Jeremiah 5. 9)* Among these captives were Daniel, Hananiah, Mishael, and Azariah.

It seems quite likely that these four and the other Israelites became homesick for Judah, their homeland.

When we ask Jesus Christ to forgive our sins and to be the Lord and Savior of our lives, we identify ourselves with Him. Being His children puts us at conflict with the world, its people, and its values. *"18'If the world hates you, you know that it hated Me before it hated you. 19If you were of the world, the world would love its own. Yet because you are not of the world, but I chose you out of the world, therefore the world hates you.'"* *(John 15.18–19)* However, as children of God, we need to remember that we, like the captive Israelites in Babylon, are not at home in this world. God has something much better in store for us. *"But now they desire a better, that is, a heavenly country. Therefore God is not ashamed to be called their God, for He has prepared a city for them."* (Hebrews 11.16) Our eternal home is with God in Heaven as "fellow citizens" with our Christian friends and loved ones. *"Now, therefore, you are no longer strangers and foreigners, but fellow citizens with the saints and members of the household of God."* (Ephesians 2.19)

Are we homesick today for our promised home in Heaven? We should be since this life is not the end but the beginning of our journey. We are just passing through this world on our way to a glorious eternity!

Daniel 1.8–14

Verse 8- But Daniel purposed in his heart that he would not defile himself with the portion of the king's delicacies, nor with the wine which he drank; therefore he requested of the chief of the eunuchs that he might not defile himself.

Daniel decided *in his heart* not to eat the king's provisions, which surely would have seemed to be a reckless decision since it was inexcusable to disobey the king's orders. However, Daniel did not want to "defile" his body with substances that God specified in the Law of Moses not to eat. The Hebrew word translated as *defile* means "to pollute; to stain" and carries with it a spiritual emphasis more than a physical one.[5] Although the request that Daniel made of the eunuch was in direct opposition to what the king had ordered the eunuch to do, Daniel stood firmly upon his convictions.

Verse 9- Now God had brought Daniel into the favor and goodwill of the chief of the eunuchs.

God softened the heart of the chief of the eunuchs toward Daniel, and therefore, the chief granted Daniel special privilege, even though Daniel was a captive stranger that the chief had only known for a short time. God used Daniel and his friends to influence their authorities. God is all-powerful and often uses even the unbeliever to accomplish His will. Any benevolence granted to Daniel by the chief was, as this verse confirms, a direct result of God's intervention.

Verse 10- And the chief of the eunuchs said to Daniel, "I fear my lord the king, who has appointed your food and drink. For why should he see your faces looking worse than the young men who are your age? Then you would endanger my head before the king."

The chief of the eunuchs feared disobeying the king's command and the consequences that would come upon him as a result. One of the consequences that the chief dreaded most, as indicated by his response, was execution by beheading. The face is often the first place that indicates a person's state of healthiness, and Ashpenaz feared that the king might be able to look upon the faces of Daniel and his friends and see that they had been disobedient. Ashpenaz was afraid that their faces would look whiter, more drawn, or in some other way less healthy than the other young men who were in this group.

Verses 11, 12- ¹¹So Daniel said to the steward whom the chief of the eunuchs had set over Daniel, Hananiah, Mishael, and Azariah, ¹²"Please test your servants for ten days, and let them give us vegetables to eat and water to drink.

Daniel appealed to the proper authorities through the proper channels. He was not able to convince Ashpenaz, the chief of the eunuchs, but he did not lose heart. Instead, Daniel petitioned the steward who was placed directly in charge of his group.

Daniel pleaded with the steward to consider his petition, at least for a trial period. Willing to put his conviction to the test if the steward would permit this ten-day trial, Daniel requested only vegetables and water during this time to prove his God.

Verse 13- "Then let our appearance be examined before you, and the appearance of the young men who eat the portion of the king's delicacies; and as you see fit, so deal with your servants."

Daniel invited the steward to compare his and his friends' appearances with those that had eaten the king's food after the duration of ten days. He did not suggest that their faces would appear healthier than those who had eaten the king's provisions; he merely encouraged the steward to wait ten days and see for himself. At that time, the steward could determine what the king's men would serve the Israelites from thereon.

Daniel's trust in God's faithfulness was so steadfast that he agreed with whatever action the steward deemed appropriate at the end of the ten-day trial, whether that meant submissive compliance with the king's diet or even punishment for their conduct. This is the first of many examples where Daniel boldly placed his life in God's hands, regardless of the outcome, with uncompromising obedience.

Verse 14- So he consented with them in this matter, and tested them ten days.

The steward eventually permitted the request, so Daniel, Hananiah, Mishael, and Azariah ate only vegetables and water for ten days.

Notes/Applications

In this passage, Daniel decided *in his heart* not to eat the food of the king's table. The heart is often considered the very core of a person, and in this verse, the description *in his heart* refers to Daniel's total commitment to God's law rather than to an emotional decision that he made based upon his own preferences. Like Daniel, our decisions must be made *in the heart* if we are to remain committed to those decisions. *"With my whole heart I have sought You; oh, let me not wander from Your commandments!" (Psalm 119.10) "'For the LORD does not see as man sees; for man looks at the outward appearance, but the LORD looks at the heart.'" (1 Samuel 16.7b)* If we rely upon our human emotions or intellect, we will find ourselves aligned with the world's practices and against God's precepts.

Although Daniel knew that God would not want him to eat the king's food, he did not act defiantly against the king's orders. Instead, Daniel asked for permission to refrain from eating this food. Christians are not to rebel against the orders of those placed in authority over us. *"⁵Bondservants, be obedient to those who are your masters according to the flesh, with fear and trembling, in sincerity of heart, as to Christ; ⁶not with eyeservice, as men-pleasers, but as bondservants of Christ, doing the will of God from the heart." (Ephesians 6.5–6)* If these orders contradict God's Word, we should try to change policies and procedures but do so with a godly attitude and spirit.

Daniel meekly stood upon his convictions. Likewise, we need to decide *in our hearts* to live according to God's instructions in His Holy Word. In what areas of our lives do we need to abandon our own desires and fully, with our whole heart, mind, and soul, commit to applying God's principles to our lives?

Daniel 1.15–21

Verse 15- And at the end of ten days their features appeared better and fatter in flesh than all the young men who ate the portion of the king's delicacies.

At the end of the ten-day trial period, Daniel, Hananiah, Mishael, and Azariah actually appeared healthier and "fatter in flesh" than any of the other Jewish children who ate of the king's diet because these four obeyed the guidelines the Lord had given regarding eating proper foods. Certainly, Daniel chose this particular diet out of obedience to God rather than according to his own personal taste:

> *[1]When you sit down to eat with a ruler, consider carefully what is before you; [2]and put a knife to your throat if you are a man given to appetite. [3]Do not desire his delicacies, for they are deceptive food. (Proverbs 23.1–3) Do not incline my heart to any evil thing, to practice wicked works with men who work iniquity; and do not let me eat of their delicacies. (Psalm 141.4)*

Verse 16- Thus the steward took away their portion of delicacies and the wine that they were to drink, and gave them vegetables.

Because the results at the end of the ten days so favored Daniel and his three friends, the steward allowed them to continue with their special diet and did not require them to partake of the king's provisions. Although according to verse eleven, it is a possibility that Daniel still might not have secured Ashpenaz's approval, he did have the consent of the one who had been placed directly over this particular group of Jewish captives. In addition, Daniel did not fear the possible consequences of his actions because he knew that what he was doing was correct by God's standards. Similarly, the steward was not afraid to continue providing their simple diet because he had seen the positive results, so the steward's life would not be threatened. He trusted that both Ashpenaz and Nebuchadnezzar would be pleased.

Verse 17- As for these four young men, God gave them knowledge and skill in all literature and wisdom; and Daniel had understanding in all visions and dreams.

Daniel, Hananiah, Mishael, and Azariah already possessed knowledge and intelligence in the sight of Ashpenaz, who went into Israel looking for such qualities in those who were chosen to serve the king, but God gave these four young men these qualities in liberal portion.

The verse also states that Daniel possessed something extra—the gift of understanding in all visions and dreams. As we will see throughout this book, Daniel sought God for proper interpretation of visions and dreams. It was not something he was able to do on his own; it was a gift from God to be used for God's glory.

Verse 18- Now at the end of the days, when the king had said that they should be brought in, the chief of the eunuchs brought them in before Nebuchadnezzar.

We know from verse five that these Israelites had lived in captivity for three years when their period of grooming and training ended. During this period, they had been served the finest food, exercise, and training in all matters of education and culture. They had been given the best preparation the world could offer, and at the end of the three years, Ashpenaz brought them before Nebuchadnezzar so that the king could select the finest among them for his court.

Verse 19- Then the king interviewed them, and among them all none was found like Daniel, Hananiah, Mishael, and Azariah; therefore they served before the king.

The king conversed with the captives. He likely asked them particular questions to gain the necessary information to evaluate each candidate's worthiness. Obviously, Nebuchadnezzar controlled the situation, and because it took three years to groom and educate these men, we can presume that these questions were very difficult. It was an oral examination.

Out of all of the young captives interviewed, none compared to Daniel, Hananiah, Mishael, and Azariah. They excelled above all the other participants. The goal explained in verse five—the training of all the Jewish captives in order to find the most commendable individuals worthy to serve before the king—had been fulfilled in these four Israelites.

> **DIG DEEPER:** *COOPERATIVE CAPTIVES*
>
> It appears that the Israelite captives were treated relatively well by their Babylonian captors. They were given the choicest food and drink available and were educated to be exceptional scholars. Is this why there was apparently little or no resistance by the Jewish captives? Probably not. More likely, they were aware of the words of the prophet Jeremiah, who foretold of their coming captivity and warned them not to resist but to go willingly. *(Jeremiah 21.7-9, 22.1-5, 24.5-7, and 29.4-7)*

Verse 20- And in all matters of wisdom and understanding about which the king examined them, he found them ten times better than all the magicians and astrologers who were in all his realm.

The Lord continued to bless the obedience of his four servants, Daniel, Hananiah, Mishael, and Azariah. The king apparently tested their wisdom and knowledge in many different aspects, and in "all matters," these four, whose wisdom and intelligence were from God, were found to be far superior to any of the king's magicians and astrologers, whose intelligence was of the world. Therefore, Daniel and his friends were, even by the king's worldly standards, the most intelligent men in the Babylonian Empire. The king was certainly thrilled to have these four great men in his court, and many times, as we will see throughout the study of Daniel, Nebuchadnezzar praised God for them.

Verse 21- Thus Daniel continued until the first year of King Cyrus.

Though we are not sure about Hananiah, Mishael, and Azariah, this verse states that "Daniel continued," which means that he remained in the king's court. This is not intended to suggest that Daniel's presence in the king's court did not exceed beyond the first year of Darius, for we know from other Scriptures that it did:

> *¹It pleased Darius to set over the kingdom one hundred and twenty satraps, to be over the whole kingdom; ²and over these, three governors, of whom Daniel was one, that the satraps might give account to them, so that the king would suffer no loss. ³Then this Daniel distinguished himself above the governors and satraps, because an excellent spirit was in him; and the king gave thought to setting him over the whole realm. (Daniel 6.1–3)*

Furthermore, we can also conclude from other biblical records that Daniel's position was not always as prominent nor his reputation as well-known as when he served under Nebuchadnezzar. *(Daniel 5.10–16)*

King Cyrus came to power at the end of the seventy years of the Jewish exile. *(Jeremiah 25.11–12; Jeremiah 29.10; Ezra 1.1–3)* Daniel, therefore, had remained in the court for at least seventy years and at this point would have been around eighty-six years old. However, the cunning, ungodly forces that tried to abolish his godly example within the king's court many times threatened Daniel's life.

Notes/Applications

Does God really care how we spend our money? Do the foods we eat really matter to God? Does God really care which person we marry? Does He care how we earn a living? We may think that God does not care about these personal areas of our lives. However, not only does God care, He calls us to be obedient to Him by applying the principles in His Word to every area of our lives—the little things and the big things. *"And whatever you do in word or deed, do all in the name of the Lord Jesus, giving thanks to God the Father through Him."* *(Colossians 3.17)* Obedience to God means that, out of our love for Him, we follow Him in all that we say and do.

In this chapter, four of the Jewish captives did not partake of the king's foods because they knew that this was in conflict with the guidelines God had previously given them. To us, eating the king's meats might seem trivial. What harm would have been done if Daniel and his friends had eaten the king's delicacies? Would they have been struck by lightning? Probably not, since there are no indications that such consequences ever befell the other Israelite children. However, in the Hebrew law, God specifically instructed His children not to eat from the king's table because these meats were considered unclean. Notice that as a result of Daniel and his friends' obedience in this seemingly simple matter God made them physically healthier than the other captive children and ten times wiser than the king's magicians and astrologers. Therefore, if they had disobeyed God, these four would have probably robbed themselves of God's blessings.

Certainly, we are saved by God's grace, and the Christian walk is not a formula. Doing x and y may not always yield result z. However, God's Word outlines several basic principles that we should follow in order to live obedient, godly lives. Although our works do not save us, they do reveal for Whom we are working. *"15What then? Shall we sin because we are not under law but under grace? Certainly not! 16Do you not know that to whom you present yourselves slaves to obey, you are that one's slaves whom you obey, whether of sin leading to death, or of obedience leading to righteousness." (Romans 6.15–16)*

Are there any areas of our lives that we have held back from God thinking that He does not care about trivial things or thinking that we could handle those situations on our own? Do we obey God out of our love and devotion to Him or out of a sense of duty?

19And by this we know that we are of the truth, and shall assure our hearts before Him. 20For if our heart condemns us, God is greater than our heart, and knows all things. 21Beloved, if our heart does not condemn us, we have confidence toward God. 22And whatever we ask we receive from Him, because we keep His commandments and do those things that are pleasing in His sight. (1 John 3.18–22)

According to these verses, what spiritual blessings does God bestow upon those who obey Him?

Chapter Two

Daniel 2.1–7

Verse 1- Now in the second year of Nebuchadnezzar's reign, Nebuchadnezzar had dreams; and his spirit was so troubled that his sleep left him.

This chapter presents the first recorded dream of King Nebuchadnezzar. These were special dreams that God sent in the form of a vision, although Nebuchadnezzar did not recognize their source. This vision occurred during the second year of Nebuchadnezzar's reign as king of Babylon, which rewinds the clock a few years from where the first chapter of Daniel concluded. Therefore, we also know that Daniel and the other Jewish captives had not yet completed their three years of training by this point.

From the phrasing of this verse, we can infer that Nebuchadnezzar dreamed several intense dreams that disturbed his spirit. *Spirit*, in this context, comes from the Hebrew word *ruwach*, which means "breath" and by implication expresses the essence of life.[1] Whenever he laid his head down at night to sleep, Nebuchadnezzar's rest was interrupted by these terrible dreams, and as a result, his whole being was troubled.

Verse 2- Then the king gave the command to call the magicians, the astrologers, the sorcerers, and the Chaldeans to tell the king his dreams. So they came and stood before the king.

Nebuchadnezzar summoned the service of the Chaldeans, core magicians, astrologers, and sorcerers to interpret the meaning of his dreams. These men were viewed as the intellectual elite of their culture, but they sought their wisdom from ungodly sources.

> **DIG DEEPER:** *ALL THE KING'S MEN*
>
> The term *magicians* comes from the Hebrew word *chartom*, which means "drawers of magical lines and circles," such as those who drew diagrams to explain a "divine" thing. *Astrologers*—from the Hebrew word *ashshaph*, which means, "a conjurer"—were priests who received their enlightenment by reading the stars.[2] The sorcerers cast spells, practiced occult magic, and performed visual "miracles." Throughout biblical history, "wise men" of this sort, who obtained their power from ungodly sources, have never been able to match the true power of Almighty God. *(Genesis 41; Exodus 8; Daniel 4)*

Verse 3- And the king said to them, "I have had a dream, and my spirit is anxious to know the dream."

The king admitted that he recently had a dream, and although he could not remember it, the dream troubled him deeply. When the king said, "My spirit is anxious to know the dream," he confirmed that his agitation drove his compelling desire to know its meaning. Surely, his summoning of these wise men for such a seemingly trivial matter revealed the king's desperation. Therefore, he demanded that the wisest men in his kingdom tell him what his dream concerned.

Verse 4- Then the Chaldeans spoke to the king in Aramaic, "O king, live forever! Tell your servants the dream, and we will give the interpretation."

The Chaldeans spoke to the king first. Speaking to him in the Syrian language, they said, "O king, live forever," which was, as evidenced throughout this book, a traditional greeting of a servant toward a reigning potentate. They then urged the king to tell them his dream so that they could interpret it for him. Appeasing the king would have been simple under these circumstances since each Chaldean could have offered his own interpretation of the dream with no regard for accuracy. The problem, however, persisted because the Chaldeans did not know what the king had dreamed and, therefore, could not even suggest an interpretation for him.

Verse 5- The king answered and said to the Chaldeans, "My decision is firm: if you do not make known the dream to me, and its interpretation, you shall be cut in pieces, and your houses shall be made an ash heap.

It seems that the Chaldeans' response spurred Nebuchadnezzar's aggravation because these were, supposedly, the wisest men in his kingdom. Nebuchadnezzar impatiently reiterated his need for someone to recount the dream's details. The king then threatened the Chaldeans by saying that he would kill them by cutting them into pieces and that he would also destroy their homes if they could not tell him his dream. Apparently, he fully intended to carry out his threats.

Verse 6- "However, if you tell the dream and its interpretation, you shall receive from me gifts, rewards, and great honor. Therefore tell me the dream and its interpretation."

The king enticed the Chaldeans with promises of gifts, money, and public praise as a reward for revealing the events of his dream and its interpretation. The wise men were surely tempted by these promises of wealth and stature, which certainly captivated them with visions of the public honor that might be bestowed upon them. If possible, they likely would have fabricated a reply, whether true or not. However, even with serious threats upon their lives, they refrained from lying to the king, for if they were found to be deceitful, they would have undoubtedly lost their lives. Though Nebuchadnezzar waved great temptations as well as threats before the Chaldeans, these men were unable to do what only God could do.

Verse 7- They answered again and said, "Let the king tell his servants the dream, and we will give its interpretation."

Probably by this point, the material rewards offered by the king seemed inconsequential to the Chaldeans, who now only sought to escape from the predicament with their lives. Because of their inability to answer the king accurately, the Chaldeans stalled for more time. They again begged the king to tell them his dream, so they could interpret it for him. Still, Nebuchadnezzar simply could not remember the dream, and his wise men's response only further irritated him, according to later verses.

Notes/Applications

According to these verses, Nebuchadnezzar sought the advice of his wise men, whereas the wise men sought the king's praise. Even today, people barter away their souls for the approval of others.

The need for acceptance is deeply seeded within the heart of man. Everyone wants to be recognized as someone of significance. However, man's need for acceptance can only be met by the Heavenly Father. He alone fully understands this need. He alone is equipped to meet this need because He alone has the capability to love unconditionally.

Therefore, individual performance does not determine one's importance. A Christian's identity and sense of worth lies not in his works. As believers, our worth is reflected in the price that God incurred when He bought our redemption through the sacrifice of His Son, the Lord Jesus Christ. *"For you were bought at a price; therefore glorify God in your body and in your spirit, which are God's." (1 Corinthians 6.20)*

Have we grown tired of performing for the approval of others? Our search for significance ends when we remember that being "precious in His sight" renders us forever priceless to the One who really matters.

Daniel 2.8–15

Verse 8- The king answered and said, "I know for certain that you would gain time, because you see that my decision is firm:

Nebuchadnezzar sensed that the Chaldeans struggled for time. The king reiterated that the remembrance of the dream escaped him, and although the Chaldeans believed the king, they desperately delayed the process to prolong their lives. Neither Nebuchadnezzar nor the Chaldeans realized it, but God eliminated Nebuchadnezzar's remembrance of the dream to give Daniel the opportunity to glorify his God—the one true God.

Verse 9- "If you do not make known the dream to me, there is only one decree for you! For you have agreed to speak lying and corrupt words before me till the time has changed. Therefore tell me the dream, and I shall know that you can give me its interpretation."

Nebuchadnezzar rightly accused the Chaldeans of scrambling for more time. Therefore, he no longer trusted anything they said. The king was quickly losing his patience, though he appeared rather void of patience from the beginning. Nevertheless, he granted the Chaldeans and wise men one last opportunity and commanded them to tell him his dream immediately.

Verse 10- The Chaldeans answered the king, and said, "There is not a man on earth who can tell the king's matter; therefore no king, lord, or ruler has ever asked such things of any magician, astrologer, or Chaldean.

The Chaldeans finally confessed their inability to the king. They daringly suggested that Nebuchadnezzar unrealistically required something that no man on earth could do. They argued that regardless of the authority given to a particular person—whether king, lord, or other ruler—he should know better than to ask for the impossible, even from the wisest men in the world.

Verse 11- "It is a difficult thing that the king requests, and there is no other who can tell it to the king except the gods, whose dwelling is not with flesh."

The Chaldeans contended that it was indeed a rare and weighty request. They attempted to reason with Nebuchadnezzar despite his irrational expectations. The wise men admitted that only the "gods whose dwelling is not with flesh" could solve this mystery. In admitting that none of the resources at their disposal were able to help them answer the king's request, they were also inadvertently admitting that they had no access to such a true god, if indeed they even believed one existed. Unwittingly, Nebuchadnezzar and the Chaldeans set the stage for Daniel to honor the only true God when they acknowledged that this revelation could not be accomplished by man.

Verse 12- For this reason the king was angry and very furious, and gave a command to destroy all the wise men of Babylon.

At this point, Nebuchadnezzar completely lost control of his emotions. In his rage, he set forth a command to kill all of Babylon's wise men because they could not do what was asked of them. The king decided to destroy them all without any regard for the unreasonableness of his request.

Verse 13- So the decree went out, and they began killing the wise men; and they sought Daniel and his companions, to kill them.

Upon the king's command, the decree that ordered the deaths of every wise man throughout Babylon was enacted. The consequences of this order also fell upon Daniel, his three friends, and the other young Jewish men who belonged to the king's court, even though the king had apparently never consulted them regarding the dream. We also know that this was more than just a ploy to coerce these wise men; the killing had already begun. Therefore, Daniel and his three friends were in imminent danger.

Verses 14, 15- 14Then with counsel and wisdom Daniel answered Arioch, the captain of the king's guard, who had gone out to kill the wise men of Babylon; 15he answered and said to Arioch the king's captain, "Why is the decree from the king so urgent?" Then Arioch made the decision known to Daniel.

Alarmed by the decree, Daniel addressed Arioch, the captain of the king's guard. Arioch, whose name means "lion-like," was in charge of executing the wise men throughout the Babylonian Empire.[3] Daniel, who spoke with godly wisdom and discernment, inquired about the reason for the hastiness of the decree and the deliberate speed with which the mandate was being carried out. Arioch informed Daniel that no one had successfully advised the king regarding the dream itself, which certainly eliminated any hope of its interpretation.

Notes/Applications

In these passages, Nebuchadnezzar became so furious with the wise men's inability to tell him his dream that he sentenced them to death. Obviously, by allowing his temper to cloud his rationale, the king acted hastily.

Have we ever hastily said or done something in anger that we later regretted? Are the consequences to losing our tempers usually worth the emotional relief that we feel by venting those feelings? Decisions that we make while we are angry are generally hasty ones. After our anger subsides, we may change our mind about a situation, but we can never change the ramifications of what we said or did in the midst of the tantrum. *"A wrathful man stirs up strife, but he who is slow to anger allays contention."* (Proverbs 15.18)

People often use the excuse of "righteous anger" to justify their incensed emotions, but God is very clear about His aversion to anger. *"But now you yourselves are to put off all these: anger, wrath, malice, blasphemy, filthy language out of your mouth."* (Colossians 3.8) We need to maintain control of our emotions and always strive to exemplify the meek—strength under control—and loving Spirit of Christ within us. *"He who is slow to anger is better than the mighty, and he who rules his spirit than he who takes a city."* (Proverbs 16.32)

Daniel 2.16–21

Verse 16- So Daniel went in and asked the king to give him time,
that he might tell the king the interpretation.

When Daniel approached the king, he assured Nebuchadnezzar
that, if given time, he would interpret the king's dream. According to
following verses, the king granted Daniel's request for additional time
and also temporarily lifted his decree against Babylon's wise men
until Daniel was either found to be helpful in the matter or found to
be another fraud merely stalling for time. As a result of this exchange
between Daniel and Nebuchadnezzar, Daniel delayed the fulfillment
of the decree against the wise men of Babylon.

Verses 17, 18- 17Then Daniel went to his house, and made the
decision known to Hananiah, Mishael, and Azariah, his compan-
ions, 18that they might seek mercies from the God of heaven con-
cerning this secret, so that Daniel and his companions might not
perish with the rest of the wise men of Babylon.

To interpret the dream, Daniel first needed to know the dream,
and he knew that he must seek those answers from God. Daniel did
not know *when* God would help him, but he knew that in God's time
he would receive divine guidance. Therefore, as soon as the king
granted Daniel the time, Daniel went back to his house and confided
in his brothers of faith—Hananiah, Mishael, and Azariah—seeking
their prayer support. Together, they prayed for God to reveal the
king's dream.

The four young men asked God for mercy, although they knew
they did not deserve it. Nevertheless, they sought the answer to this
secret in order to be delivered from the decree with the rest of the
Babylonian wise men. Daniel made no public display of his prayers
to God. He simply returned to his house and gathered his three
friends, whereupon they collectively, fervently prayed, believing God
for the answer that would come.

Verse 19- Then the secret was revealed to Daniel in a night vision. So Daniel blessed the God of heaven.

In a vision that night, while Daniel's mind was free from the cares and concerns of the day, God gave Daniel the message of Nebuchadnezzar's dream, which is the first recorded use of Daniel's God-given gift of understanding visions and dreams. *"As for these four young men, God gave them knowledge and skill in all literature and wisdom; and Daniel had understanding in all visions and dreams." (Daniel 1.17)* He knew the source of the vision, so he could take no credit for the dream. Daniel simply rendered himself as God's instrument, and he blessed the Lord God of Heaven *before* he shared the secret with the king.

Verse 20- Daniel answered and said: "Blessed be the name of God forever and ever, for wisdom and might are His.

Daniel's first reaction to God's revelation of the king's dream was to thank the Lord, the faithful God who answered their prayers, granted them mercy, and spared their lives. Daniel exclaimed, "Blessed be the name of God," thereby exalting God's holy name; he declared that God's name should be revered "forever and ever," thereby acknowledging God's infinitude and eternality. Daniel also attributed all wisdom and strength to God alone.

Verse 21- "And He changes the times and the seasons; He removes kings and raises up kings; He gives wisdom to the wise and knowledge to those who have understanding.

Daniel praised God for His vast and perfect power as the One in control of time and seasons. *"And He said to them, 'It is not for you to know times or seasons which the Father has put in His own authority.'" (Acts 1.7)* He declared that God sovereignly determines all earthly authorities, even the wicked leaders of the world. Again, Daniel acknowledged that God alone bestows discernment and insight upon those who are perceived as wise and knowledgeable. *"For the LORD gives wisdom; from His mouth come knowledge and understanding." (Proverbs*

2.6) "He who instructs the nations, shall He not correct, He who teaches man knowledge?" (Psalm 94.10)

Notes/Applications

In verse sixteen, Daniel appealed for time to find the answers that the king so desperately sought. The king granted Daniel's request, so Daniel returned home and listened for God's voice. In the stillness of the night, God answered Daniel's prayer.

We, too, must learn to stop, look, and listen for God's guidance. *"Be still, and know that I am God." (Psalm 46.10a)* In his insightful book, *Victorious Christian Living,* Allen Redpath challenges the believer to "dare to stand still" until he knows the direction that God would have him to go:

> *Never, never, never trust your own judgment in anything. When common sense says that a course is right, lift your heart to God, for the path of faith and the path of blessing may be in a direction completely opposite to that which you call common sense. When voices tell you that action is urgent that something must be done, immediately refer everything to the tribunal of Heaven. Then, if you are still in doubt, dare to stand still. If you are called on to act, and you do not have time to pray, don't act. If you are called on to move in a certain direction and cannot wait until you have peace with God about it, don't move. Be strong enough and brave enough to dare to stand and wait on God, for none of them that wait on God shall ever be ashamed. That is the only way to outmatch the devil.[4]*

No one who waits upon God ever regrets doing so. He will not miss the boat, train, bus, or any opportunity, but he may very well bypass the heartache and confusion that accompany hasty actions. Recognizing that God is faithful and trustworthy to answer each of our prayers according to His perfect will and in His perfect timing, do we dare to stand still until we know His will?

Daniel 2.22–28

Verse 22- "He reveals deep and secret things; He knows what is in the darkness, and light dwells with Him.

Daniel continued praising the Lord for answering their prayers and for sparing their lives. God is light, and He knows what is "in the darkness," those things unknown to any other. Daniel knew that God held in the palm of His hand the answers to each of life's questions, but he also knew that God would disclose only the things that He wished to reveal. What a blessing that God had chosen to divulge such secrets to him!

Verse 23- "I thank You and praise You, O God of my fathers; You have given me wisdom and might, and have now made known to me what we asked of You, for You have made known to us the king's demand."

In a nation of many false gods, Daniel audaciously served the only true God, the God of his fathers, Who had been faithful to His people from generation to generation. He magnified God as the One Who had given him the wisdom and strength to appear boldly before Nebuchadnezzar. The plural pronoun "us" used in this verse describes how Daniel thanked God for unveiling "what *we* asked of You." Daniel recognized that it was an answer to several prayers and not just his own.

Verse 24- Therefore Daniel went to Arioch, whom the king had appointed to destroy the wise men of Babylon. He went and said thus to him: "Do not destroy the wise men of Babylon; take me before the king, and I will tell the king the interpretation."

After Daniel offered praise and thanksgiving to the Lord, he went directly to Arioch, the man who was given the assignment of executing the death decree, and asked Arioch to take him before the king so that he could recite the interpretation of the dream. Arioch certainly must have thought Daniel was insane because he, too, knew what the king had requested and that an interpretation could not be accomplished unless the dream was known. He, like the others in the king's court, realized no human could accomplish this miracle.

Verse 25- Then Arioch quickly brought Daniel before the king, and said thus to him, "I have found a man of the captives of Judah, who will make known to the king the interpretation."

There are several possible reasons that Arioch promptly took Daniel to see the king. Arioch surely understood how desperately Nebuchadnezzar wanted to learn his dream. In having the possible solution to the king's problem within his grasp, Arioch promptly responded for the sake of the king's peace of mind or, more likely it seems, for selfish gain, since he told the king, "*I* have found," when in fact Daniel had volunteered his services. Arioch, with visions of possible rewards showered upon him, probably hoped to appease the king. Another possible reason that Arioch rushed Daniel before the king would be that he, like the others, knew the resulting death sentence of the king's unreasonable request. Perhaps even this chief executioner, aware of his role in the executions, was anxious to spare lives that he would otherwise be required to take. Whatever the reason, Arioch quickly took Daniel before the king.

Verse 26- The king answered and said to Daniel, whose name was Belteshazzar, "Are you able to make known to me the dream which I have seen, and its interpretation?"

Nebuchadnezzar, seemingly unable to believe such good news, asked Daniel if he was truly able to reveal the dream and explain its interpretation. The king, now a skeptic, had likely given up on knowing his dream and its interpretation, for he had ordered the deaths of every wise man in Babylon for the failures of a few.

Verse 27- Daniel answered in the presence of the king, and said, "The secret which the king has demanded, the wise men, the astrologers, the magicians, and the soothsayers cannot declare to the king.

Daniel first stated things Nebuchadnezzar already knew. For example, the king was unable to find the answers he sought from the Chaldeans, astrologers, magicians, and soothsayers, and none of these men could recount the forgotten dream or reveal its interpretation. Daniel again referred to the dream as a "secret" to emphasize that its truth existed beyond the realm of human knowledge.

Verse 28- "But there is a God in heaven who reveals secrets, and He has made known to King Nebuchadnezzar what will be in the latter days. Your dream, and the visions of your head upon your bed, were these:

Daniel, however, also assured the king that the God of the Israelites, the only *true* God, held the key to such secrets and had unveiled this mystery to Daniel. Before Daniel explained the dream and its interpretation to the king, he revealed a small clue about the dream's interpretation and the time to which it referred. However, the period of time that is called the "latter days" cannot be clearly identified, though it seems apparent by the interpretation of the vision given later that this description refers to the end of the world.

Notes/Applications

Daniel proclaimed that God was the source of knowledge and wisdom. Although *knowledge* and *wisdom* are synonyms, they still vary in their definitive meanings. The *American Heritage Dictionary* defines *knowledge* as "the state or fact of knowing; understanding gained through experience or study; learning," and it defines *wisdom* as "understanding what is true, right, or lasting; common sense; good judgement; scholarly learning."[5]

How can a person know and consistently practice true, right, and lasting discernment outside of the absolute authority of an eternal and unchanging God? Many people can retain the knowledge of facts, but only those who intently seek to apply biblical principles can attain true wisdom. True wisdom comes from God alone and cannot be manifested in an individual unless he rids himself of all humanistic predispositions and becomes fully dependent upon the Lord. *"20Where is the wise? Where is the scribe? Where is the disputer of this age? Has not God made foolish the wisdom of this world? 21For since, in the wisdom of God, the world through wisdom did not know God, it pleased God through the foolishness of the message preached to save those who believe."* (1 Corinthians 1.20-21)

God promises that He will generously give us discernment in our daily situations if we humble ourselves and seek His ways. *"If any of you lacks wisdom, let him ask of God, who gives to all liberally and without reproach, and it will be given to him."* (James 1.5) However, so many times we postpone or even avoid asking God for understanding. We look instead to the society around us and think that social reform, money, relationships, or something else can provide us with a plan or a purpose for our existence, but these are temporary, earthly imitations of the genuine spiritual truth.

Which of these adequately satisfies thirst: a glass of pure water or a glass of sour vinegar? The answer is obvious. Likewise, our souls thirst for what only God can supply. Therefore, we must not settle for the world's "misunderstanding" but seek God's answers with our whole heart, mind, body, and soul. *"Receive my instruction, and not silver, and knowledge rather than choice gold."* (Proverbs 8.10)

Daniel 2.29–35

Verse 29- "As for you, O king, thoughts came to your mind while on your bed, about what would come to pass after this; and He who reveals secrets has made known to you what will be.

Daniel explained that the dream occurred while Nebuchadnezzar was in his bed, presumably while he was asleep, and that it concerned future events. He then clarified that God Himself imparted this dream to Nebuchadnezzar as a warning of certain future events.

Verse 30- "But as for me, this secret has not been revealed to me because I have more wisdom than anyone living, but for our sakes who make known the interpretation to the king, and that you may know the thoughts of your heart.

Daniel immediately admitted that this dream had not been revealed to him based upon any superior intelligence that he possessed as one greater than the other wise men. Rather, he emphasized the dream had been given to him so that the king would finally understand the things that greatly troubled him and, in turn, would show mercy to Daniel and to his companions.

Verse 31- "You, O king, were watching; and behold, a great image! This great image, whose splendor was excellent, stood before you; and its form was awesome.

Daniel began to tell the dream to Nebuchadnezzar, explaining in great detail what the king had seen in his dream. Nebuchadnezzar had seen a "great" and "awesome" image, magnificent, beautiful, and enormous in measure.

Verses 32, 33- "32This image's head was of fine gold, its chest and arms of silver, its belly and thighs of bronze, 33its legs of iron, its feet partly of iron and partly of clay.

Next, Daniel described the image to the king. The head was molded of refined gold, its upper torso and arms of silver, its lower torso and upper legs of brass, its lower legs of iron, and its feet partly of iron and partly of clay. The completed description of this image revealed a composite of materials whose value and strength progressively diminished from head to toe.

Verse 34- "You watched while a stone was cut out without hands, which struck the image on its feet of iron and clay, and broke them in pieces.

A stone not made with human hands pummeled the image by crushing its feet into countless fragments.

Remember that the image consisted of gold, silver, brass, iron, and clay. What would happen if an enormous structure were actually made of these materials and constructed in this order? The specific gravity of any given material is a ratio by which that material's mass is compared to the mass of an equal volume of water.[6] More specifically, gold's specific gravity is 19.32 (or is 19.32 times heavier than the same volume of water), silver is 10.47, brass is 8.92, iron is 7.92, and clay is 1.93.[7] Gold, therefore, is about 10 times heavier than clay. Consequently, this image was extremely top-heavy with a poor foundation. If one actually attempted to build such an object in the physical world, it could not stand.

Verse 35- "Then the iron, the clay, the bronze, the silver, and the gold were crushed together, and became like chaff from the summer threshing floors; the wind carried them away so that no trace of them was found. And the stone that struck the image became a great mountain and filled the whole earth.

The whole image collapsed into dust, beginning with the clay and iron feet and ending with the head of gold. What was once an imposing image was quickly reduced to pieces "like chaff" blown "from the summer threshing floors." When wheat is threshed, chaff is the naked husk of the wheat that, because of its virtual weightlessness, is blown away by the wind. When this occurred in the dream, the wind scattered the remaining dust to places where it would never be found. The stone that destroyed the image became a mountain that filled the whole earth.

> **DIG DEEPER:** *THE STONE*
>
> Throughout the Scriptures, the Lord Jesus Christ is referred to as the "Cornerstone" spoken of in Psalm 118.22. *(Matthew 21.42–44; 1 Peter 2.7–8)* Christ, the perfect embodiment of the Law, has never filled the whole earth, but He will one day when He returns. *(Revelation 2.27–29)*

Notes/Applications

God revealed the dream to Daniel but not according to Nebuchadnezzar's or even to Daniel's timeline. It is obvious that God's plan for revealing the dream and its interpretation served a far greater purpose than appeasing Nebuchadnezzar's restlessness. According to verses twenty-nine and thirty, why did God reveal this information to Daniel?

We are not much different than Nebuchadnezzar. We, too, grow impatient. Still, our Lord reminds us to grow anxious for nothing. *"Be anxious for nothing, but in everything by prayer and supplication, with thanksgiving, let your requests be made known to God."* (Philippians 4.6) When we long to see a purpose for life's predicaments and when it seems that we have waited and waited for our prayers to be answered, we must trust that Father God knows our needs better than we do. Certainly, He will provide for our needs better than we can ever provide for ourselves. *"Wait on the LORD; be of good courage, and He shall strengthen your heart; wait, I say, on the LORD!"* (Psalm 27.14)

What burdens weigh heavily on our hearts today? May we commit each of those needs to Him in prayer and thank Him for the assurance that according to His perfect timing He will meet our needs.

Daniel 2.36–42

Verse 36- "This is the dream. Now we will tell the interpretation of it before the king.

Daniel completed his account of Nebuchadnezzar's dream by telling the king that "we" would explain the interpretation. In using this phrasing, Daniel alluded to his three companions, whose prayers had also been answered by the revelation of the king's dream and its interpretation.

Verse 37- "You, O king, are a king of kings. For the God of heaven has given you a kingdom, power, strength, and glory;

Daniel directly addressed Nebuchadnezzar, describing him as a king among kings. *"For thus says the Lord GOD: 'Behold, I will bring against Tyre from the north Nebuchadnezzar king of Babylon, king of kings, with horses, with chariots, and with horsemen, and an army with many people.'" (Ezekiel 26.7)* At this point in history, Nebuchadnezzar had only recently begun his reign as Babylon's king. By the end of his reign, however, he had made the Babylonian Empire the most powerful kingdom in the world, with its dominion stretching over other powerful nations such as Egypt, Arabia, and Syria. Everyone and everything in the region submitted to the authority of Nebuchadnezzar.[8] Nevertheless, Daniel strongly reminded the king that the God of Heaven had given the king this empire and all the benefits that came with it.

Verse 38- "and wherever the children of men dwell, or the beasts of the field and the birds of the heaven, He has given them into your hand, and has made you ruler over them all—you are this head of gold.

While emphasizing Nebuchadnezzar's God-ordained power, Daniel told the king that he was not only ruler of all people but that he also had dominion over the animals of the earth and the birds of the air. God divinely appointed Nebuchadnezzar as commander and controller over all of creation. Daniel then explained that the golden head of the image in the dream represented Nebuchadnezzar and his empire.

Verse 39- "But after you shall arise another kingdom inferior to yours; then another, a third kingdom of bronze, which shall rule over all the earth.

The duration of Nebuchadnezzar's reign would be limited. Nebuchadnezzar was not told how another kingdom would succeed his own, only that one would and that it would have an inferior governmental structure, as indicated by the silver chest and arms in the image of the king's vision. History has since proven this empire to be the kingdoms of the Medes and the Persians. The Medo-Persian Empire was a limited monarchy, meaning that the king of this empire would not have full control to do as he pleased but was accountable to other leaders.

Nebuchadnezzar was then told that a third world empire, represented in the image by the brass belly and thighs, would follow the second one. This kingdom, we now know, was the Greco-Macedonian Empire. The government of Alexander the Great, the epitome of the Greco-Macedonian Empire at its height of power, was a limited monarchy ruled by military aristocracy. As brass is weaker than silver, the type of leadership of this third kingdom would prove to be inferior to that of the kingdom before it.

Verse 40- "And the fourth kingdom shall be as strong as iron, inasmuch as iron breaks in pieces and shatters everything; and like iron that crushes, that kingdom will break in pieces and crush all the others.

The iron legs of the image represented the fourth kingdom, the Roman Empire. This seems to be the general governing style that has prevailed; it is the model for many present-day forms of government that are autocratic democracies, wherein the people determine, by the election of their leaders, those who govern them. We are told in this verse that iron, as when fashioned into tools, can subdue all things. The implication here is that this fourth and final kingdom will end the dominion of the kingdoms that preceded it. Furthermore, though seemingly strong and powerful, we will see in the verses that follow that this fourth kingdom's strength was compromised by the inherent weaknesses that accompany this type of government.

Verse 41- "Whereas you saw the feet and toes, partly of potter's clay and partly of iron, the kingdom shall be divided; yet the strength of the iron shall be in it, just as you saw the iron mixed with ceramic clay.

It is important to remember the prophetic nature of Nebuchadnezzar's dream. In fact, the fulfillment of the dream's prophecy has not yet occurred. The iron and clay mixture represents the ultimate deterioration and loss of strength of the fourth empire. As long as there is at least some iron in the mixture, some strength remains. As illustrated by this particular description of the feet of Nebuchadnezzar's image, the weaker the foundation of a structure, the weaker the integrity of the structure as a whole will also be. This symbolizes the Roman style of government with its divided authority, whereby the strength of its authority is undermined.

Verse 42- "And as the toes of the feet were partly of iron and partly of clay, so the kingdom shall be partly strong and partly fragile.

The Roman Empire fell, but its form of government remains strong around the world. However, what is often perceived as the strength of this type of government—the power of the general public in its influence over its leaders—will ultimately lead to its demise because man will always make selfish decisions on his own behalf rather than for the benefit of the people. Man, who from birth is at contention with God, will always rule himself contrary to God's ways. This image, therefore, illustrates the decline in mankind's regard for God and an increased disobedience to His laws and His will.

Notes/Applications

In order for an orchestra to play harmoniously, every musician must follow the same leader—the conductor. If even one musician plays his own music in his own timing, the result sounds like chaotic jumble rather than a harmonious blending. The last type of government depicted in the image is a system of shared authority, represented by the weakest element in the image's construction because, as with an orchestra that is out of sync, this system of rule produces confusion.

As Christians, we must submit to God's supremacy by recognizing that He has ordained every detail of our lives, including the earthly rulers who administer over us. *"For there is no authority except from God, and the authorities that exist are appointed by God." (Romans 13.1b)* The authority figures in our lives—church leaders, employers, spouses, teachers, and so forth—hold us accountable to the laws and standards of our society. Frankly, if we think that we please God yet constantly rebel against the boundaries that He has ordained, we deceive ourselves. Being submissive, however, is not synonymous with being weak. Quite the contrary is true. By respecting the authority figures in our lives, we ultimately honor God, our highest authority:

> *[13]Therefore submit yourselves to every ordinance of man for the Lord's sake, whether to the king as supreme, [14]or to governors, as to those who are sent by him for the punishment of evildoers and for the praise of those who do good. [15]For this is the will of God, that by doing good you may put to silence the ignorance of foolish men— [16]as free, yet not using liberty as a cloak for vice, but as bondservants of God. (1 Peter 2.13–16)*

Daniel 2.43–49

Verse 43- "As you saw iron mixed with ceramic clay, they will min-gle with the seed of men; but they will not adhere to one another, just as iron does not mix with clay.

These individual kingdoms will be weakened when they "min-gle" with their respective societies. In this context, *mingle* means "mixed or blended" as to form a new compound.[9] Therefore, these ten kingdoms represented by the ten toes of the image will dilute their own power by the interaction with and influence from the people over whom they are supposed to govern.[10] It seems apparent that the inevitable result of governmental democracies is the watering down of the governing authorities by the surging influence of the common people.

Verse 44- "And in the days of these kings the God of heaven will set up a kingdom which shall never be destroyed; and the kingdom shall not be left to other people; it shall break in pieces and con-sume all these kingdoms, and it shall stand forever.

Almighty God will usher in His indestructible kingdom after all the other kingdoms have been destroyed. Rulership of God's king-dom will not be left to any man, and this kingdom, a holy monarchy whose King is Jesus, the Christ, will endure forever.

Verse 45- "Inasmuch as you saw that the stone was cut out of the mountain without hands, and that it broke in pieces the iron, the bronze, the clay, the silver, and the gold—the great God has made known to the king what will come to pass after this. The dream is certain, and its interpretation is sure."

The ten kingdoms, represented by ten toes, will be ten earthly kingdoms, world powers that will be completely demolished with one great blow by the Stone. Apparent by what the Stone accom-plishes and by its description of not having been formed by human hands, the great stone that crushes this image symbolizes Jesus

Christ, the Son of God.[11] Therefore, Jesus Christ will subdue all the earth and will be in complete, perfect control:

> [42]*Jesus said to them, 'Have you read in the Scriptures: "The stone which the builders rejected has become the chief cornerstone. This was the Lord's doing, and it is marvelous in our eyes"? [43]Therefore I say to you, the kingdom of God will be taken from you and given to a nation bearing the fruits of it. [44]And whoever falls on this stone will be broken; but on whomever it falls, it will grind him to powder.'* (Matthew 21.42–44)

Daniel concluded the interpretation of the dream by telling the king, "The great God has made known to the king what will come to pass after this." Daniel assured Nebuchadnezzar of the validity of the dream and its interpretation.

Verse 46- Then King Nebuchadnezzar fell on his face, prostrate before Daniel, and commanded that they should present an offering and incense to him.

The king fell on his face as though worshipping Daniel, which was certainly an uncharacteristic way for a "king of kings," as Nebuchadnezzar had been titled, to behave toward a common man. Evidently, Nebuchadnezzar believed all that Daniel had told him. Surely, the king was so relieved to understand this dream that had deeply burdened him that he expressed his gratitude to Daniel by lavishly rewarding him with abundant luxuries.

Verse 47- The king answered Daniel, and said, "Truly your God is the God of gods, the Lord of kings, and a revealer of secrets, since you could reveal this secret."

Despite the rewards that Nebuchadnezzar bestowed upon Daniel, the king acknowledged that Daniel himself did not deserve the credit. Nebuchadnezzar recognized the source of the revelation, Daniel's God, Who had proven Himself to be the true God of gods.

DIG DEEPER: *GOD OF GODS*

Nebuchadnezzar saw how God worked in Daniel's life, and it provoked him to call Daniel's God "the God of gods." *(Deuteronomy 10.17)* Imagine the impact that we Christians could have on the world if we allowed God to boldly demonstrate His power through us the way that Daniel did! *(Matthew 5.16; Colossians 4.5–6)*

Verse 48- Then the king promoted Daniel and gave him many great gifts; and he made him ruler over the whole province of Babylon, and chief administrator over all the wise men of Babylon.

The king offered Daniel many "great gifts," which included a prestigious position as ruler over the province of Babylon, second only to Nebuchadnezzar and over all of the wise men. This extremely distinguished position would have honored any man, let alone a captive Jew.

Daniel was able to rule with wisdom because he daily relied upon God, and despite his vast material possessions, Daniel never denied his dependence upon the Lord.

Verse 49- Also Daniel petitioned the king, and he set Shadrach, Meshach, and Abed-Nego over the affairs of the province of Babylon; but Daniel sat in the gate of the king.

Daniel did not forget his three friends—Shadrach, Meshach, and Abednego—who had prayed with him for God to reveal the dream and to spare lives through His mercy. They had certainly endured many hard times together. Therefore, Daniel appealed to Nebuchadnezzar that they, too, be rewarded, so the king obliged and also recompensed them for their faithfulness by appointing them as ministers over the affairs of Babylon.

Daniel, however, "sat in the gate of the king," a phrase which, according to the Old Testament and other historical references, described the king's court.[12] Nebuchadnezzar ruled autocratically or with absolute power, yet he yielded much of this power to Daniel, the first in command under him.

Notes/Applications

Daniel did not allow the king's rewards to obstruct his relationship with God because he knew that all of his possessions were imparted to him by God's mercy. Many people who have great riches think that they do not need God. However, material wealth is only temporary and, except for God's grace, can vanish instantly. Money cannot buy health, happiness, peace, or most importantly, an entrance into Heaven.

What would others say is the most important thing to us? What would others say motivates us to do the things that we do? Is it so that we can impact more people for the Lord or so that we can have more? Success is not a matter of how much time, talent or money we possess because none of these goods determines our usefulness to God. God created each of us for a special purpose—to have a fellowship–relationship with Him. When we seek intimacy with Him more than any other earthly commodity, we purchase a genuine treasure that appreciates in value throughout eternity:

[17]*'Because you say, "I am rich, have become wealthy, and have need of nothing"—and do not know that you are wretched, miserable, poor, blind, and naked—*[18]*I counsel you to buy from Me gold refined in the fire, that you may be rich; and white garments, that you may be clothed, that the shame of your nakedness may not be revealed; and anoint your eyes with eye salve, that you may see.* [19]*As many as I love, I rebuke and chasten. Therefore be zealous and repent.* [20]*Behold, I stand at the door and knock. If anyone hears My voice and opens the door, I will come in to him and dine with him, and he with Me.' (Revelation 3.17–20)*

Chapter Three

Daniel 3.1–7

Verse 1- Nebuchadnezzar the king made an image of gold, whose height was sixty cubits and its width six cubits. He set it up in the plain of Dura, in the province of Babylon.

At some point during his reign, Nebuchadnezzar erected a golden image, and though the years of the king's reign are not cited, it can be inferred that this occurred after Daniel and his three friends had been appointed to their positions of leadership (chapter 2). The king set up this idol in an open field, so those who came to worship it would see it from a great distance. Some expositors have speculated that Nebuchadnezzar had this image erected in response to Daniel's interpretation of the vision recorded in chapter two, and they have concluded that the king constructed this image entirely of gold to portray his empire as a permanent kingdom rather than a temporary one.[1]

This image measured approximately ninety feet tall and nine feet wide, using calculations of one cubit equaling about eighteen inches. The measurement ratio given in this verse suggests that the statue was unusually slim in proportion to its height, which leads

some scholars to believe that the measurement of the image's eleva-
tion possibly included the dimensions of a pedestal upon which the
symmetrical idol stood.[2] In addition, the statue was probably not
made of solid gold because an image of such proportions, even if
creating and pouring such a mold were feasible, would have been
virtually immovable due to its excessive tonnage.[3] Rather, it is more
likely that the image was plated with gold as was the custom for such
massive structures. *(1 Chronicles 29.4; Isaiah 40.19)* It must have certainly been an impressive image, although larger statues of ancient
times, such as the Colossus at Rhodes, did exist.[4]

**Verse 2- And King Nebuchadnezzar sent word to gather together
the satraps, the administrators, the governors, the counselors, the
treasurers, the judges, the magistrates, and all the officials of the
provinces, to come to the dedication of the image which King Nebuchadnezzar had set up.**

The king summoned every person in the kingdom that served in
an official capacity to attend the dedication of the image. *Satrap* is
an archaic Persian word that refers to a provincial governor who
ruled over a distinct region, either a small prominent city or a larger
territorial district.[5] A captain, who most often served in a military
capacity, was also a leader over certain groups of people. However,
one can only speculate what the precise responsibilities of each of
these official positions included, but with relative certainty, we can
ascertain that this gathering was comprised of Babylon's elite.

**Verse 3- So the satraps, the administrators, the governors, the
counselors, the treasurers, the judges, the magistrates, and all the
officials of the provinces gathered together for the dedication of
the image that King Nebuchadnezzar had set up; and they stood
before the image that Nebuchadnezzar had set up.**

This verse essentially repeats verse two except in the action of
the sentence. In the previous verse, these men were *to be* present
together, and in this verse, they *were gathered* before the enormous
statue erected by King Nebuchadnezzar.

Verses 4, 5- ⁴Then a herald cried aloud: "To you it is commanded, O peoples, nations, and languages, ⁵"that at the time you hear the sound of the horn, flute, harp, lyre, and psaltery, in symphony with all kinds of music, you shall fall down and worship the gold image that King Nebuchadnezzar has set up;

The herald's duty was to proclaim the king's decrees and to guarantee that the commands were heard and understood by the people. Whereas he might have repeated the message in several languages to ensure that every captive group in Babylon understood the command, it is just as likely, since these captives were trained to be among the elite of the kingdom, that the herald spoke in Chaldean.

Once Babylon's officials assembled for the dedication of the image, the herald announced the king's message. Only this multitude of gathered officials actually heard the decree, but the mandate extended to each and every inhabitant of Babylon, as evidenced in the address to all "peoples, nations, and languages." Upon hearing the decree, these officials were to relay the message to their respective subordinates and would enforce the decree within their specific realm of authority.

These instruments are individually listed probably as a representative cross-section of the most common instruments of that time and culture, though modern versions of the horn, flute, and harp are popular instruments still today. The lyre and psaltery were similar harp-like stringed instruments.[6] The herald then clearly explained the proclamation and its relevance to these instruments. Whenever the people of the Babylonian Empire heard any kind of music, they were to "fall down and worship the golden image."

Verse 6- "and whoever does not fall down and worship shall be cast immediately into the midst of a burning fiery furnace."

The consequence for disobeying the king's decree was severe. Anyone found refusing to fall down and worship the golden image was to be thrown immediately into a fiery furnace. This form of capital punishment was not altogether uncommon in Babylon. *(Jeremiah*

29.22) These furnaces may have been the same large ovens used to bake bricks and melt gold, though it is just as likely, based upon Nebuchadnezzar's evident proneness to extremes, that the king had built these furnaces solely for this purpose.[7] Whatever the situation, it seems that the furnaces were continually stoked to consume anyone that did not comply with the king's command.

Verse 7- So at that time, when all the people heard the sound of the horn, flute, harp, and lyre, in symphony with all kinds of music, all the people, nations, and languages fell down and worshiped the gold image which King Nebuchadnezzar had set up.

After the king's declaration, the playing of the music began, and as commanded, people of all nationalities and languages immediately fell down and worshipped the golden image. In light of what we have learned about the king's personality and by virtue of the severity of the punishment, we can presume that Nebuchadnezzar intended this to be as strict and uncompromising a decree as any he had ever given.

Notes/Applications

These passages serve as the first example of how Nebuchadnezzar had witnessed and testified to God's great power yet eventually returned to his own selfish, prideful ways. Nebuchadnezzar became so intoxicated with egotism that it ultimately led to his ruin.

"Pride goes before the fall" has become a common cliché, yet this is not only a warning. It is a biblical promise. *"Pride goes before destruction, and a haughty spirit before a fall." (Proverbs 16.18)* Simply stated, pride is a condition where a person, consumed by his own desires, does not acknowledge God's supremacy or live in obedience to God's principles. Pride, like a parasite that eats away at its host, blinds us to God's abundant grace and more importantly to our need for His healing touch upon our sin-sickened lives. *"[21]'For from within, out of the heart of men, proceed evil thoughts, adulteries, fornications, murders, [22]thefts, covetousness, wickedness, deceit, lewdness, an evil eye, blas-*

phemy, pride, foolishness. ^{23}*All these evil things come from within and defile a man.'" (Mark 7.21–23)* Essentially, pride, the root of other sinful desires, is a symptom that reveals our depravity and need for a complete heart transplant by the Master Physician, the Lord Jesus Christ.

Obviously, this absorption with self infects every one of us. None of us is immune from it. Therefore, our primary way to battle the spread of pride to every area of our life and to keep it from destroying us, as it did Nebuchadnezzar, is to give God total glory on a daily basis for Who He is and for what He has done. What are some aspects of God's character for which we can offer our praise? For what blessings can we offer God our thanksgiving today?

Daniel 3.8–15

Verse 8- Therefore at that time certain Chaldeans came forward and accused the Jews.

Apparently, some Chaldeans knew of the Jews' devotion to God and His laws because they seized this opportunity to find fault in the Israelites. Ironically, these Chaldeans would not have noticed certain Jews' refusal to bow if they had been worshipping the image as the king previously commanded. These Chaldeans evidently went to the king to incriminate the Jews, who are specifically identified in later verses as Shadrach, Meshach, and Abednego.

Verse 9- They spoke and said to King Nebuchadnezzar, "O king, live forever!

The Chaldeans spoke with Nebuchadnezzar about the matter, though they knew the king favored these Jews because they were Daniel's friends. They began with the customary greeting by saying, "O king, live for ever." This statement by these Chaldeans may or may not have been sincere. The repetitiveness of this greeting throughout the book of Daniel suggests that such was simply "standard operating procedure" when a subject approached the king.

Verse 10- "You, O king, have made a decree that everyone who hears the sound of the horn, flute, harp, lyre, and psaltery, in symphony with all kinds of music, shall fall down and worship the gold image;

The Chaldeans repeated to the king his own decree as if to ensure its inevitable enforcement against those in defiance, regardless of status. They also gave Nebuchadnezzar total credit for creating the decree. He was the king and had final, complete authority.

Verse 11- "and whoever does not fall down and worship shall be cast into the midst of a burning fiery furnace.

The Chaldeans also reiterated the king's predetermined penalty against those that violated the decree. Certainly, Nebuchadnezzar had not forgotten such specifics, considering the time and energy required in constructing the image. Rather, the Chaldeans seemed to provoke the king to wrath to ensure their desired results for Shadrach, Meshach, and Abednego.

Verse 12- *"There are certain Jews whom you have set over the affairs of the province of Babylon: Shadrach, Meshach, and Abed-Nego; these men, O king, have not paid due regard to you. They do not serve your gods or worship the gold image which you have set up."*

The Chaldeans then pinpointed three Jews that the king had appointed to positions of authority over the province of Babylon and who now refused to obey this decree. They accused Shadrach, Meshach, and Abednego likely because they were despised as Jewish captives who had been promoted to high positions of authority.[8] Apparently, the Chaldeans reserved no gratitude toward these three men who had played an integral role in saving the lives of all the wise men of the kingdom *(chapter 2)*.

Interestingly, this is one of only two chapters in the book of Daniel where Daniel's name is not mentioned. In the other chapter (twelve), the text is obviously written by Daniel who was describing a future time period and, therefore, did not refer to himself. Did Daniel, God's instrument, worship this pagan idol? Surely not. Some commentators suggest that he may have been away from Babylon on the king's business during this time.[9] It seems more probable, though, that Daniel had been promoted to a position of authority above the Chaldeans and was, therefore, beyond their reproach and out of their immediate observation.[10]

Furthermore, this account specifically records the charges against Shadrach, Meshach, and Abednego but does not necessarily negate the possibility that few, several, or many other captive Jews also refused to bow to the image. It is not improbable that many Jews

could have been found in defiance and even executed in the same
fiery furnace for their convictions. However, the fact that these three
served as members of the king's court makes this specific account so
relevant.

Verse 13- Then Nebuchadnezzar, in rage and fury, gave the com-
mand to bring Shadrach, Meshach, and Abed-Nego. So they
brought these men before the king.

The king became enraged with the things he heard. How could
these same Israelites that he previously promoted from the disgrace
of captivity to the prominence of authority dare to defy his decree?
Nebuchadnezzar commanded the men of his court to bring
Shadrach, Meshach, and Abednego before him so that he could personally question them.

Verse 14- Nebuchadnezzar spoke, saying to them, "Is it true,
Shadrach, Meshach, and Abed-Nego, that you do not serve my
gods or worship the gold image which I have set up?

Nebuchadnezzar bluntly asked Shadrach, Meshach, and Abed-
nego if they had refused to serve his gods and worship the golden
image. More importantly, however, he probably questioned the intention of their actions. He was very fond of these men because they
were Daniel's friends, so perhaps at this point they could have simply
denied the allegations, and the king might have spared them.

Verse 15- "Now if you are ready at the time you hear the sound of
the horn, flute, harp, lyre, and psaltery, in symphony with all kinds
of music, and you fall down and worship the image which I have
made, good! But if you do not worship, you shall be cast immedi-
ately into the midst of a burning fiery furnace. And who is the god
who will deliver you from my hands?"

The king offered them another chance before they responded to
his first question. He prompted the three Jews toward the answer that
he wanted to hear by repeating the punishment for those who

refused to obey the decree. Surely, most men would have been frightened into begging the king's forgiveness with the assurance that it
would never happen again. But not these men. Nebuchadnezzar
assumed that not even their God could deliver them from his punishment when he said, "Who is the god who will deliver you from my
hands?"

Notes/Applications

Though they did not realize it, Shadrach, Meshach, and Abed-
nego were being watched by ungodly spies who desired to slander
them. Often this is the case with us as well. Many evil forces lie in
wait hoping to find fault in Christians who claim to be "changed,"
and these observers exploit those situations for selfish gain.

If we live Christ-centered lives, it is probable that some will hate
us because we live according to God's principles. In fact, it is more
than probable. The Scriptures promise that this kind of persecution
will certainly befall us. Therefore, we can count it joy to know that
persecution for our faith can be an indicator that we are living
Christ-centered lives:

*18'If the world hates you, you know that it hated Me before it hated
you. 19If you were of the world, the world would love its own. Yet
because you are not of the world, but I chose you out of the world,
therefore the world hates you.' (John 15.18–19) Yes, and all who
desire to live godly in Christ Jesus will suffer persecution. (2 Timothy
3.12)*

Also, just as Nebuchadnezzar did with Shadrach, Meshach, and
Abednego, the world may sometimes offer us an escape from peril
by demanding that we conceal or even deny our faith, but we must
not cower from proclaiming what we believe. Blending in with the
world can be enough to keep others from seeing the Spirit that
should be evident in our lives. *"And do not be conformed to this world,
but be transformed by the renewing of your mind, that you may prove what is
that good and acceptable and perfect will of God." (Romans 12.2)* The world
constantly observes us with its private, accusing eyes. However,

regardless of whether or not we think we are under the skeptical, watchful eyes of others, we should always strive to be Christ-like in speech and in action in order to impact our world for Christ:

> *13'You are the salt of the earth; but if the salt loses its flavor, how shall it be seasoned? It is then good for nothing but to be thrown out and trampled underfoot by men. 14You are the light of the world. A city that is set on a hill cannot be hidden. 15Nor do they light a lamp and put it under a basket, but on a lampstand, and it gives light to all who are in the house. 16Let your light so shine before men, that they may see your good works and glorify your Father in heaven.' (Matthew 5.13–16)*

Daniel 3.16–22

Verse 16- Shadrach, Meshach, and Abed-Nego answered and said to the king, "O Nebuchadnezzar, we have no need to answer you in this matter.

Shadrach, Meshach, and Abednego immediately and boldly answered the king. They must have known that their response would not please him; nevertheless, the three Jews asserted that they were not afraid to answer the king truthfully.

> **DIG DEEPER:** *BE NOT ASHAMED*
>
> As exemplified by the lives of Shadrach, Meshach, and Abednego, the Lord calls us to serve and obey Him with uncompromising boldness. *(Hebrews 13.6)* Let us never be ashamed of the One who has delivered our souls from a fiery fate! *(Luke 9.23–26; Romans 1.16)*

Verse 17- "If that is the case, our God whom we serve is able to deliver us from the burning fiery furnace, and He will deliver us from your hand, O king.

The three Jews then explained why they were not afraid to answer truthfully. Again, they remained respectful in how they addressed the king, but they purposely declared that if God so chose He could save them from the furnace and from the hand of Nebuchadnezzar.

Verse 18- "But if not, let it be known to you, O king, that we do not serve your gods, nor will we worship the gold image which you have set up."

The faith and allegiance to God that these three possessed empowered them to proclaim that even if God did not deliver them from the furnace they still would not worship the king's gods or bow to his golden idol. Their emphasis in saying "but if not" demonstrated their unconditional faith in whatever God's will was for their lives.

They did not disrespect their earthly king, but they would not disobey their Heavenly King, no matter the consequences.

Verse 19- Then Nebuchadnezzar was full of fury, and the expression on his face changed toward Shadrach, Meshach, and Abed-Nego. He spoke and commanded that they heat the furnace seven times more than it was usually heated.

We may assume by his reaction that Nebuchadnezzar took the response of Shadrach, Meshach, and Abednego as a blow to his pride because they chose to be obedient to their God rather than to Nebuchadnezzar as their king. Ironically, the king had once bowed before these three who participated with Daniel in interpreting the king's former dream, but Nebuchadnezzar now punished Daniel's friends for worshipping the same God, the true God, who had answered their prayers by revealing the meaning of Nebuchadnezzar's vision.

Consequently, the king became so enraged with the three men that "his face changed toward Shadrach, Meshach, and Abednego." This phraseology indicates a natural flush that changed Nebuchadnezzar's complexion, or it might express the extreme disfavor with which he suddenly regarded the three Jews. Based upon his reaction, probably both interpretations are intertwined in the king's sentiments.

Nebuchadnezzar's fury soared, so the punishment he had deemed suitable for those who disobeyed his decree no longer sufficed. As a result, he ordered his servants to heat the furnace seven times hotter than usual, although its normal temperature would have been hot enough to consume anything within it. This was done solely for the king's satisfaction in thinking that he could multiply the men's punishment.

Verse 20- And he commanded certain mighty men of valor who were in his army to bind Shadrach, Meshach, and Abed-Nego, and cast them into the burning fiery furnace.

Nebuchadnezzar instructed the mightiest men in his service to restrain Shadrach, Meshach, and Abednego, so they could not escape. They were bound, probably hand and foot, and then thrown into the fiery furnace.

What went through their minds as they were being bound and while they waited for the furnace to reach its increased temperatures? Might they have wondered how soon God would deliver them? With every passing moment that drew them closer to being thrown into the furnace, did they question whether God really intended to deliver them at all?

Verse 21- Then these men were bound in their coats, their trousers, their turbans, and their other garments, and were cast into the midst of the burning fiery furnace.

The three men's mobility and movement were restricted as they were tied up with their own clothing, which would have the same effect as being restrained in straight jackets. To be bound in this manner would also cause them to burn more quickly.

Verse 22- Therefore, because the king's command was urgent, and the furnace exceedingly hot, the flame of the fire killed those men who took up Shadrach, Meshach, and Abed-Nego.

The heat from the furnace was so intense that the men who threw Shadrach, Meshach, and Abednego into the fire perished just by being so near to it. Certainly by that point, the fire should have also immediately consumed Shadrach, Meshach, and Abednego.

Ironically, by having the furnace heated seven times hotter than usual, the king inadvertently added to the glory that God would receive for delivering Shadrach, Meshach, and Abednego from such intense circumstances. There would be no doubt as to the validity of the miracle, and Nebuchadnezzar would never be able to discredit the marvel by saying that the furnace had not been made hot enough.

Notes/Applications

What a remarkable faith Shadrach, Meshach, and Abednego had! They knew their God, the God of their fathers, could save them from the furnace. However, God, in His sovereignty, allowed them to be sentenced to the fiery chambers. So what happened? Did God abandon them? Did they curse God as they approached the intense heat of the blazing furnace? It appears that their faith did not waiver even as they stood face to face with the fire.

The Bible defines faith as "the substance of things hoped for, the evidence of things not seen." *(Hebrews 11.1)* The issue here was not the amount of faith that Daniel's friends possessed but the object of their faith. Even when the object—Almighty God—could not be seen with the naked eye, they trusted that He would accomplish His plan for them through this ordeal. Ultimately, God did not save them *from* the furnace, but He certainly saved them *within* the furnace.

God delivered Shadrach, Meshach, and Abednego in a way unimaginable by human design but in a way that glorified Himself even more greatly. God still wants to work this way in our lives today. Despite our pressing circumstances, God is accomplishing His dynamic plan and perfect will for our lives, and He will not leave us alone in the belly of the furnace. We can walk confidently into fiery trials because God Himself stands with us in the midst of the fire. *"The fear of man brings a snare, but whoever trusts in the LORD shall be safe." (Proverbs 29.25) "But without faith it is impossible to please Him, for he who comes to God must believe that He is, and that He is a rewarder of those who diligently seek Him." (Hebrews 11.6)*

What is the object of our faith? Is it powerful enough to save us in the midst of fiery trials and loving enough to stand with us in them?

Daniel 3.23–30

Verse 23- *And these three men, Shadrach, Meshach, and Abed-Nego, fell down bound into the midst of the burning fiery furnace.*

As these three were thrown into the furnace's fierce heat, they were at the mercy of God. The fire not only had no effect upon their bodies, but it did not burn the clothing that chained them either! They fell down in the midst of the furnace, still bound but completely unscathed from the extreme heat of the roaring flames surrounding them.

Verse 24- *Then King Nebuchadnezzar was astonished; and he rose in haste and spoke, saying to his counselors, "Did we not cast three men bound into the midst of the fire?" They answered and said to the king, "True, O king."*

Evidently, the king took a spectator's seat nearby because we are told that he quickly jumped to his feet while observing this spectacle. Many of his counselors and leaders accompanied him as we will read in verse twenty-seven. It seems as though the king intended to make sport of this horrible display.

Nebuchadnezzar obviously thought that his eyes deceived him because he asked those around him to confirm that they had thrown three men into the fires of the furnace. Those accompanying the king assured him that he was correct.

Verse 25- *"Look!" he answered, "I see four men loose, walking in the midst of the fire; and they are not hurt, and the form of the fourth is like the Son of God."*

Nebuchadnezzar exclaimed that he saw *four* men loose and walking amidst the furnace and unaffected by the fire. The four in the furnace were not harmed in the least, but we also know that they were not in some type of protective bubble because these verses tell us that they walked around "in the midst of the fire."

How could all of this be, and who was this fourth person? Even Nebuchadnezzar, a prideful leader who served false gods, recognized the identity of this fourth person as the very Son of God, Whose presence redeemed the captives from the furnace's death grip. Such an appearance of the Lord in the Old Testament prior to His earthly birth in Bethlehem is called a "Christophany." Apparently, the Son of God had loosened the garments and ropes and enabled the captives to walk around freely within the furnace.

Regardless of the things Shadrach, Meshach, and Abednego might have been thinking prior to being thrown into the fire, what were they thinking at this moment? Surely, they praised the miraculous, awesome God that they served! He had proven Himself to be far more powerful than they could have ever imagined! The Lord could have caused the great flames to be extinguished, yet this miracle brought even more glory to Him.

Verse 26- Then Nebuchadnezzar went near the mouth of the burning fiery furnace and spoke, saying, "Shadrach, Meshach, and Abed-Nego, servants of the Most High God, come out, and come here." Then Shadrach, Meshach, and Abed-Nego came from the midst of the fire.

Nebuchadnezzar approached the mouth of the furnace, still unable to believe what he saw, and called for the Jews to come out of the furnace. As he neared the entrance of the furnace, he called each of the three men individually by name and corporately as "servants of the Most High God." Because of the conviction and determination displayed by these three, God received the glory.

Verse 27- And the satraps, administrators, governors, and the king's counselors gathered together, and they saw these men on whose bodies the fire had no power; the hair of their head was not singed nor were their garments affected, and the smell of fire was not on them.

Many important leaders witnessed this incredible spectacle. The fire had not touched Shadrach, Meshach, or Abednego in the least. Neither their skin nor clothes were burned. Not a hair on their heads was singed, and their clothes did not even smell of smoke! It was as if they were never even near the flames!

Verse 28- Nebuchadnezzar spoke, saying, "Blessed be the God of Shadrach, Meshach, and Abed-Nego, who sent His Angel and delivered His servants who trusted in Him, and they have frustrated the king's word, and yielded their bodies, that they should not serve nor worship any god except their own God!

After Nebuchadnezzar inspected the men, he blessed the God Who saved them. As previously stated, this absolute monarch could seemingly do anything in the world that he pleased. However, God will allow man, even an absolute earthly monarch, to go only as far as His sovereign will permits.

The king fully and accurately acknowledged the role of God's providence in the entire situation. The God of Israel had not only spared the lives of these men, but more importantly, He delivered them because they demonstrated obedience to Him by not worshipping other gods.

Verse 29- "Therefore I make a decree that any people, nation, or language which speaks anything amiss against the God of Shadrach, Meshach, and Abed-Nego shall be cut in pieces, and their houses shall be made an ash heap; because there is no other God who can deliver like this."

Nebuchadnezzar immediately made another decree, and in so doing, seemingly rescinded the earlier decree that required all people to worship his golden image. However, this was not a decree that required the worship of the God of Shadrach, Meshach, and Abednego, but simply a mandate that forbade anyone to speak against their God. Anyone found speaking against the God of the Israelites would be cut into pieces and would have his home utterly destroyed by fire.

As a witness to God's ultimate power over the elements of the earth and protective power over these faithful servants, Nebuchadnezzar experienced a slight adjustment in his thinking because he realized that no other god could have delivered these men like this all-powerful God.

Verse 30- Then the king promoted Shadrach, Meshach, and Abed-Nego in the province of Babylon.

Shadrach, Meshach, and Abednego already held high positions in the government, according to chapter two. In the Chaldean language of the original texts, the word for *promoted* as used here is *tselach,* which means, "to advance," indicating that they prospered while serving in Nebuchadnezzar's court.[11]

Notes/Applications

This passage is another example of Nebuchadnezzar's fluctuating "spirituality." Remember that at the end of chapter two the king praised God for revealing his dream and its translation to Daniel, but in earlier passages of this chapter, he resorted back to his prideful ways by erecting an enormous golden image and commanding the people to worship it. Now again, Nebuchadnezzar seemed to have taken a turn toward the "Most High God" because of the incredible miracle that he witnessed at the fiery furnace.

Nebuchadnezzar's lack of spiritual steadiness is not unlike that of many people today who feast upon religious smorgasbords. The world is full of "spiritualites," individuals who sample a little bit of this religion and a little bit of another one, mix it together, and label it "truth." Some even claim to be Christians, and although they may intellectually believe in the existence of a Supreme Being—and may even call it a "belief in God"—they have never experienced an authentic conversion of the heart. They have never admitted that they are sinners in need of the saving redemption that only the Lord

Jesus Christ has the power and authority to give. Naturally, when seemingly spiritual people are ungrounded in their faith, they will ultimately return to a worldly lifestyle, which appeals to human desires. *"But it has happened to them according to the true proverb: 'A dog returns to his own vomit,' and, 'a sow, having washed, to her wallowing in the mire.'" (2 Peter 2.22)*

There is a vast difference between knowing about God and Christ's teachings, even between witnessing miraculous signs and wonders first-hand, and accepting the truth that Jesus Christ, God's Son, is the only way to eternal life in Heaven. Have we partaken of the Bread of Life and accepted His Living Water? *"⁵¹'I am the living bread which came down from heaven. If anyone eats of this bread, he will live forever.'" (John 6.51b) "¹³'Whoever drinks of this water will thirst again, ¹⁴but whoever drinks of the water that I shall give him will never thirst. But the water that I shall give him will become in him a fountain of water springing up into everlasting life.'" (John 4.13–14)* Feast on the Bread of Life today.

Chapter Four

Daniel 4.1–7

Verse 1- Nebuchadnezzar the king, To all peoples, nations, and languages that dwell in all the earth: Peace be multiplied to you.

Thus far, Daniel recorded his account of Nebuchadnezzar's reign in the third person narrative voice, but in chapter four, a distinct shift in the point of view occurs. Verse four leaves little doubt that King Nebuchadnezzar narrated this chapter as his own personal experience. The reason that Daniel chose to include this account instead of his own version is unknown, though conclusions may be drawn from reading other chapters of Daniel. The most logical conclusion might be that it was such a rarity for an absolute monarch to recognize his own character flaws, to confess the error of his ways, and to surrender his authority to a higher One.[1] Therefore, Nebuchadnezzar's testimonial account strengthens the impact of this story's lesson in humility. To open this narration, the king delivered a general greeting in which he wished peace to the inhabitants of the entire world.

Verse 2- I thought it good to declare the signs and wonders that the Most High God has worked for me.

Nebuchadnezzar explained that he chose to tell his version of this story because he wanted to attest to Almighty God's marvelous works in his life.

Verse 3- How great are His signs, and how mighty His wonders! His kingdom is an everlasting kingdom, and His dominion is from generation to generation.

The king testified of God's miraculous signs and power. Nebuchadnezzar had obviously been influenced by the living example of Daniel, Shadrach, Meshach, and Abednego and especially by the appearance of the Son of God in the fiery furnace. In essence, the king had witnessed God's complete control over creation and human experience, and as a result, had obtained at least some understanding of Jehovah and His attributes. Yet, the evidence of the king's actions recorded in later verses reveals an incomplete comprehension of Almighty God as the highest authority. Sixteenth-century theologian John Calvin states, "He [Nebuchadnezzar] seemed to receive with the greatest modesty what God had manifested by his dream through Daniel's interpretation of it, yet he professed with his mouth what he did not really possess."[2]

Verse 4- I, Nebuchadnezzar, was at rest in my house, and flourishing in my palace.

Nebuchadnezzar expressed the contentment and peacefulness he felt within the security of his home. He currently prospered in material wealth, and his mind was clear of any anxieties.

Verse 5- I saw a dream which made me afraid, and the thoughts on my bed and the visions of my head troubled me.

Similar to a previous episode, Nebuchadnezzar experienced another dream. This second recorded vision abruptly interrupted the king's serenity and shattered his self-confidence. In addition, the king was not merely disturbed by this dream as he had been by the first dream but was also reduced to a state of uncharacteristic trembling and fear.

Verse 6- Therefore I issued a decree to bring in all the wise men of Babylon before me, that they might make known to me the interpretation of the dream.

Unlike his first vision, Nebuchadnezzar remembered the events of this dream; however, he did not understand their meaning, so he still needed to have the dream interpreted. He apparently had not learned from his earlier mistake, for he repeated it. Without first consulting Daniel individually, Nebuchadnezzar again summoned Babylon's wise men to appear before him and to venture an interpretation for this awesome dream.

Verse 7- Then the magicians, the astrologers, the Chaldeans, and the soothsayers came in, and I told them the dream; but they did not make known to me its interpretation.

We are told which groups of the king's wise men came to help him—the magicians, astrologers, Chaldeans, and soothsayers. When Nebuchadnezzar previously needed their assistance, they assured him that if he told them his dream they could then interpret its meaning for him. This time, however, the king was fully capable to recount the details of his dream, yet the wise men could still not render an interpretation. The Lord prevented these worldly men from posing false explanations of the dream's meaning because He would once again fulfill His plan through His servant Daniel.

Notes/Applications

Although Daniel resolved the conflict of Nebuchadnezzar's first dream, Nebuchadnezzar again summoned the wise men of the kingdom before speaking to Daniel individually. The king obviously had not learned from his past experience of relying upon the magicians in his court to accomplish what only Almighty God could do.

Do we judge Nebuchadnezzar too harshly? Do we not also sometimes commit the same sins time and time again? As Christians, those saved from sin's mire, why do we continue to make the same mistakes over and over before learning our lessons? Even the Apostle Paul, who many would label as the "ultimate Christian," struggled with this boggling question:

14For we know that the law is spiritual, but I am carnal, sold under sin. 15For what I am doing, I do not understand. For what I will to do, that I do not practice; but what I hate, that I do. 16If, then, I do what I will not to do, I agree with the law that it is good. 17But now, it is no longer I who do it, but sin that dwells in me. 18For I know that in me (that is, in my flesh) nothing good dwells; for to will is present with me, but how to perform what is good I do not find. 19For the good that I will to do, I do not do; but the evil I will not to do, that I practice. 20Now if I do what I will not to do, it is no longer I who do it, but sin that dwells in me. 21I find then a law, that evil is present with me, the one who wills to do good. 22For I delight in the law of God according to the inward man. 23But I see another law in my members, warring against the law of my mind, and bringing me into captivity to the law of sin which is in my members. 24O wretched man that I am! Who will deliver me from this body of death? 25I thank God—through Jesus Christ our Lord! So then, with the mind I myself serve the law of God, but with the flesh the law of sin. (Romans 7.14–25)

We must never forget that we are sinners saved by God's grace; His grace alone has pardoned us from the penalty of sin, which is eternal damnation in the lake of fire. *(Matthew 25.41,46; Revelation 20.10,15)* However, while on this earth, our spirit continues to battle against the innate desires of our sinful nature, and our adversary, the devil, preys upon our vulnerabilities to keep us from being living examples of God's transforming grace. Ultimately, in our own strength, we have no human power over our sin nature. Our ability to resist temptation comes from the Holy Spirit that lives within us. Therefore, we must daily abide in the Holy Spirit in order to overcome sin. *"16I say then: walk in the Spirit, and you shall not fulfill the lust of the flesh. 17For the flesh lusts against the Spirit, and the Spirit against the flesh; and these are contrary to one another, so that you do not do the things that you wish. 25If we live in the Spirit, let us also walk in the Spirit." (Galatians 5.16–17, 25)*

Since it seems that we constantly fail God by continually sinning, should we stop trying to live obediently? Of course not. He wants His children to have repentant hearts, to stop trying in our own strength, and to start trusting Him. *"6Knowing this, that our old man was crucified with Him, that the body of sin might be done away with, that we should no longer be slaves of sin. 7For he who has died has been freed from sin." (Romans 6.6–7)*

Daniel 4.8–16

Verse 8- But at last Daniel came before me (his name is Belteshaz-zar, according to the name of my god; in him is the Spirit of the Holy God), and I told the dream before him, saying:

God allowed Nebuchadnezzar to exhaust his human resources before the king "at last" turned to Daniel, the only vehicle through which Nebuchadnezzar knew he could reach God. The king recognized that Daniel, whom he called Belteshazzar, possessed the Spirit of the Holy God. We continually see the progression of Nebuchadnezzar's spiritual awareness and understanding. He now recognized the Spirit of the Holy God, but we have no evidence that he had abandoned polytheism for sole devotion to Jehovah God. In fact, in this verse, Nebuchadnezzar's profession "according to the name of *my* god" suggests a continued allegiance to the Babylonian patron god, Bel. Some biblical evidence indicates that Nebuchadnezzar later became a believer in Jehovah God, but again, at this point, the king probably did not fully commit himself to monotheism, the worship of one god.

Verse 9- "Belteshazzar, chief of the magicians, because I know that the Spirit of the Holy God is in you, and no secret troubles you, explain to me the visions of my dream that I have seen, and its interpretation.

As previously stated, the Babylonians worshipped many gods, but obviously, the king observed a difference in Daniel, which he only knew to refer to as "the Spirit of the Holy God." At this point, Nebuchadnezzar expressed some awareness as to the scope and absolute power of the Living God that Daniel served. Nebuchadnezzar, however, still held much pride in his heart, so he did not honor God's supremacy as it applied to his own life.

Verses 10, 11- "¹⁰These were the visions of my head while on my bed: "I was looking, and behold, a tree in the midst of the earth, and its height was great. ¹¹The tree grew and became strong; its height reached to the heavens, and it could be seen to the ends of all the earth.

Nebuchadnezzar began recounting his dream. He first recollected a scene of an enormous tree that stood in the middle of the earth. Initially, the height of the tree was great, but nevertheless, it continued growing until it touched the heavens. This awesome tree could be seen from all over the world.

Verse 12- Its leaves were lovely, its fruit abundant, and in it was food for all. The beasts of the field found shade under it, the birds of the heavens dwelt in its branches, and all flesh was fed from it.

The king further stated that the tree's leaves were beautiful. In addition, this mammoth tree provided life and comfort to the entire earth's population. A vast supply of fruit that could adequately feed everyone and everything on earth flourished upon the tree, so no living being faced starvation. Also, various animals rested under the tree's shade while the birds of the air found their rest within the tree's branches.

Verses 13, 14- "¹³I saw in the visions of my head while on my bed, and there was a watcher, a holy one, coming down from heaven. ¹⁴He cried aloud and said thus: 'Chop down the tree and cut off its branches, strip off its leaves and scatter its fruit. Let the beasts get out from under it, and the birds from its branches.

The king continued. A watcher, also called "a holy one," descended from Heaven. Most scholars identify this being as a heavenly angel sent by God to communicate a message.[3] The being sounded God's command to destroy the tree, cut off its limbs, shake off its leaves, and scatter its fruit. Consequently, the animals would no longer find shade beneath the tree, nor would the birds find shelter within its branches.

Verse 15- Nevertheless leave the stump and roots in the earth, bound with a band of iron and bronze, in the tender grass of the field. Let it be wet with the dew of heaven, and let him graze with the beasts on the grass of the earth.

The tree's stump and roots, however, were to remain untouched. The command required preservation of the stump by wrapping it with iron and brass in order to hold it together, thereby ultimately ensuring its potential for regeneration. Although the tree trunk and limbs were hewn down, the stump would remain rooted in the ground and receive refreshment from Heaven's dew, and *his* existence would be as a beast in the grass of the fields. Notice the pronoun used in this verse is *him* instead of *it*, although the dream was supposedly about an inanimate tree.

Verse 16- Let his heart be changed from that of a man, let him be given the heart of a beast, and let seven times pass over him.

The tree's heart would then be transformed from a man's heart to that of a beast. *Times* as used in this verse is translated from the Chaldean word *iddan*, which connotes one year, so this condition would last for seven years.[4]

Notes/Applications

King Nebuchadnezzar, ruler over the entire known world at the time, basked in his worldly achievements and considered himself untouchable in his position over creation. However, Nebuchadnezzar's exploits failed in comparison to Almighty God's greatness. We may smugly criticize the king for placing his confidence in something so insecure as himself, but we, too, often hinge our security upon our personal prosperity.

On England's southern coastal shoreline stand the White Cliffs of Dover, which divide land and water. Seemingly, no amount of superhuman power could destroy these enormous fixtures—timeless, secure, and immovable. However, reality greatly contrasts human perception. Fine sediments of granite, sandstone, and white chalk compose these stone walls, so each ocean wave, like a sculptor's chiseling tool, slowly but certainly exfoliates pieces away from the face of these massive structures. With the naked eye, we may not see this erosion occur, but it happens nonetheless. Therefore, what appears to be solid, eternal rock is actually constructed of very fragile particles.

Our lives are much the same. We build our lives upon what we perceive to be solid foundations—our positions, possessions, and families. However, it only takes a culmination of the daily grind's recurring waves or one tidal wave of tragedy, and everything upon which we have placed our security washes away.

Nebuchadnezzar lost his possessions and also his humanity before realizing that the foundation upon which he had built his life paled in comparison to the constant, steadfast strength of Almighty God. Likewise, we may have to be stripped of our worldly layers in order to see the naked truth, which is that God, by His grace, makes us who we are and gives us what we have:

[24]'If I have made gold my hope, or said to fine gold, "You are my confidence"; [25]if I have rejoiced because my wealth was great, and because my hand had gained much; [26]if I have observed the sun when it shines, or the moon moving in brightness, [27]so that my heart has been secretly enticed, and my mouth has kissed my hand; [28]this also would be an iniquity deserving of judgment, for I would have denied God who is above.' (Job 31.24–28)

Daniel 4.17–24

Verse 17- '*This decision is by the decree of the watchers, and the sentence by the word of the holy ones, in order that the living may know that the Most High rules in the kingdom of men, gives it to whomever He will, and sets over it the lowest of men.*'

The messenger continued proclaiming the sentence. It was not a suggestion but a final, irrevocable command. Nebuchadnezzar understood the weight of such decrees, for he himself had often sanctioned them. God Almighty established this decree to proclaim to mankind that He alone reigns supremely over every being, so nothing on earth occurs without His permission. From the lowest servant to the highest king, God places and removes rulers from positions of authority according to His perfect will, and He personally demonstrated this divine authority to Nebuchadnezzar through an experience the king would never forget.

DIG DEEPER: *EARTHLY AUTHORITY*

Throughout history, government leaders ascend to earthly power only by God's providence although such leaders, generally speaking, rarely acknowledge the hand of God in their destinies. *(Daniel 2.21; Romans 13.1; Colossians 1.16)* Almighty God is sovereign and supreme. Therefore, it is important that we never forget that our earthly rulers serve in their roles under the absolute sovereignty of God.

Verse 18- "*This dream I, King Nebuchadnezzar, have seen. Now you, Belteshazzar, declare its interpretation, since all the wise men of my kingdom are not able to make known to me the interpretation; but you are able, for the Spirit of the Holy God is in you.*"

Nebuchadnezzar finished describing his dream, and after reiterating that the other wise men had failed to interpret the dream, he asked for Daniel's explanation.

Verse 19- Then Daniel, whose name was Belteshazzar, was astonished for a time, and his thoughts troubled him. So the king spoke, and said, "Belteshazzar, do not let the dream or its interpretation trouble you." Belteshazzar answered and said, "My lord, may the dream concern those who hate you, and its interpretation concern your enemies!

Daniel's thoughts deeply disturbed him. Perhaps, he realized that the dream's interpretation would displease the king and was briefly dumbfounded about what to say. He was not afraid for himself but, rather, for the king. In contrast, perhaps the king was already somewhat relieved by the prospect of knowing the dream's meaning. He told Daniel not to be so worried by the dream, as though he knew its interpretation could not be so dreadful. Daniel, as if thinking aloud, verbalized his wish that the judgment depicted in this dream would befall the king's enemies rather than the king himself.

Verses 20, 21- [20]The tree that you saw, which grew and became strong, whose height reached to the heavens and which could be seen by all the earth, [21]whose leaves were lovely and its fruit abundant, in which was food for all, under which the beasts of the field dwelt, and in whose branches the birds of the heaven had their home—

Daniel then began interpreting the king's dream. The towering tree, as previously stated, reached high into the heavens and could be seen from anywhere on the earth. He then repeated the idyllic scene of the tree—a tree clothed with beautiful leaves and enough fruit to feed all of creation. Also, beneath the shade of the tree, animals lounged, and the birds of the air rested within its branches.

Verse 22- it is you, O king, who have grown and become strong; for your greatness has grown and reaches to the heavens, and your dominion to the end of the earth.

Daniel interpreted the first part of the dream by explaining that the tree represented King Nebuchadnezzar, whose greatness had flourished so much that his dominion extended high into the heavens and unto the ends of the earth. As indicated by the dream, mankind and animals harmoniously coexisted during Nebuchadnezzar's reign, which meant that every aspect of creation prospered under his rule. Certainly at this point, the king must have been very pleased with the interpretation of this dream.

Verse 23- And inasmuch as the king saw a watcher, a holy one, coming down from heaven and saying, 'Chop down the tree and destroy it, but leave its stump and roots in the earth, bound with a band of iron and bronze in the tender grass of the field; let it be wet with the dew of heaven, and let him graze with the beasts of the field, till seven times pass over him';

We now understand why Daniel previously became so troubled. He repeated the scene in which the king saw a holy messenger descend from Heaven, cut down and destroy the tree, yet protect the stump with bands of iron and brass. *Watcher* as used in this verse stems from the Chaldean word *iyr,* which means an angel or guardian. *Holy one* translates from the Chaldean word *qaddiysh,* which means "saint."[5] This being, therefore, was an angel sent directly from God to Nebuchadnezzar.

Notice that the tree's roots remained in the ground to maintain the life of the stump. Although this preservation of the tree's roots would sustain only a minimal amount of life, the essence of life, nonetheless, would endure. Daniel then repeated that the stump became wet with the night's dew and dwelled as a beast in the grassy field for seven years.

Verse 24- this is the interpretation, O king, and this is the decree of the Most High, which has come upon my lord the king:

Daniel was charged with the difficult task of relaying the interpretation of this last sequence of Nebuchadnezzar's dream. He prefaced this portion of the interpretation by reemphasizing that it was a message from Almighty God and not of human concoction. Daniel, therefore, stressed that, although the news was sobering it was from a higher power and beyond his control.

Notes/Applications

Daniel was a man of integrity. Perhaps, he somewhat feared the king's response to the dream's dismal interpretation, but Daniel ultimately knew that God would protect him and bless his honesty. *"My defense is of God, who saves the upright in heart." (Psalm 7.10)*

Integrity is a lost commodity in today's marketplace. Unfortunately, many people underestimate its worth. At one time, a person's word legally and, more importantly, morally bound him, but today the world is complicated by legalities. Although it is only wise for people to protect their agreements in writing, just think how different society would be if we knew that another person's word was trustworthy. Think how different it would be if that person knew the same about our word.

How do we respond to situations when proclaiming truth may not win us favor? When proclaiming truth may even endanger our lives? As Christians, no matter the cost, we are to be, like Daniel, a people of integrity before our Holy God. May each of us be able to say confidently as the psalmist David said, *"I have walked in my integrity: I have trusted also in the Lord; therefore I shall not slide." (Psalm 26.1)*

Daniel 4.25–30

Verse 25- They shall drive you from men, your dwelling shall be with the beasts of the field, and they shall make you eat grass like oxen. They shall wet you with the dew of heaven, and seven times shall pass over you, till you know that the Most High rules in the kingdom of men, and gives it to whomever He chooses.

Daniel further explained that Nebuchadnezzar would eventually be removed from his palace and exiled into the fields to live among the animals as one of them. As the oxen and cattle, he would partake of the field's grasses for his nourishment. The degradation of his condition would humiliate him because even an animal would seek shelter in the dampness of the night. For seven years, the king would dwell outdoors both day and night and wake up saturated with the morning dew. This is a picture of the dominant world leader being humbled into submission to Almighty God's authority because Nebuchadnezzar refused to give God total credit for granting him the position as ruler over all the known earth.

Verse 26- And inasmuch as they gave the command to leave the stump and roots of the tree, your kingdom shall be assured to you, after you come to know that Heaven rules.

Daniel offered the king some encouraging news as well: a tree can grow again if the stump is protected. The tree's main trunk cannot grow again, but a new shoot can sprout from the stump. Therefore, God offered a promise that Nebuchadnezzar would not lose his life, and restoration would follow God's judgment, which perfectly illustrates God's mercy and grace. Daniel assured Nebuchadnezzar that once he honored God as divine ruler over all creation, including his own life, he would return to the throne as a changed, humbled king.

Verse 27- Therefore, O king, let my advice be acceptable to you; break off your sins by being righteous, and your iniquities by showing mercy to the poor. Perhaps there may be a lengthening of your prosperity."

Daniel fervently warned Nebuchadnezzar that this sentence would transpire because of the king's stubbornness and pride, and he counseled the king to repent of his sin so that judgment might be avoided. Although most citizens of Babylon prospered under Nebuchadnezzar's rule, Daniel suggested that Nebuchadnezzar might demonstrate a change of heart by extending mercy to the poor. This benevolent deed in and of itself could never earn Nebuchadnezzar God's gift of grace, but this act of humility could outwardly display the king's sincerity, and if the king heeded this warning, he might have continued living peacefully in his accustomed manner.

Verse 28- All this came upon King Nebuchadnezzar.

This is a transition verse in the text. The king obviously did not heed Daniel's advice, so the fulfillment of the prophecy eventually came to pass.

Verse 29- At the end of the twelve months he was walking about the royal palace of Babylon.

Apparently, God extended the king a grace period of twelve months to consider what Daniel had told him and to repent of his ways, which illustrates for us God's patience and forbearance with sinful man. God first warned Nebuchadnezzar, then He gave the king ample time to heed the warning.

Verse 30- The king spoke, saying, "Is not this great Babylon, that I have built for a royal dwelling by my mighty power and for the honor of my majesty?"

Obviously, the king did not embrace Daniel's warnings. If anything, Nebuchadnezzar reveled even more in his own accomplishments. While walking in his palace, he arrogantly boasted, "*I* have built this great Babylon by the might of *my* power and for *my* honor." Undoubtedly, the king had accomplished many great things during his reign, but none of these things had been done to glorify God. Nebuchadnezzar ignored God's warning and obsessed even more with his own magnificence, so God fulfilled the fate prophesized by his servant Daniel.

Notes/Applications

Daniel predicted the tumultuous times ahead for King Nebuchadnezzar and urged the king to acknowledge God's supremacy. However, the king arrogantly ignored Daniel's wise counsel, refused to humble himself, and credited himself with the prosperity of the empire.

Humility requires the lowering or lessening of oneself, but very few of us want to be lowered and lessened. The reason is because humility goes against our prideful nature. Despite God's blessings upon us, we expect more. In fact, most of us think that we *deserve* more—more happiness, financial prosperity, and freedom—when in fact, the attainment of such things is not our right but our privilege.

A prideful heart is a form of idolatry because it places the individual on a pedestal glorifying self without recognizing God's authority over everything and everyone. *"Before destruction the heart of a man is haughty, and before honor is humility." (Proverbs 18.12)* God gives us the opportunity to humble ourselves, but we can be assured that if we, like Nebuchadnezzar, continue in our stubborn self-absorption, either through direct or indirect circumstances, God Himself will humble us, even if that means removing the pedestal out from under us:

> *"³'The pride of your heart has deceived you, you who dwell in the clefts of the rock, whose habitation is high; you who say in your heart, "Who will bring me down to the ground?" ⁴Though you ascend as high as the eagle, and though you set your nest among the stars, from there I will bring you down,' says the LORD." (Obadiah 1.3–4)*

What will it take to bring our hearts under submission to Almighty God? What must we lose before we are humbled? Are we seeking a spirit of humility? We can begin acquiring a humbled spirit by recognizing and thanking God for His blessings. *"A man's pride will bring him low, but the humble in spirit will retain honor." (Proverbs 29.23)*

Daniel 4.31–37

Verse 31- While the word was still in the king's mouth, a voice fell from heaven: "King Nebuchadnezzar, to you it is spoken: the kingdom has departed from you!

The prophecy foretold in the dream transpired. As the king reveled in his own achievements, even as the words of the previous verse departed from his lips, the audible voice of God Almighty spoke to him. God told Nebuchadnezzar that as of that very moment the kingdom had been taken away from him.

Verse 32- And they shall drive you from men, and your dwelling shall be with the beasts of the field. They shall make you eat grass like oxen; and seven times shall pass over you, until you know that the Most High rules in the kingdom of men, and gives it to whomever He chooses."

The Lord then reminded Nebuchadnezzar of Daniel's exact words concerning the prophetic vision. Certainly, this reminder haunted Nebuchadnezzar because he realized that he had been cautioned yet had ignored the warnings.

Verse 33- That very hour the word was fulfilled concerning Nebuchadnezzar; he was driven from men and ate grass like oxen; his body was wet with the dew of heaven till his hair had grown like eagles' feathers and his nails like birds' claws.

Within the same hour that the Lord had spoken to the king, the prophecy became reality. The king's associates banished him from his palace when insanity overtook him.[6] Nebuchadnezzar's deranged condition was a result of his disobedience to a direct command from the Lord God. However, as Daniel predicted, the people of the king's court did not attempt to kill the king because God's hand still protected Nebuchadnezzar's life.

As also predicted, while in the fields, Nebuchadnezzar ate grass like the animals, the hair on his body became long like the feathers of an eagle, his fingernails grew like the claws of a bird, and in every other way, he became more like a beast than a human. At this point, Nebuchadnezzar lived among the creatures over which he had once ruled. He actually became lower than these beasts because he could not even survive by instinct. His survival was based entirely upon God's grace and provision for him. Notice and ponder the stark contrast between what this man had once been and his current existence.

We might wonder if thoughts of his past prominence tormented the king, but evidently, he did not even have the rationale to reason in such a manner. This, in itself, exemplifies God's grace even in the midst of His judgment. If God had allowed Nebuchadnezzar to continue in his prideful ways, like a time bomb, the king would have surely self-destructed. However, our just and compassionate God sentenced Nebuchadnezzar to this seven-year exile to ultimately break through Nebuchadnezzar's prideful will. Through this experience, God transformed Nebuchadnezzar into the king and person that God wanted him to be.

Verse 34- And at the end of the time I, Nebuchadnezzar, lifted my eyes to heaven, and my understanding returned to me; and I blessed the Most High and praised and honored Him who lives forever: for His dominion is an everlasting dominion, and His kingdom is from generation to generation.

The progression of Nebuchadnezzar's spiritual journey manifested itself at this point. Seven years of dismal existence served as a milestone along that journey. God lowered Nebuchadnezzar until the king accepted rather than just acknowledged God's supremacy. At the end of the seven years, the period of God's judgment was fulfilled, and Nebuchadnezzar lifted his eyes to God, whereupon God immediately restored the king's rationale. Just as prophesied, the king finally, wholeheartedly confessed Jehovah as the only true eternal God. More specifically, he blessed and praised God as the One Who personifies supremacy and sovereign control over everyone and everything.

Verse 35- All the inhabitants of the earth are reputed as nothing; He does according to His will in the army of heaven and among the inhabitants of the earth. No one can restrain His hand or say to Him, "What have You done?"

Nebuchadnezzar learned that every man on earth, from servant to king, lives under subjection to God's sovereign will. No man ever has or ever will gain power that is not ordained by the Lord. The king also admitted that God accomplishes His plan in Heaven and earth regardless of man's approval or disapproval:

> [20]*But indeed, O man, who are you to reply against God? Will the thing formed say to him who formed it, 'Why have you made me like this?'* [21]*Does not the potter have power over the clay, from the same lump to make one vessel for honor and another for dishonor?* [22]*What if God, wanting to show His wrath and to make His power known, endured with much longsuffering the vessels of wrath prepared for destruction,* [23]*and that He might make known the riches of His glory on the vessels of mercy, which He had prepared beforehand for glory,* [24]*even us whom He called, not of the Jews only, but also of the Gentiles? (Romans 9.20–24)*

Verse 36- At the same time my reason returned to me, and for the glory of my kingdom, my honor and splendor returned to me. My counselors and nobles resorted to me, I was restored to my kingdom, and excellent majesty was added to me.

As soon as Nebuchadnezzar humbly surrendered himself to the truth, God returned his humanity to him. The king had certainly experienced sheer torment more horrific than imaginable. Babylon's imperial monarch had been reduced to a terrible existence for seven years. However, his repentance served as a catalyst to restore him in the eyes of God and in the eyes of man. God returned unto Nebuchadnezzar his sanity, his position, his honor, and his splendor. The leaders of his government again looked to him as the king of Babylon, their leader.[7] However, God in His graciousness not only returned everything that the king had prior to these seven years of judgment, but He also added unto Nebuchadnezzar more blessings and majesty than the king had ever possessed.

Verse 37- Now I, Nebuchadnezzar, praise and extol and honor the King of heaven, all of whose works are truth, and His ways justice. And those who walk in pride He is able to put down.

For the first time in his life, Nebuchadnezzar sincerely worshipped the living God. He paid God the respect that only God deserves. This offering of praise surely carried a tone of humility, sincerity, repentance, and thankfulness! At the end of this verse, Nebuchadnezzar even personally testified to what he considered the life lesson of this experience: God humbles those who are full of pride. Though Nebuchadnezzar had not attained perfection, it appears that he had awakened spiritually because he now sought the guidance of Jehovah, the one, true, holy, and living Lord God.

Notes/Applications

Ironically, an attitude of self-promotion consumes pride-filled people, yet these prideful attitudes ultimately lead to destruction. Nebuchadnezzar's seven years of tribulation was God's judgment upon this king's prideful heart. Many times, our hearts must also be subjected to the refining fires of God's judgment to further transform us into His image.

When a metal such as gold or silver is subjected to fire, the physical properties of the metal change. Not only are the metal's elements purified, the metal's structure is strengthened as well. Likewise, in order to bring our unrepentant, proud hearts into submission, we too must pass through the refining fires of judgment and chastisement guided by the hand of our Holy Father. God may allow tribulation, such as personal loss, abuse, financial pressure, or illness, to occur in our lives and to test us in every way imaginable. As the intensity of the trial increases, we may question God's plan. At times, we may even doubt His love for us. However, God's purpose for each trial is not to make our lives miserable. Our gracious God uses adversity to correct us, to restore us, and to strengthen our faith in Him. For the child of God, a seemingly dismal situation can actually be a blessing because it ultimately deepens his relationship with Him. *"¹⁰'Behold, I have refined you, but not as silver; I have tested you in the furnace of affliction. ¹¹For My own sake, for My own sake, I will do it; for how should My name be profaned? And I will not give My glory to another.'"* (Isaiah 48.10–11)

After He cleanses the impurities of our sinful nature from our lives with His refining fire, Father God then lovingly draws us, as He did Nebuchadnezzar, into a dynamic, intimate fellowship-relationship with Him. We emerge from these fires tried, toughened, and true as God's precious treasure. *"'For whom the Lord loves He chastens, and scourges every son whom he receives.'"* (Hebrews 12.6)

Do we desire to know God intimately enough to accept the refining process that is sometimes necessary?

Chapter Five

Verse 1- Belshazzar the king made a great feast for a thousand of his lords, and drank wine in the presence of the thousand.

The events recorded in this chapter occurred about twenty years after the events of the previous chapter. Traditionally, biblical historians date the year as 538–539 BC. Approximately seventy years had passed since Nebuchadnezzar initially besieged Jerusalem and brought the Israelite captives to Babylon, so at this point, Daniel would probably have been in his mid-eighties.[1]

The events recorded in this chapter characterize Belshazzar as a corrupt, self-absorbed, and abusive ruler. Months earlier, the armies of the Medes and Persians had captured and imprisoned his father, Nabonidus, who was the king of the Babylonian Empire.[2] Belshazzar, the ruler over the city of Babylon, hosted this great feast and did not concern himself with the welfare of his father. The king invited a thousand of his lords, who were men of great prominence in the city. In an arrogant display of blatant contempt, Belshazzar drank wine in their presence, which for a king was strongly discouraged since excessive wine compromised mental capacities. A king needed to remain alert against the threat of invasion. *"⁴It is not for kings, O Lemuel, it is not for kings to drink wine, nor for princes intoxicating drink. ⁵Lest they drink and forget the law, and pervert the justice of all the afflicted."* *(Proverbs 31.4–5)*

The presence of women at this feast also indicates that this gathering was purely hedonistic. Belshazzar planned the event strictly as a social banquet and not for any official purposes. Sadly, the carousing sacrilege performed at this feast serves as Belshazzar's only claim to notoriety.[3]

Verse 2- While he tasted the wine, Belshazzar gave the command to bring the gold and silver vessels which his father Nebuchadnezzar had taken from the temple which had been in Jerusalem, that the king and his lords, his wives, and his concubines might drink from them.

Apparently, Belshazzar felt lightheaded and, as a result, behaved recklessly. As was standard military practice, when Nebuchadnezzar overtook the city of Jerusalem, he confiscated the gold and silver vessels from the Jewish temple and placed them within the temples of the Babylonian pagan gods.[4] Years later, unlike Nebuchadnezzar, his forefather, Belshazzar's command to have these vessels brought to him for such unthinkable intentions aroused the wrath of Holy God.

Belshazzar's father, Nabonidus, was Nebuchadnezzar's son-in-law; therefore, Belshazzar was actually the grandson of Nebuchadnezzar. Consequently, the word *father* in this verse likely denotes a general familial relationship, such as *father's father* or *forefather.*[5]

The foolishness of Belshazzar's pagan acts is compounded by the fact that the armies of the Medes and the Persians, which had already captured King Nabonidus, were enclosing upon the city gates while these sacrilegious festivities occurred within the palace.[6] Belshazzar's disregard for this imposing threat further magnified his pompous sense of invincibility.

Verse 3- Then they brought the gold vessels that had been taken from the temple of the house of God which had been in Jerusalem; and the king and his lords, his wives, and his concubines drank from them.

As commanded, servants fetched the vessels for the king, and he, his princes, wives, and concubines drank wine from them. This verse emphasizes again that these vessels originated from God's temple in Jerusalem. Although the vessels held no intrinsic holy value, they had been designed for exclusive use by the Jewish priests in the temple of the Holy God and had been dedicated to Him, thereby making them sanctified vessels.

Verse 4- They drank wine, and praised the gods of gold and silver, bronze and iron, wood and stone.

The partiers performed extensive sacrilegious acts with these vessels. In addition, Belshazzar's drunken guests probably competed to exceed each other's flagrantly sacrilegious displays. When Belshazzar took Jehovah's vessels and toasted the Babylonian idols of gold, silver, brass, iron, wood, and stone, he promoted pagan practices that were an affront to God. Sadly, despite the personal witness of Nebuchadnezzar, his forefather, Belshazzar arrogantly showed no reverence for the Living God, and in fact, his outward behavior displayed his internal rebellion against the Most High God.

Verse 5- In the same hour the fingers of a man's hand appeared and wrote opposite the lampstand on the plaster of the wall of the king's palace; and the king saw the part of the hand that wrote.

God did not allow this sacrilege to continue for long. As the king and his court binged and caroused, a man's fingers suddenly appeared and wrote on the wall. These fingers inscribed a section of the wall that was illuminated by a light, so its message could be clearly seen. Historically, common practice warranted the writing of a king's past titles, victories, and exploits upon a wall at such feasts for the purpose of paying tribute to the king.[7] Therefore, the presence of a message on this wall was not unusual, but the means by which the message appeared there was unprecedented. Certainly, all eyes fell upon the ghostly fingers writing on the wall.

Verse 6- Then the king's countenance changed, and his thoughts troubled him, so that the joints of his hips were loosened and his knees knocked against each other.

When the king saw this marvel, he quickly became somber. In fact, the experience frightened him to the point of physical debilitation. His legs buckled and shook so badly that his knees quivered. Perhaps, the king's countenance dropped, or maybe, the blood drained from his face until he was completely pale. Regardless, Belshazzar's facial expressions displayed the amazing, horrifying effect of this wonder. He was physically and emotionally weakened from witnessing this phenomenon.

Verse 7- The king cried aloud to bring in the astrologers, the Chaldeans, and the soothsayers. The king spoke, saying to the wise men of Babylon, "Whoever reads this writing, and tells me its interpretation, shall be clothed with purple and have a chain of gold around his neck; and he shall be the third ruler in the kingdom."

Belshazzar then summoned the Babylonian wise men, whose faith rested in false gods that were unable to assist the king in matters beyond the realm of human reason. In doing so, Belshazzar repeated the same mistake made by his grandfather Nebuchadnezzar. We may safely presume, based upon the history of oral tradition, that the unique events surrounding Nebuchadnezzar's dreams and Daniel's interpretations of those dreams had been communicated from one generation to the next.[8] Therefore, we might conclude that Belshazzar would have learned from his grandfather's experiences. However, Belshazzar, as Nebuchadnezzar before him, attempted to entice the wise men with material rewards. Whoever could interpret the writing on the wall would be rewarded with a purple robe and a gold necklace and would receive a position as the third ruler in Babylon.

This promise of authority as the *third* ruler in the kingdom insinuates that Belshazzar did not recognize the approaching armies of the Medes and Persians as a serious threat. Therefore, this great feast was not, as some scholars have theorized, a suicidal fling in the abandonment of hope because the king's behavior in this and other verses indicates the contrary.[9] He was simply partying and oblivious to reality.

Verse 8- Now all the king's wise men came, but they could not read the writing, or make known to the king its interpretation.

God would not allow the wise men of Babylon to render an interpretation. God wanted Belshazzar and those with him to know that this marvel, though seemingly unbelievable, was very real. God blocked their understanding, so none could interpret this mysterious secret written upon the wall.

DIG DEEPER: *DIVINE KNOWLEDGE*

As his grandfather Nebuchadnezzar had done, Belshazzar sought the help of the Chaldeans and of the other wise men, but none of them could interpret the meaning of the writing on the wall because they relied upon their pagan gods for such knowledge. Satan might be the god of this world, but he is not all-knowing nor does he have any powers except those temporarily granted to him by God. Real truth and wisdom come from God alone. *(1 Corinthians 4.5; 1 John 4.4–6; Psalm 94.7–15)*

Notes/Applications

Although Belshazzar repeated some of the same sins that his grandfather Nebuchadnezzar had committed, Belshazzar progressed even deeper into the pits of idolatry. After demanding that the temple's golden vessels be brought to him, he and his guests worshiped their pagan gods and sacrilegiously drank wine from these vessels.

"God is a jealous God," means that He does not share His rightful glory as the only true, living God with false gods. *"For the LORD your God is a consuming fire, a jealous God."* (Deuteronomy 4.24) But how does His jealousy differ from ours?

Our human jealousy derives from our insecurities or from the idea that we deserve something more or better than what we have. God's jealousy, however, is based upon His supremacy—His holiness, perfection, goodness, justice, mercy, and grace. Essentially, we commit infidelity when we place ourselves, other things, or other people above Him. *"For I am jealous for you with godly jealousy."* (2 Corinthians 11.2a) God alone deserves all of our honor and praise because He alone is worthy of it. Therefore, our sincere love for Him is communicated when we honor Him as the exclusive, sole object of our worship. God is long-suffering, but He will tolerate our irreverence for only so long before His judgment will follow:

> ³*'You shall have no other gods before Me. ⁴You shall not make for yourself a carved image, or any likeness of anything that is in heaven above, or that is in the earth beneath, or that is in the water under the earth; ⁵you shall not bow down to them nor serve them. For I, the LORD your God, am a jealous God, visiting the iniquity of the fathers on the children to the third and fourth generations of those who hate Me.' (Exodus 20.3–5)*

What has been the object of our worship? People, family, material wealth, work, religion, pleasure, or selfish desires? Anyone or anything that we seek more than we seek Him becomes the focus of what we worship and serve.

Daniel 5.9–16

Verse 9- Then King Belshazzar was greatly troubled, his countenance was changed, and his lords were astonished.

The king's condition worsened because he was greatly terrified. *Countenance* in this verse comes from the Chaldean word *ziyv,* which means, "brightness or cheerfulness."[10] Belshazzar's cheerfulness, his disposition, changed so remarkably that it amazed and alarmed those in his midst.

Verse 10- The queen, because of the words of the king and his lords, came to the banquet hall. The queen spoke, saying, "O king, live forever! Do not let your thoughts trouble you, nor let your countenance change.

The queen, after hearing about the incident, lent her assistance. Most evidence suggests that this was not Belshazzar's wife, but a queen mother, perhaps the wife of Nabonidus or an earlier king. The strongest evidence that this queen was not a bride of Belshazzar is that she "came to the banquet hall," which implies that she was not counted among his wives who, according to verse three, were already gathered at the great feast. Furthermore, whatever her identity and relationship to Belshazzar, her words indicate that she was personally acquainted with Nebuchadnezzar.[11] After addressing Belshazzar with the customary greeting, the queen attempted to comfort him by encouraging him not to let this experience burden him.

Verse 11- "There is a man in your kingdom in whom is the Spirit of the Holy God. And in the days of your father, light and understanding and wisdom, like the wisdom of the gods, were found in him; and King Nebuchadnezzar your father—your father the king—made him chief of the magicians, astrologers, Chaldeans, and soothsayers.

The queen assured Belshazzar that one man in the kingdom possessed the "Spirit of the Holy God" and could help the king. The queen's description of this man did not necessarily confirm, however, that she worshipped this man's God. Though noting the unique power of this man's God, she probably did not acknowledge this Holy God as the only true God. She also recalled that, in the days of Nebuchadnezzar, this man displayed supernatural wisdom unlike that of the wise men currently in the king's presence. This man possessed so much wisdom, in fact, that Nebuchadnezzar had appointed him as chief over the kingdom.

Verse 12- "Inasmuch as an excellent spirit, knowledge, understanding, interpreting dreams, solving riddles, and explaining enigmas were found in this Daniel, whom the king named Belteshazzar, now let Daniel be called, and he will give the interpretation."

The queen then described with more detail the ways in which this person surpassed the other wise men in the kingdom. She finally revealed this man's identity as Daniel, who Nebuchadnezzar had renamed Belteshazzar. After reminding Belshazzar of Daniel's accomplishments for Nebuchadnezzar, she convinced Belshazzar to beckon Daniel to interpret these writings. Whether consciously or subconsciously, the queen credited Daniel as a truly godly man.

Verse 13- Then Daniel was brought in before the king. The king spoke, and said to Daniel, "Are you that Daniel who is one of the captives from Judah, whom my father the king brought from Judah?

As the queen advised, Belshazzar finally summoned Daniel to appear before him. The king confirmed Daniel's identity as a captive Jew, seemingly "to keep Daniel in servile obedience."[12] Again, Belshazzar's reference to his *father* Nebuchadnezzar indicates an ancestral link and not a direct father-son relationship.

Verse 14- "I have heard of you, that the Spirit of God is in you, and that light and understanding and excellent wisdom are found in you.

Belshazzar repeated what the queen told him about Daniel. Again, Daniel's close relationship to God characterized him. These compliments, however, did not spark haughtiness in Daniel because he had observed firsthand what pride could do in a man's life. He remained focused upon the source of his blessings.

Verse 15- "Now the wise men, the astrologers, have been brought in before me, that they should read this writing and make known to me its interpretation, but they could not give the interpretation of the thing.

Belshazzar told Daniel, almost in the form of a challenge, that the other wise men in Babylon had already appeared before the king, but none of them successfully deciphered the meaning of the writing on the wall.

Verse 16- "And I have heard of you, that you can give interpretations and explain enigmas. Now if you can read the writing and make known to me its interpretation, you shall be clothed with purple and have a chain of gold around your neck, and shall be the third ruler in the kingdom."

Belshazzar expressed that his particular interest in Daniel resulted from the queen's comments about Daniel's gift for interpretations. The king then offered Daniel the same rewards that he previously promised to the other wise men. If Daniel could decode the writing, he would receive a purple robe, a golden necklace, and the third highest position in Babylon directly under Belshazzar. However, these offerings did not tempt Daniel, one who had already enjoyed the greatest levels of worldly material wealth and positions of authority. Such earthly commendations meant nothing to him, especially coming from such a heretical ruler as Belshazzar.

Notes/Applications

It is obvious from this passage that Daniel lived such a God-centered life that he was remembered for it even generations after his years of active service in Nebuchadnezzar's court. He left a legacy in the kingdom of Babylon that testified of God's character as a supreme yet personal God.

What do we want others to remember us for years after we are gone? Far greater than the wealth that we have acquired or the accomplishments that we have achieved, we should strive to leave a legacy of godly servitude. Only those things that we do for the kingdom of God will be of any eternal value in Heaven and are also likely the only things worth remembering on earth. *"But lay up for yourselves treasures in heaven, where neither moth nor rust destroys and where thieves do not break in and steal.'" (Matthew 6.20)*

Daniel 5.17–24

Verse 17- Then Daniel answered, and said before the king, "Let your gifts be for yourself, and give your rewards to another; yet I will read the writing to the king, and make known to him the interpretation.

Daniel politely declined Belshazzar's gifts and told the king to give the rewards to someone else. Daniel recognized the temporal value of these gifts, especially from such a wicked king whose reign neared its end. He, nevertheless, agreed to read the writing and to decipher its meaning for Belshazzar, though not out of obligation as one of the king's subjects but because he understood his role as God's instrument.[13]

Verses 18, 19- "[18]O king, the Most High God gave Nebuchadnezzar your father a kingdom and majesty, glory and honor. [19]And because of the majesty that He gave him, all peoples, nations, and languages trembled and feared before him. Whomever he wished, he executed; whomever he wished, he kept alive; whomever he wished, he set up; and whomever he wished, he put down.

Before rendering the interpretation, Daniel reminded Belshazzar that Almighty God gave the kingdom of Babylon to Nebuchadnezzar, Belshazzar's forefather, and with this position came prestige, wealth, and power, but also much responsibility. The sovereign source of Nebuchadnezzar's great status was the Most High God, Who determines all things, including the beginning and end of every king's reign.

Verse 20- "But when his heart was lifted up, and his spirit was hardened in pride, he was deposed from his kingly throne, and they took his glory from him.

Daniel further explained how Nebuchadnezzar's pride had blinded him to Almighty God's omnipotence. King Nebuchadnezzar had become so filled with haughtiness that God dethroned him for a

time. The throne, however, was not the greatest treasure that Nebuchadnezzar had lost; his greatest forfeiture was his identity as a
human being.

*Verse 21- "Then he was driven from the sons of men, his heart was
made like the beasts, and his dwelling was with the wild donkeys.
They fed him with grass like oxen, and his body was wet with the
dew of heaven, till he knew that the Most High God rules in the
kingdom of men, and appoints over it whomever He chooses.*

Daniel thoroughly recapped Nebuchadnezzar's condition as an
insane, scavenging wild animal, which remained for seven years
until Nebuchadnezzar professed God as the ultimate ruler over
everything and everyone, including all earthly leaders.

*Verse 22- "But you his son, Belshazzar, have not humbled your
heart, although you knew all this.*

Daniel brazenly pointed out that Belshazzar displayed the same
prideful tendencies that had destroyed his grandfather, Nebuchadnezzar. In addition, Daniel reprimanded Belshazzar for refusing to
humble himself despite knowing the history of his grandfather's
reign.

*Verse 23- "And you have lifted yourself up against the Lord of
heaven. They have brought the vessels of His house before you, and
you and your lords, your wives and your concubines, have drunk
wine from them. And you have praised the gods of silver and gold,
bronze and iron, wood and stone, which do not see or hear or
know; and the God who holds your breath in His hand and owns
all your ways, you have not glorified.*

Daniel then admonished the king for his deliberate disregard of
God's supremacy, holiness, and righteousness. Rather than leading
the nation with integrity and dignity, Belshazzar passed the temple
vessels among his guests, who toasted their false gods. They dishonored the only true, all-seeing, all-hearing, and all-knowing God upon

Whose mercy their every breath solely depended. Daniel stressed that the Lord God who Belshazzar so recklessly dishonored with contemptuous irreverence actually determined every second of Belshazzar's life and directed his every step. Furthermore, Almighty God held Belshazzar accountable for defaming the temple goods but, more importantly, for what this disgrace revealed—a defiant heart against Jehovah God. Just as the gavel of divine justice fell upon Nebuchadnezzar, it would also fall upon Belshazzar to a far greater extent because he did not heed the lessons of the past.

Verse 24- "Then the fingers of the hand were sent from Him, and this writing was written.

After rebuking the king for his wicked behavior, Daniel prepared to give the literal interpretation of the wall's writing. Unlike past writings that might have adorned the king's wall, the Lord's fingers wrote this message.

Notes/Applications

Whether positively or negatively, history does repeat itself. Unfortunately, instead of learning from past mistakes, one generation often duplicates the iniquities of its forefathers. Belshazzar refused to humble his heart before Almighty God despite knowing the events of his grandfather's reign. Belshazzar's lewdness, therefore, ultimately surpassed Nebuchadnezzar's foolishness because Belshazzar ignored the testimony of his grandfather:

> [20]*For since the creation of the world His invisible attributes are clearly seen, being understood by the things that are made, even His eternal power and Godhead, so that they are without excuse,* [21]*because, although they knew God, they did not glorify Him as God, nor were thankful, but became futile in their thoughts, and their foolish hearts were darkened. (Romans 1.20–22)*

We, too, are individually accountable for what we do with Christ. If we come from an anti-God or atheistic background, we must break the cycle of our fathers' and mothers' sins and become the Christian seed planted in our family and society:

> *6That the generation to come might know them, the children who would be born, that they may arise and declare them to their children, 7that they may set their hope in God, and not forget the works of God, but keep His commandments; 8and may not be like their fathers, a stubborn and rebellious generation, a generation that did not set its heart aright, and whose spirit was not faithful to God. (Psalm 78.6–8)*

If we come from a rich Christian heritage, we should be thankful, but we must not depend upon the accomplishments of our forefathers. We ourselves must move forward in our faith. Let us not be slaves to the sins or achievements of our forefathers. Let us be pioneers and break new ground in our spiritual journey.

Daniel 5.25–31

Verse 25- "And this is the inscription that was written: MENE, MENE, TEKEL, UPHARSIN.

The inscription was comprised of the Chaldean words "MENE, MENE, TEKEL, UPHARSIN," which causes us to wonder why the king's wise men were unable to interpret the message.[14] Apparently, they could read the words but were unable to comprehend their implications, so despite the knowledge and intellect of the king's "wisest" men, the Lord blocked their understanding of what these words meant, so the writing probably appeared to be nothing more than a mass of senseless words.

Verse 26- "This is the interpretation of each word. MENE: God has numbered your kingdom, and finished it;

MENE is a Chaldean word that means "numbered." As Daniel stated, God numbered the days of the Babylonian Empire, and more specifically of Belshazzar's reign, and He now declared it finished. Ironically, the same wall that generally featured flattering legends of the king's magnificence now publicized this mysterious inscription, which foretold his fall. Furthermore, historically, a monarch's death marked the end of his reign, thereby "finishing" his kingdom, so this message not only predicted the end of Belshazzar's reign but the end of his life as well.

Verse 27- "TEKEL: You have been weighed in the balances, and found wanting;

The word *TEKEL* means "weighed." Daniel explained that God had deliberated and deemed that Belshazzar failed to measure up to God's standards. Belshazzar, too immature as a king to deal with such weighty matters or too consumed by worldliness, lacked the character traits necessary to be a good leader. As previously stated, no other historical contributions highlighted Belshazzar's ruling record other than this account of the blasphemous feast. In addition, although his father had been a prisoner for several months, Belshazzar evidently made little or no attempt to rescue him. Therefore, God rendered Belshazzar as spiritually bereft and also irresponsible as a king.

Verse 28- "PERES: Your kingdom has been divided, and given to the Medes and Persians."

The word *PERES* is the same as *UPHARSIN,* which means "to divide." So, in summary, the wall's inscription actually said, "numbered, numbered [again], weighed, and divided." This statement meant nothing to most people, including the king's men, especially since God confounded their understanding. Daniel, however, knew that God had prescribed this message to alert Belshazzar that his kingdom was quickly nearing its end. Although this king had been given many resources, he had recklessly squandered them. He ruled so poorly, in fact, that God ultimately divided the Babylonian kingdom and gave it to a different race of people, the Persians and the Medes.

Verse 29- Then Belshazzar gave the command, and they clothed Daniel with purple and put a chain of gold around his neck, and made a proclamation concerning him that he should be the third ruler in the kingdom.

Belshazzar fulfilled his promise to Daniel. The king's servants clothed Daniel in a purple robe, placed a golden chain around his neck to signify his authority and leadership, and appointed him as third ruler over Babylon.

Daniel ascended to prominent positions early in his life when he first came to Babylon under Nebuchadnezzar, and now again, during his later years, Daniel was promoted to a high position, which he evidently retained throughout the Medo-Persian Empire. However, Daniel must have tasted the bittersweet reality of knowing the imminent end of the Babylonian Empire.

Verse 30- That very night Belshazzar, king of the Chaldeans, was slain.

As predicted, during that same night, King Cyrus' armies attacked and murdered Belshazzar, called here the "king of the Chaldeans":

> [22]'A sound of battle is in the land, and of great destruction. [23]How the hammer of the whole earth has been cut apart and broken! How Babylon has become a desolation among the nations! I have laid a snare for you; [24]you have indeed been trapped, O Babylon, and you were not aware; you have been found and also caught, because you have contended against the Lord. [25]The LORD has opened His armory, and has brought out the weapons of His indignation; for this is the work of the Lord God of hosts in the land of the Chaldeans.' (Jeremiah 50.22–25) [40]'I will bring them down like lambs to the slaughter, like rams with male goats. [41]Oh, how Sheshach is taken! Oh, how the praise of the whole earth is seized! How Babylon has become desolate among the nations!' (Jeremiah 51.40–41)

Verse 31- And Darius the Mede received the kingdom, being about sixty-two years old.

God closed the curtain on the Babylonian Empire and instituted the next great kingdom—the Medo-Persian Empire. Darius the Mede succeeded Belshazzar as viceroy of Babylon, and few historians doubt his identity as the same Darius mentioned in chapters six, nine, and eleven of Daniel.[15] Darius was sixty-two years old when King Cyrus the Persian granted him jurisdiction as governor over the district previously known as the Babylonian Empire.

Notes/Applications

When God surveyed the spiritual condition of Belshazzar's heart, he found that instead of having a heart filled with humility, Belshazzar's heart was puffed with pride. Therefore, in God's eyes, Belshazzar was found lacking. But how did Belshazzar fall short? When people looked at him, they probably saw a man that had everything a person could desire—kingship, money, friends, food, wine, and pleasure. However, when God looked at this king, He found a spirit void of His Holy Spirit.

Unlike a human judge who may be swayed by his own opinions, biases, or emotions, God is a righteous, holy, and perfect judge. *"Honest weights and scales are the LORD's; all the weights in the bag are His work." (Proverbs 16.11)* When we look at others, we may draw conclusions based upon their appearance or accomplishments, but when God judges each of us, He does not consider one's house, job, financial status, educational level, or family name. The Lord looks internally to the core of our being. *"But the LORD said to Samuel, 'Do not look at his appearance or at the height of his stature, because I have refused him. For the LORD does not see as man sees; for man looks at the outward appearance, but the LORD looks at the heart.'" (1 Samuel 16.7)* God judges us based upon the condition of our heart and motives. He welcomes us when we approach Him with a broken spirit, a spirit fully surrendered to Him, acknowledging Him for Who He truly is. *"The sacrifices of God are a broken spirit, a broken and a contrite heart—these, O God, You will not despise." (Psalm 51.17)*

If we take a personal inventory of ourselves, what do we see? Do we see what God sees when He looks at us?

Lord, thank you for the righteousness of Jesus Christ by which my spiritual lacking or wanting no longer condemns me. When you look at me, may You find a humbled spirit and a repentant heart that are pleasing in Your sight.

Chapter Six

Daniel 6.1–7

Verse 1- It pleased Darius to set over the kingdom one hundred and twenty satraps, to be over the whole kingdom;

Historical evidence indicates that Darius the Mede was not the conqueror of Babylon but was appointed as ruler over the kingdom by King Cyrus the Persian.[1] Though this chapter refers to Darius as "king," his sanctioned command, his job description, resembled that of Belshazzar, who presided over Babylon under the authority of Nabonidus.

Darius established a ruling counsel in Babylon, which consisted of 120 satraps who governed the various regions of Babylon's kingdom. As in chapter three, *satrap* is an archaic Persian word that refers to a provincial governor who ruled over a distinct region, either a small prominent city or a larger territorial district.[2] In essence, the Medo-Persian government structure diluted the monarch's authority, fostered greater differences in opinions, decisions, styles, and ideas and, as a result, created the perfect atmosphere for political corruption where one group or person struggled for power over another.

Verse 2- and over these, three governors, of whom Daniel was one, that the satraps might give account to them, so that the king would suffer no loss.

Three presidents supervised the 120 satraps to oversee the financial management of the king's assets. Darius established this chain of command to avoid involvement with the routine, menial problems associated with leading a great dominion and also as a means to protect his monetary interests. Basically, he delegated many of his financial tasks to these three presidents and then along to the 120 satraps, so Darius served more as an administrator than as an absolute monarch.[3] Daniel, chosen to be one of these three presidents, likely gained this position because of his honest, trustworthy, and godly character, whereas many of the king's subjects took advantage of their positions of authority by robbing the king and then hiding their actions with altered records.

Verse 3- Then this Daniel distinguished himself above the governors and satraps, because an excellent spirit was in him; and the king gave thought to setting him over the whole realm.

Daniel's godliness pervaded into his every word and action, which kept him unspoiled by the wealth and position he had gained. Darius favored Daniel over the other two presidents because Daniel had proven himself to be trustworthy. To reward Daniel for his honorable stewardship, Darius considered promoting him to an even higher position of authority.

Verse 4- So the governors and satraps sought to find some charge against Daniel concerning the kingdom; but they could find no charge or fault, because he was faithful; nor was there any error or fault found in him.

Whenever one person or group is esteemed above others, it often leads to jealousy among the less favored. Likewise, the other two presidents and the satraps probably despised Daniel because Darius so greatly respected him. Certainly, Daniel's ethnic heritage as a captive Israelite must have further fueled their resentment. These men searched for some justifiable reason to discredit Daniel's impeccable reputation as a fit ruler, but they found none. This does not imply that Daniel was perfect. It simply means that these conspirators found no suitable reason to disqualify Daniel from the position. Because Daniel gave God total control of his life, his sins—at least in the sight of the worldly eyes that sought to judge him—were insignificant, so he was beyond human reproach.

Verse 5- *Then these men said, "We shall not find any charge against this Daniel unless we find it against him concerning the law of his God."*

Since they were unable to find justifiable reasons to discredit Daniel, these resentful rulers concocted a scheme to incriminate Daniel and to provoke his dismissal. They maliciously fabricated a charge against Daniel by targeting his greatest attribute—his relationship with God. They knew that Daniel prayed three times a day in his room as he sought God's guidance for his life, so they decided to entrap him by creating legislation that would conflict with the laws of Daniel's God.

Verses 6, 7- *⁶So these governors and satraps thronged before the king, and said thus to him: "King Darius, live forever! ⁷All the governors of the kingdom, the administrators and satraps, the counselors and advisors, have consulted together to establish a royal statute and to make a firm decree, that whoever petitions any god or man for thirty days, except you, O king, shall be cast into the den of lions.*

A representative group of the conspirators, possibly even just a minority of the court who had access to the king, assembled before Darius. After addressing the king with the customary greeting, these men claimed that every official throughout the kingdom had conferred on the matter when, in actuality, they likely misrepresented the true number of officials that had concurred. Even if all 122 of the other rulers had agreed on the matter, they had not consulted Daniel, Darius' most esteemed ruler, and so it was with deception that these conspirators approached the king.[4]

Once before the king, they explained their proposal for a new decree, which prohibited anyone from petitioning any god or person other than the king for thirty days, seemingly ample time to entrap Daniel. The conspirators then announced their prescribed punishment for breaking their proposed law. Anyone found guilty of violating this law would be thrown into the lion's den, a common method of execution during this time in history.[5] The king's men wished to execute this law and its punishment immediately.

Obviously, these men cleverly devised this recommendation to manipulate the king with flattery. Such a decree certainly inflated Darius' ego. Scripture does not emphasize that Darius was an egotistical king, as were Nebuchadnezzar and Belshazzar, but to varying measures, all people succumb to the sin of pride, and these men obviously preyed upon Darius' natural prideful inclinations. Furthermore, Darius probably viewed the proposal as a gesture of respect and honor since the decree had been formulated by his appointed leaders and not by him.

Notes/Applications

Many souls hunger for the living hope that they see in the lives of believers. However, like the conspirators who sought to entrap Daniel, there are others in this world—perhaps strangers, coworkers, peers, or even family members—who vehemently oppress those who claim the name of Christ. *"²Deliver me from the workers of iniquity, and save me from bloodthirsty men. ³For look, they lie in wait for my life; the mighty gather against me, not for my transgression nor for my sin, O LORD."* (Psalm 59.2–3)

Corrie ten Boom, a committed Christian, suffered imprisonment in a German concentration camp for hiding Jews in her home during World War II. Boom states, "In countries where Christians suffer great tribulation, even persecution, I have seen how the Lord used weak people and children as channels of streams of living water. Their own strength was not enough, but they trusted Him who filled them with the Spirit—not of fear, 'but of power, and of love, and of a sound mind.'"[6]

As Christians, no matter our age or level of spiritual maturity, the attacks of others wound us. However, we need to change our focus and perception, so we can perceive these struggles for what they truly are—moments that demand our total dependency upon God.

We do not have to fear persecution because, although none of us desire to be incriminated by others, what better charge could be laid to our account than to be identified as a follower of the Lord Jesus Christ? *"28And not in any way terrified by your adversaries, which is to them a proof of perdition, but to you of salvation, and that from God. 29For to you it has been granted on behalf of Christ, not only to believe in Him, but also to suffer for His sake." (Philippians 1.28–29)* The only area of Daniel's life that incriminated him was his intimate relationship with his Heavenly Father. Can the same be said of us? *"For to me, to live is Christ, and to die is gain." (Philippians 1.21)*

Daniel 6.8–14

Verse 8- "Now, O king, establish the decree and sign the writing, so that it cannot be changed, according to the law of the Medes and Persians, which does not alter."

The presidents and satraps then asked the king to sign the recommendation into law, making it legally binding. The conspirators knew that the decree could not be overturned once the king signed it, but they also cunningly made the decree short-term (thirty days) since Medo-Persian laws were otherwise irreversible. James M. Freeman, author of *Manners and Customs of the Bible,* explains the confining nature of Medo-Persian law: "The strict etiquette of the Persian court obliged the king never to revoke an order once given, however much he might regret it, because in so doing he would contradict himself, and, according to Persian notions, the law could not contradict itself."[7] *"If it pleases the king, let a royal decree go out from him, and let it be recorded in the laws of the Persians and the Medes, so that it will not be altered." (Esther 1.19a)* A law, however, could be "neutralized" by executing another decree that stated the opposite of the previous one.

Verse 9- Therefore King Darius signed the written decree.

Darius, upon the urging of his officials and with a heightened sense of importance, signed the decree into law without considering the ramifications of his compliance.

Verse 10- Now when Daniel knew that the writing was signed, he went home. And in his upper room, with his windows open toward Jerusalem, he knelt down on his knees three times that day, and prayed and gave thanks before his God, as was his custom since early days.

It did not take long for news of the decree to reach Daniel. Perhaps, the conspirators even sent men to notify Daniel as soon as the decree was sealed. However, despite the decree's deadly ramifications, Daniel did not evade the issue or change his practice. Peering through his window toward Jerusalem, Daniel continued praying to Jehovah three times a day. He proved his commitment and faithfulness to God by praying openly and boldly according to Jewish custom.[8] *"I will worship toward Your holy temple, and praise Your name for Your lovingkindness and Your truth; for You have magnified Your word above all Your name." (Psalm 138.2)*

Verse 11- Then these men assembled and found Daniel praying and making supplication before his God.

Some of the satraps, maybe even the presidents themselves, arrived outside Daniel's window and saw him praying just as expected, so they now collected their witnesses and evidence against Daniel.

Verse 12- And they went before the king, and spoke concerning the king's decree: "Have you not signed a decree that every man who petitions any god or man within thirty days, except you, O king, shall be cast into the den of lions?" The king answered and said, "The thing is true, according to the law of the Medes and Persians, which does not alter."

The conspirators approached Darius, yet before they informed him of their findings, they repeated to him the decree because they knew that he highly favored Daniel. The men again clarified the king's obligation to execute the punishment. Darius then not only confirmed the validity of the decree but also reaffirmed that "according to the law of the Medes and Persians" neither this law nor its punishment could be rescinded.

Verse 13- So they answered and said before the king, "That Daniel, who is one of the captives from Judah, does not show due regard for you, O king, or for the decree that you have signed, but makes his petition three times a day."

The conspirators finally disclosed Daniel's identity as one who had transgressed the law, and not just once but three times a day.

They also undermined Daniel by referring to him as "one of the captives from Judah." They further alleged that Daniel had disregarded the king and his decrees by breaking this law.

Verse 14- And the king, when he heard these words, was greatly displeased with himself, and set his heart on Daniel to deliver him; and he labored till the going down of the sun to deliver him.

After hearing from his officials, Darius, who was vexed with hastiness, realized the impact of his rash decision and his helplessness to postpone enforcement of the decree's punishment. Although he knew he had been swindled, he could not annul the matter, so he spent the rest of his day trying to circumvent the law, thereby hoping to spare Daniel's life.

Notes/Applications

Daniel did not wait until the crisis, the signing of the decree, to begin his prayer life. Even before the crisis, his prayers were perpetually lifted to the God that he so intimately knew, and despite the bleak circumstances, Daniel faithfully prayed expectantly. *"Rejoicing in hope, patient in tribulation, continuing steadfastly in prayer." (Romans 12.12)* Certainly, if Daniel thought that God would not hear his prayers and answer them, this wise man would not have squandered his time. Daniel, however, knew that omnipotent God would act in a mighty way. Therefore, the frequency of Daniel's petitions did not demonstrate a lack of faith. On the contrary, Daniel's earnest prayers displayed his obedience to the Lord and his faith that Almighty God answers the prayers of His people. *"The effective, fervent prayer of a righteous man avails much." (James 5.16b)*

Perhaps, we yearn for a meaningful and dynamic prayer life but think that we do not know where to begin. Some situations completely baffle us, and we are unsure how to approach God, so we cease praying altogether. However, this is the wrong course of action. Even when Heaven seems silent, we must faithfully converse with God. When we approach Him in sincerity, even when we cannot eloquently communicate our needs, His Holy Spirit intervenes and does this for us:

> *26bLikewise the Spirit also helps in our weaknesses. For we do not know what we should pray for as we ought, but the Spirit Himself makes intercession for us with groanings which cannot be uttered. 27Now He who searches the hearts knows what the mind of the Spirit is, because He makes intercession for the saints according to the will of God. (Romans 8.26b–27)*

God not only hears our mouths speaking; He hears our hearts as well, so if nothing else, we can go before His throne and simply express our loss for words.

Is prayer our immediate response or our last resort to the situations that we face? Have we faithfully spent time in prayer with the King of kings on a daily basis? Do we fervently pray believing that God will work mightily according to His will? *"And whatever things you ask in prayer, believing, you will receive."' (Matthew 21.22)*

Daniel 6.15–22

Verse 15- Then these men approached the king, and said to the king, "Know, O king, that it is the law of the Medes and Persians that no decree or statute which the king establishes may be changed."

The conspirators assembled before King Darius and reminded him about the mandatory punishment for violators of the decree. Although they sensed the king's resentment, they, nonetheless, pressured him to enforce the sentence against Daniel.

Verse 16- So the king gave the command, and they brought Daniel and cast him into the den of lions. But the king spoke, saying to Daniel, "Your God, whom you serve continually, He will deliver you."

Darius had Daniel thrown into the lion's den. Notice Darius' statement at the end of this verse: "Your God, whom you serve continually, He will deliver you." Could it be that Darius recognized a difference between his idol gods that could not see, hear, move, or think and the one, true God that Daniel served? Based upon Daniel's example, Darius evidently believed in the capability of Daniel's God to extend mercy and deliverance to this servant. What an influence Daniel's consistent prayer life and spiritual walk must have been to convey the Lord's power and strength so clearly even to a king who did not serve Jehovah as his God!

Verse 17- Then a stone was brought and laid on the mouth of the den, and the king sealed it with his own signet ring and with the signets of his lords, that the purpose concerning Daniel might not be changed.

The king's men placed a stone over the mouth of the den to prohibit any attempt of escape, and then the king sealed the stone with his own signet, as did the lords of his court. A *signet* was an engraved seal that marked the identity of the sealer. The seal authenticated official documents, so in effect, the king's official seal of approval marked this stone to discourage anyone from attempting to free Daniel.[9]

Verse 18- *Now the king went to his palace and spent the night fasting; and no musicians were brought before him. Also his sleep went from him.*

After closing the den, Darius returned to his quarters for an atypical night. The king spent the night in isolation. He did not partake of food or have his musicians play for him, and according to this verse, he did not sleep at all that night.

Verse 19- *Then the king arose very early in the morning and went in haste to the den of lions.*

This verse does not state that the king *awoke* because as the previous verse stated Darius never slept. The king *arose* early the next morning and hurried to the lion's den, implying that he hoped Daniel was still alive.

Verse 20- *And when he came to the den, he cried out with a lamenting voice to Daniel. The king spoke, saying to Daniel, "Daniel, servant of the living God, has your God, whom you serve continually, been able to deliver you from the lions?"*

We can only speculate if Darius truly believed that Daniel had survived the night. When the king called out in a sorrowful voice, his disposition seemed to be one of defeat. As he called into the pit, Darius referred to Daniel as a "servant of the living God." He then asked if Daniel's God had been able to deliver His servant from death.

Verses 21, 22- [21]*Then Daniel said to the king, "O king, live forever!* [22]*"My God sent His angel and shut the lions' mouths, so that they have not hurt me, because I was found innocent before Him; and also, O king, I have done no wrong before you."*

Although the king most likely did not expect a response, from the depths of the lion's den, an answer emerged. What an enormous relief it must have been for Darius to hear Daniel's voice! Daniel responded, "O king, live forever," in the simple, respectful manner that he always addressed the other kings before Darius. Daniel answered Darius by testifying that "God sent His angel" to shut the mouths of the lions. Remarkably, Daniel was not just alive but was altogether unharmed! It was, without doubt, God's awesome power protecting Daniel's life.

Daniel also assured the king that he had done nothing to harm him. Although Daniel failed to abide by the king's law, the conspirators manipulated Darius into establishing this decree, which disobeyed the greater law of God. Therefore, if Daniel obeyed Darius' law, he transgressed the laws of God.

Notes/Applications

King Darius allowed his governors and satraps to flatter him and manipulate him into hurriedly signing the decree. Obviously, the king could have avoided much anguish if he had evaluated the situation before taking action.

A heart and mind yielded to the will of God will make deliberate decisions rather than hasty ones. *"The thoughts of the righteous are right, but the counsels of the wicked are deceitful." (Proverbs 12.5)* We may recognize the need to commit the "big" things to the Lord but think that we can handle the "small" things ourselves. But how do we know the impact that any decision has upon our lives? Truthfully, if we do not seek God in the seemingly trivial matters, we probably do not search for His wisdom in the important decisions either. However, yielding to the Holy Spirit in this manner is not a one-time occurrence on our Christian journey.

We are so easily distracted by the temporal cares of this fast-paced world that we must begin taking every matter before the throne of God, thereby seeking His will and direction in every situation and listening for His voice. We must then not impart on a different course until we know that we have heard *His* voice—not the world's and not our own. Simply stated, we must surrender our will to His. *"⁵Trust in the LORD with all your heart, and lean not on your own understanding; ⁶in all your ways acknowledge Him, and He shall direct your paths."* *(Proverbs 3.5–6)*

Hasty decisions have consequences, and the impact of any decision endures far beyond the present. However, if we wait for God's direction before we act, we will spare ourselves of the consequential guilt and unrest that accompany trying to do the impossible, which is running ahead of God. *"⁸'For My thoughts are not your thoughts, nor are your ways My ways,' says the LORD. ⁹'For as the heavens are higher than the earth, so are My ways higher than your ways, and My thoughts than your thoughts.'"* *(Isaiah 55.8–9)*

Daniel 6.23–28

Verse 23- Then the king was exceedingly glad for him, and commanded that they should take Daniel up out of the den. So Daniel was taken up out of the den, and no injury whatever was found on him, because he believed in his God.

The king rejoiced because Daniel survived. Violation of the decree required that a sentence be served in the lions' den but failed to stipulate the duration of time spent there, so Darius ordered his men to remove Daniel from the pit. Although Daniel was checked for injuries, not a single scratch was found on him. Certainly, Daniel's accusers never comprehended that he would survive a single hour in the den, let alone emerge completely unscathed after spending an entire night there. The only reason for this, as stated at the end of the verse, related to Daniel's unreserved conviction in the power of Almighty God. Daniel's release, therefore, marvelously testified of God's care for those that sincerely love and faithfully obey Him.

> **DIG DEEPER:** *DELIVERANCE*
>
> Because of Daniel's uncompromising commitment to God, his captors cast him into a lions' den to die for his "crimes." However, once again, the Lord directed Daniel's course and miraculously spared his life. Throughout the Scriptures, Almighty God has demonstrated His faithfulness toward His children who remain obedient to Him despite trying circumstances. *(Exodus 14; Acts 16)*

Verse 24- And the king gave the command, and they brought those men who had accused Daniel, and they cast them into the den of lions—them, their children, and their wives; and the lions overpowered them, and broke all their bones in pieces before they ever came to the bottom of the den.

Finally—justice! Ironically, Darius sentenced Daniel's accusers, their wives, and their children to the lions' den—the same execution they had designed for Daniel. This proclamation likely did not include all 120 satraps because the absence of several ruling authorities would have caused considerable upheaval, leaving the kingdom militarily vulnerable. However, the group thrown to the lions certainly included the most determined of the conspirators—probably the same people who first approached Darius regarding the decree.

This verse confirms other scriptural implications. It may seem unjust to punish the immediate families of these men, but the king felt justified in responding this way. This, in essence, illustrates the domino effect that an individual's sin has on others. Since these men extended no mercy toward the servant of God, King Darius demonstrated no mercy toward Daniel's accusers or toward their families. Without a doubt, the lions thrived as hungry, vicious beasts, which were ready, willing, and able to satisfy their voracious appetites because, before the conspirators even reached the bottom of the den, the lions completely ravished them.

Verses 25, 26- ²⁵Then King Darius wrote: To all peoples, nations, and languages that dwell in all the earth: Peace be multiplied to you. ²⁶I make a decree that in every dominion of my kingdom men must tremble and fear before the God of Daniel. For He is the living God, and steadfast forever; His kingdom is the one which shall not be destroyed, and His dominion shall endure to the end.

Darius issued a new decree and forwarded it with a greeting of peace to every citizen throughout the Medo-Persian Empire. To avoid any misunderstanding, it reached every person of every nation and language and required them to revere the God of Daniel because, as Darius restated, "He is the Living God." Darius declared that God was steadfast and immovable forever and that His kingdom would never be destroyed.

The forging of this decree by Darius after witnessing a miracle of God parallels Nebuchadnezzar's declaration after Shadrach, Meshach, and Abednego had been wondrously spared from their certain deaths within the fiery furnace. *"Therefore I make a decree that any people, nation, or language which speaks anything amiss against the God of*

Shadrach, Meshach, and Abed-Nego shall be cut in pieces, and their houses shall be made an ash heap; because there is no other God who can deliver like this.'" (Daniel 3.29) Just like Nebuchadnezzar many years before him, Darius acknowledged that God holds ultimate power over the entire earth and that His dominion will eternally prevail.

Verse 27- He delivers and rescues, and He works signs and wonders in heaven and on earth, Who has delivered Daniel from the power of the lions.

Whether or not Darius entrusted his life to God is unknown, but he testified of God's awesome, powerful works to the entire known world. In the decree, Darius explained that God continually presides over all matters in the universe as displayed by His deliverance of His servant Daniel.

Verse 28- So this Daniel prospered in the reign of Darius and in the reign of Cyrus the Persian.

Daniel, well into his eighties at this point, lived a healthy life and prospered during the reign of King Cyrus the Persian, directly under the authority of Darius the Mede because Daniel continued in his spiritual walk of faithful service to Almighty God!

Notes/Applications

Some people pose the argument that Daniel survived the lions' lair because the lions were sick or were not hungry. However, Scripture explains that an angel shut the mouths of the lions. Daniel once again experienced the miraculous power of God, thereby testifying to an earthly king the transforming, miraculous power of the Heavenly King.

Whether our lions' den consists of emotional, familial, financial, physical, or spiritual strife, we can know that in the midst of the spiritual warfare, our God can shut the lions' mouths.

We may not always be spared from the lions' lair, but God will perform a miracle within us that glorifies Himself and strengthens us during our spiritual journey. Like Daniel, we will be a living testament of Almighty God's immeasurable, miracle-working power. *"Ah, Lord GOD! Behold, You have made the heavens and the earth by Your great power and outstretched arm. There is nothing too hard for You."* (Jeremiah 32.17) With God Almighty, the impossible is possible. *"With men this is impossible, but with God all things are possible."* (Matthew 19.26b) *"For with God nothing will be impossible."* (Luke 1.37)

Chapter Seven

Daniel 7.1–7

Verse 1- In the first year of Belshazzar king of Babylon, Daniel had a dream and visions of his head while on his bed. Then he wrote down the dream, telling the main facts.

The first six chapters in the Book of Daniel recount Daniel's intervention in the lives of kings and of God's miraculous intervention in the lives of Daniel and his Israelite brothers. While studying these passages, we are awed by the miracles of our loving, sovereign God expressed through the testimony of His obedient and faithful servant Daniel.

During the last half of the book of Daniel, beginning with this chapter, a much different tone surfaces compared to the first half of the book. The separation in the text is clear, almost as though the book were written in two sections, one which could be entitled *History* and the other *Prophesies*. Whereas chapters one through six describe Daniel's interpretations of the visions and dreams of Babylon's leaders, chapters seven through twelve recount specific prophetic visions that God bestowed directly upon Daniel. In the first year of Belshazzar's reign, which historians place between 556 BC and 553 BC, God sent a vision to Daniel.[1] Placed within the chronological sequence outlined in the first six chapters of the book, this vision happened sometime between the events recorded in chapters four and five. Therefore, at the conclusion of chapter six, we now take a fourteen-year step backwards to examine Daniel's prophetic vision concerning the end-time events awaiting the Jewish race and the entire world.

God had formerly used Daniel as a tool to interpret the dreams of the kings he had served, but this chapter features the first recorded account of Daniel himself having a dream or a vision.

In addition, this vision appeared to Daniel in the form of a dream, so when he awoke, Daniel recorded the details of the vision because he wanted to accurately document what God had revealed through these prophetic visions.

Verse 2- *Daniel spoke, saying, "I saw in my vision by night, and behold, the four winds of heaven were stirring up the Great Sea.*

Daniel conveyed his dream by describing the four winds of Heaven that rushed upon a great sea. Many interpretations regarding the symbolism of the "four winds" and the "Great Sea" exist. However, the most logical explanation suggests that the four winds represent nothing more than actual gusts of wind. The description of four specific winds also suggests that these opposing winds converged upon the sea from different directional origins, most likely the four major orientations of the earth—north, east, south, and west. The emphasis on these winds being "of heaven" implies that they were both created and guided by Almighty God Himself to fulfill His providential, sovereign will. This imagery of winds used to accomplish God's purposes appears in other scriptural texts as well and usually signals God's approaching judgment upon wayward people:

> 'Against Elam I will bring the four winds from the four quarters of heaven, and scatter them toward all those winds; there shall be no nations where the outcasts of Elam will not go.' (Jeremiah 49.36)

Thus says the LORD: 'Behold, I will raise up against Babylon, against those who dwell in Leb Kamai, a destroying wind.' (Jeremiah 51.1) But the LORD sent out a great wind on the sea, and there was a mighty tempest on the sea, so that the ship was about to be broken up. (Jonah 1.4)

Many expositors contend that the great sea in this verse represents the entire population of mankind on a grand scale.[2] However, the literal Hebrew translation of this word means "sea" or "ocean" as we commonly understand it today.[3] Therefore, this great sea likely refers specifically to the Mediterranean Sea, which is biblically noted as the Great Sea, and the region to which this prophetic vision pertains:[4]

[6]'As for the western border, you shall have the Great Sea for a border; this shall be your western border. [7]And this shall be your northern border: from the Great Sea you shall mark out your border line to Mount Hor.' (Numbers 34.6–7) 'From the wilderness and this Lebanon as far as the great river, the River Euphrates, all the land of the Hittites, and to the Great Sea toward the going down of the sun, shall be your territory.' (Joshua 1.4)

Whether or not the *four winds* and the *great sea* hold any greater figurative significance remains uncertain, but to strongly infer that such is the case would be, at best, speculation and could, at worst, diminish the pertinence of the beasts.

Verse 3- "And four great beasts came up from the sea, each different from the other.

Four great beasts arose from the sea, though they were great only in the eyes of man. These beasts resembled mythological creatures in their appearance. We know that they were not actual animals but were images that symbolized a deeper message. Each beast varied from the others, and the following verses state that their appearances became progressively more grotesque.

Verse 4- "The first was like a lion, and had eagle's wings. I watched till its wings were plucked off; and it was lifted up from

the earth and made to stand on two feet like a man, and a man's heart was given to it.

Generally, a lion connotes strength, and the eagle represents speed. Lions tear at their prey with their sharp claws and powerful jaws, and their teeth can slice through the toughest meat. The lion is the king of all beasts, and the eagle is the king of all birds. Since ancient times, the eagle has symbolized courage and power. It possesses superb aerial skills. The bird's wings give it the ability to flee danger but also to swiftly attack its prey.

This first beast, which looked like a lion but had wings like an eagle, had four feet, yet stood upon its hind legs as a human stands upon his feet. Daniel's observations of this beast indicated that it had been weakened by some stronger force. First, the feathers of its wings were "plucked off," thereby stripping the beast of its swiftness. Second, this beast was forced to "stand on two feet like a man," so it was unable to utilize its full potential of power. Finally, no longer did it have the strong, courageous heart of a lion, but it was given the weak, timid, and fearful heart of man.

Verse 5- "And suddenly another beast, a second, like a bear. It was raised up on one side, and had three ribs in its mouth between its teeth. And they said thus to it: 'Arise, devour much flesh!'

The predatory agility of a bear lacks in comparison to a lion's coordination. A bear moves awkwardly; therefore, it must conquer with its crushing brute strength. This profound strength can literally obliterate anything in its path, so the bear's presence poses a threat and must never be underestimated. When a bear attacks, it mauls and rips the flesh of its prey.

This bear-like beast appeared to be raised up on one side, clenching between its teeth three ribs of an unidentified being. While Daniel observed this odd spectacle, a voice commanded the beast to "arise, [and] devour much flesh." Many scholars debate the identity of those who instructed this beast to arise and devour, and many good arguments are offered to support each interpretation. Since the answer does not appear to play an integral role in the overall interpretation of the vision, perhaps it is wisest to conclude that the source of this voice is the Lord Himself and that the plural pronoun use of "they" alludes to the triune existence of God. Such a rendering encompasses all other interpretations, as Calvin expresses, not because "God was the author of cruelty, but since He governs by His secret counsel the events which men carry on without method."[5] Ultimately, regardless of *who* spoke to the beast, the fulfillment of God's providential plan was enacted by the command.

Verse 6- "After this I looked, and there was another, like a leopard, which had on its back four wings of a bird. The beast also had four heads, and dominion was given to it.

A leopard is a very graceful creature—slim and swift yet strong and fierce. Noted as an agile climber and stalker of its prey, the leopard, a nocturnal creature, hunts at night when its prey may be less alert and when natural conditions allow it to surprise its victim. Although the leopard cunningly calculates an attack, once it does attack, its movements are swift yet sure, leaving its prey no time to react.

This beast resembled a leopard because it typified rapid conquests, yet this beast differed from a leopard because it was four-headed and had four wings on its back. While possessing similar abilities to those of the first beast, this beast's wings were somehow inferior since they compared to the wings of a common bird rather than those of an eagle. Daniel explained that it was given dominion, which reveals the first hint of the figurative significance of the beasts.

Verse 7- "After this I saw in the night visions, and behold, a fourth beast, dreadful and terrible, exceedingly strong. It had huge iron teeth; it was devouring, breaking in pieces, and trampling the residue with its feet. It was different from all the beasts that were before it, and it had ten horns.

The fourth beast contrasts the other beasts previously mentioned and any beast that has ever lived. The fourth beast is perhaps the most intriguing beast to study because its significance has not yet been completely fulfilled. In addition, this beast's horrible appearance and great power, described as "dreadful and terrible, exceedingly strong," paint a fearful image. It had iron teeth, representing the fierceness with which it consumed everything in its path and trampled inferior beings beneath its feet in order to bring all creation, both man and beast, under its subjection. Most significant were the ten horns upon its head.

Notes/Applications

Daniel's dream in this chapter somewhat parallels the dream in chapter two that he interpreted for Nebuchadnezzar. God used the earlier experience to increase Daniel's understanding for what he now faced. Likewise, God also uses our present situations to prepare us for the future that He has planned.

It is sometimes difficult to acknowledge God's hand in every aspect of our lives because this principle challenges our theology. We gladly accept the good times as gifts from God, but we question how He could allow the bad things to happen. Is it realistic to praise God for our fiery furnace or lions' den experiences that come in the form of losing a loved one, a job, our health, or our hope? How can we be thankful for these things? Thankfulness prevails in seeing things from God's perspective, the big picture, and knowing that God never ceases being Who He is—Sovereign God, Who equips us to persevere through today's momentary troubles. *"And we know that all things work together for good to those who love God, to those who are the called according to His purpose."* (Romans 8.28)

Everything in our lives, whether jewel or junk, is either procured by God or permitted by Him. Therefore, when we intimately know Him, we can find something in every situation for which to be thankful. *"In everything give thanks; for this is the will of God in Christ Jesus for you."* (1 Thessalonians 5.18) Nothing that happens to us today is without purpose because today prepares us for tomorrow. *"Holding fast the word of life, so that I may rejoice in the day of Christ that I have not run in vain or labored in vain." (Philippians 2.16) "Every day I will bless You, and I will praise Your name forever and ever." (Psalm 145.2)*

Daniel 7.8–14

Verse 8- "I was considering the horns, and there was another horn, a little one, coming up among them, before whom three of the first horns were plucked out by the roots. And there, in this horn, were eyes like the eyes of a man, and a mouth speaking pompous words.

As Daniel examined the ten horns, a little horn arose from within the midst of them. Although these horns had grown for a time, three of the first ten horns were uprooted immediately, seemingly as a result of the emergence of this little horn.

This little horn possessed eyes like a man and a mouth that spoke arrogant propaganda. The message was of monumental importance because the little horn's "pompous" spoutings were actually horrible words blaspheming the name of God. *"⁵And he was given a mouth speaking great things and blasphemies, and he was given authority to continue for forty-two months. ⁶Then he opened his mouth in blasphemy against God, to blaspheme His name, His tabernacle, and those who dwell in heaven." (Revelation 13.5–6)*

Verse 9- "I watched till thrones were put in place, and the Ancient of Days was seated; His garment was white as snow, and the hair of His head was like pure wool. His throne was a fiery flame, its wheels a burning fire;

Daniel watched this scene of the horrible beast with the ten horns and the little horn until the thrones—that is, the thrones of authority belonging to the kingdoms and empires represented by the beasts described in the previous verses and interpreted in verses to follow—were finally "put in place," which could more clearly be rendered "put where they belong." The existence of these great world empires will ultimately be subdued by God Almighty, the Ancient of Days.

This title, the "Ancient of Days," expresses the infinitude of God the Father, and though God the Son and God the Spirit are One with the Father in a triune existence and are, therefore, also eternal, this title seems to be reserved for God the Father. Some readers may presume that the Ancient of Days mentioned in this verse refers to the Lord Jesus simply to collaborate an interpretation that this verse refers to His Second Coming before His millennial reign. However, verse thirteen clearly identifies Jesus as the "Son of man," Who is *brought before* the Ancient of Days.

In addition, Daniel's physical description of God the Father is simple yet incomprehensible. God's pure, radiant white garments and His soft hair, white as wool, depict His wisdom, antiquity, glory, and authority. Certainly, the Holy God seated upon His throne in all of His beauty, majesty, and holiness must have been an incredible sight to behold.

Verse 10- A fiery stream issued and came forth from before Him. A thousand thousands ministered to Him; ten thousand times ten thousand stood before Him. The court was seated, and the books were opened.

This fiery stream flowed from the throne of the Ancient of Days as a vast multitude waited upon the Lord. Ten thousand times ten thousand, a seemingly endless gathering, stood in awe before the holiness of the Lord God Almighty. *"[11]Then I looked, and I heard the voice of many angels around the throne, the living creatures, and the elders; and the number of them was ten thousand times ten thousand, and thousands of thousands."* (Revelation 5.11)

Daniel, discerning the significance of the scene that he witnessed, realized that the time of judgment was at hand. He saw what were apparently books of judgment opened before the Lord. *"And I saw the dead, small and great, standing before God, and books were opened. And another book was opened, which is the Book of Life. And the dead were judged according to their works, by the things which were written in the books."* (Revelation 20.12)

Verse 11- "I watched then because of the sound of the pompous words which the horn was speaking; I watched till the beast was slain, and its body destroyed and given to the burning flame.

Daniel then observed the little horn and heard all that it spouted until a blazing flame finally consumed the little horn, presumably as a specific result of the *"pompous words"* that it spoke.

Verse 12- "As for the rest of the beasts, they had their dominion taken away, yet their lives were prolonged for a season and a time.

Daniel then briefly mentioned the fates of the three lesser beasts. Unlike the final beast, these beasts did not meet destruction simultaneously but successively. Apparently, they lost their power and no longer posed a threat, so their lives continued for a while.

Verse 13- "I was watching in the night visions, and behold, One like the Son of Man, coming with the clouds of heaven! He came to the Ancient of Days, and they brought Him near before Him.

Daniel continued explaining his visions, which should be understood to mean either the one and same vision described to this point or another vision related directly to the previous one and occurring that same night shortly after the first vision. Therefore, the plural use of the word *visions* in this verse likely indicates several parts of the same dream, and during the last segment of this vision, Daniel saw the Son of Man come "with the clouds of heaven" to the Ancient of Days. *"Then I looked, and behold, a white cloud, and on the cloud sat One like the Son of Man, having on His head a golden crown, and in His hand a sharp sickle." (Revelation 14.14)* Daniel watched as God the Son drew near to God the Father.

Verse 14- Then to Him was given dominion and glory and a kingdom, that all peoples, nations, and languages should serve Him. His dominion is an everlasting dominion, which shall not pass away, and His kingdom the one which shall not be destroyed.

The scene appeared to be a coronation. Jesus was ushered in before His Father where God would give His Son all power and dominion over the earth, not as a guiding hand that would control all manner of providence but as the direct and physically-present authority. He would literally return as supreme ruler over mankind and would begin the reign of His "everlasting dominion." Further explanation of this kingdom is provided in the interpretation of this vision in later verses.

Notes/Applications

Every mighty roar of the sea applauds God's power; every thunderstorm announces His sovereign control over all life; every blossoming flower verifies that Almighty God personally and lovingly cares for even the smallest element of His creation. *"The heavens declare the glory of God; and the firmament shows His handiwork." (Psalm 19.1)* Yes, the beauty of God's creation reflects to us only a fraction of His glory, but Daniel's vision of the Ancient of Days, Almighty God, seated upon His heavenly throne and arrayed in His eternal glory is unequaled in nature. Walters Chalmers Smith, lyricist of the classic hymn, "Immortal, Invisible," somewhat captures the magnificence of Holy God upon His eternal throne:

Immortal, invisible God only wise,
in light inaccessible hid from our eyes,
Most blessed, most glorious, the Ancient of Days,
Almighty, victorious, Thy great name we praise.

Unresting, unhasting, and silent as light,
nor wanting, nor wasting, Thou rulest in might;
Thy justice, like mountains, high soaring above;
Thy clouds, which are fountains of goodness and love.

To all, life Thou givest, to both great and small;
in all life Thou livest, the true life of all;
We blossom and flourish as leaves on the tree,
and wither and perish—but naught changeth Thee.

Great Father of glory, pure Father of light,
Thine angels adore Thee, all veiling their sight;
All praise we would render; O help us to see
'tis only the splendor of light hideth Thee![6]

Trying to imagine the beauty of the brightness that illuminates from our Father God makes us anxious for our eternal home with Him. As believers, one day, we will see our Heavenly Father and His Son, face to face in the fullness of their eternal glory. Then this life, its questions and disappointments, will make sense yet will no longer matter. *"¹²For now we see in a mirror, dimly, but then face to face. Now I know in part, but then I shall know just as I also am known." (1 Corinthians 13.12)* Thank you Heavenly Father for the promise that we have of one day seeing You face to face in all of Your glory. *"But as it is written: 'Eye has not seen, nor ear heard, nor have entered into the heart of man the things which God has prepared for those who love Him.'" (1 Corinthians 2.9)*

Daniel 7.15–20

Verse 15- "I, Daniel, was grieved in my spirit within my body, and the visions of my head troubled me.

Seeing the Son of Man and the Ancient of Days did not trouble Daniel. Rather, Daniel's distress resulted from his uncertainty regarding the significance of the beasts, specifically the last beast and the little horn. Though Daniel did not fully comprehend the symbolic meaning of the beasts, he understood that they were of grave importance, which is why, as described in the verses that follow, he sought to know the interpretation of the vision.

Verse 16- "I came near to one of those who stood by, and asked him the truth of all this. So he told me and made known to me the interpretation of these things:

Daniel approached someone standing nearby, apparently within the vision itself, and implored the meaning of the things he observed. It is a possibility that Daniel understood some of the vision since God had instilled in him the gift of interpretation and understanding. *"As for these four young men, God gave them knowledge and skill in all literature and wisdom; and Daniel had understanding in all visions and dreams." (Daniel 1.17)* Regardless, Daniel refrained from relying upon his own judgment because he hungered for God's truth by way of this "one who stood by." Daniel desired truth and wisdom, so all was made known to him.

Verse 17- 'Those great beasts, which are four, are four kings which arise out of the earth.

This vision, given to Daniel, and consequently to us, was disclosed in "capsule" form, meaning that a large amount of information appeared in a condensed presentation. The being that Daniel approached explained that these beasts represented four great kings or kingdoms that would emerge from within the earth.

Of the many varied interpretations available, and within the context and relevance of the other events recorded by Daniel, these beasts seem to correlate most closely with the same four kingdoms presented in Nebuchadnezzar's dreams and visions, and they parallel the governmental system types that these kingdoms exemplified. From that point of reference, the next two verses depict a panorama of the entire time span from the start of the Babylonian Empire to the return of the Lord Jesus Christ as King of kings.

The golden head in the image of Nebuchadnezzar's dream and the lion-like beast with eagle wings in Daniel's vision represent the first type of governmental system, the absolute monarchy of the Babylonian Empire. The silver breast and arms of Nebuchadnezzar's image and the bear-like beast in Daniel's vision represent the second form of government instituted by the Medo-Persian Empire. In addition, many historians conclude that the three ribs clenched between the bear's teeth represent the kingdoms that had been devoured by the Medes and Persians—Babylon, Egypt, and Lydia.[7] The brass thigh in the image of Nebuchadnezzar's dream and the leopard-like beast in Daniel's vision represent the third type of government system of the Greco-Macedonian Empire. The four heads of this beast likely signify the four kingdoms into which the Greco-Macedonian Empire was eventually separated—Greece, Macedonia, Syria, and Egypt. After Alexander the Great's death, the kingdom was divided between four contending successors—Lysimachus, Cassander, Seleucus, and Ptolemy.[8] The iron and clay feet of the image in Nebuchadnezzar's dream and the final, dreadful, iron-toothed beast in Daniel's vision represent a futuristic empire that has yet to occur.

Though many arguments may be developed regarding the similarities of these visions, at least one major difference between these accounts exists. The image in Nebuchadnezzar's dream illustrates the sequential deterioration of these forms of authoritative power from a human perspective. However, the vision given to Daniel apparently reveals God's view of this dilution of power because each beast seemed to lessen in power and grace but increase in grotesqueness and abnormality from the one before it.

Verse 18- 'But the saints of the Most High shall receive the kingdom, and possess the kingdom forever, even forever and ever.'

The saints, those throughout the ages who are redeemed through the atonement of Jesus Christ and faith in Almighty God, "the Most High," will inherit the final kingdom, which is the eternal, heavenly kingdom of God. What a great promise that we are given in this verse: the assurance of every believers' inheritance of God's everlasting kingdom, a world without end.

Verse 19- "Then I wished to know the truth about the fourth beast, which was different from all the others, exceedingly dreadful, with its teeth of iron and its nails of bronze, which devoured, broke in pieces, and trampled the residue with its feet;

Having resolved the matter of the previous three beasts rather expediently and realizing that the significance of the vision relied more heavily upon the interpretation of the last beast than upon the first three, Daniel sought to understand the meaning of the fourth beast. This beast represents the fourth major kingdom of the world, the Roman Empire, which philosophically continues as a model for present-day governmental systems.

Verse 20- "and the ten horns that were on its head, and the other horn which came up, before which three fell, namely, that horn which had eyes and a mouth which spoke pompous words, whose appearance was greater than his fellows.

Ten horns protruded from the head of the fourth beast. Three of the ten horns fell when "the other," the little horn with the eyes of a man, arose. This resembles an account in Revelation that equates these ten horns with ten kings. *"The ten horns which you saw are ten kings who have received no kingdom as yet, but they receive authority for one hour as kings with the beast." (Revelation 17.12)* It is possible that these ten kings or kingdoms represent the division of the end-time world under ten primary global powers that will control the earth's population. This little horn spoke blasphemous things, had much influence with his words, and appeared greater than the other horns.

Notes/Applications

Despite knowing the depravity of mankind's ever-increasing wickedness, Daniel still grieved because he viewed the fate awaiting those who refuse to submit to Almighty God.

There are no new sins. *"That which has been is what will be, that which is done is what will be done, and there is nothing new under the sun."* *(Ecclesiastes 1.9)* However, due to technological advances, fulfillment of man's evil desires is more easily accessible today than in Daniel's day. The sinful desires innate in all of us are aroused at an earlier age by vulgar and violent images. People are no longer naïve about sin. They are simply callous about it and caustic toward those who preach against it.

It is easy to give up on people and to forget that they need a Savior. However, when our Lord and Savior Jesus Christ looked upon the crowd of people, compassion filled His heart, and he referred to them as *"sheep without a shepherd."* *(Matthew 9.36)* Are we also moved with compassion for lost sheep? How grieved are we by the moral, ethical, or spiritual deterioration of our world, nation, state, community, and home?

The multitudes around us near damnation in Hell. How much does this truth burden our hearts? Enough to pray for them and tell them about the Good Shepherd? Enough to abandon our sins and to live in a way that points them to the Savior?

Daniel 7.21–28

Verse 21- "I was watching; and the same horn was making war against the saints, and prevailing against them,

As Daniel's vision continued, the messenger specifically told him that the little horn would attack the saints and overpower them for a period of time. *"It was granted to him to make war with the saints and to overcome them. And authority was given him over every tribe, tongue, and nation." (Revelation 13.7)* Therefore, the description of this little horn confirms that this figure will be a prominent charismatic leader with worldwide appeal, as the antichrist discussed in greater detail in the book of The Revelation. This, however, does not necessitate that the little horn will have global power of a political nature, though he will have enormous influence over those who are in authority—those represented by the ten horns of the fourth beast.

Verse 22- "until the Ancient of Days came, and a judgment was made in favor of the saints of the Most High, and the time came for the saints to possess the kingdom.

In the previous verse, the saints were defeated by the little horn and depicted as victims, yet in this verse, the saints ruled as victorious conquerors because God's judgment had vindicated their suffering. This sudden and absolute turn of events did not come to pass due to an innovative military strategy of the saints but, as clearly explained by this verse, because of the judgment of God Almighty, the Ancient of Days, Who will ultimately give His saints possession of the earth. The eternal kingdom of God will manifest itself at that point with the reign of the Lord Jesus Christ.

Verse 23- "Thus he said: 'The fourth beast shall be a fourth kingdom on earth, which shall be different from all other kingdoms, and shall devour the whole earth, trample it and break it in pieces.

Again, we return to the interpretation of the fourth beast or the fourth kingdom, which differed from the preceding three beasts because it was much more dreadful and much more powerful.

This beast does not represent any king or kingdom that ruled during Daniel's lifetime, but one that will preside shortly before God allows His great and final judgment to fall upon the earth. The dominating power of this kingdom will emerge as a global figure that will influence all authorities of the world. This ruler will care for no one, will be loyal to no one, and will be honest with no one. He will be indwelled with and controlled by Satan. *"So they worshiped the dragon who gave authority to the beast; and they worshiped the beast, saying, 'Who is like the beast? Who is able to make war with him?'" (Revelation 13.4)*

Verse 24- The ten horns are ten kings who shall arise from this kingdom. And another shall rise after them; he shall be different from the first ones, and shall subdue three kings.

This verse, as with its parallel scripture in Revelation, confirms the notion that the ten horns of this beast represent ten kings. *"The ten horns which you saw are ten kings who have received no kingdom as yet, but they receive authority for one hour as kings with the beast." (Revelation 17.12)* These ten kings will obtain power, but from within their midst, another one will rise to power. This ruler will differ from the others because this ruler will exercise spiritual influence in addition to the secular, political power possessed by the ten kings.

Verse 25- He shall speak pompous words against the Most High, shall persecute the saints of the Most High, and shall intend to change times and law. Then the saints shall be given into his hand for a time and times and half a time.

The little horn will spout a terrible, heretical message. His words will flagrantly blaspheme God, but nevertheless, his eloquent, powerful delivery will influence many. His charisma will attract the multitudes to him, even though his anti-God campaign will ignite unspeakable abominations in the temple in Jerusalem. *"³Let no one deceive you by any means; for that Day will not come unless the falling away comes first, and the man of sin is revealed, the son of perdition, ⁴who opposes and exalts himself above all that is called God or that is worshiped, so that he sits as God in the temple of God, showing himself that he is God." (2 Thessalonians 2.3–4)*

Almighty God will allow the little horn to reign for a predetermined period of time, which is commonly believed to be three and a half years. *"And he was given a mouth speaking great things and blasphemies, and he was given authority to continue for forty-two months." (Revelation 13.5)* During that timeframe, this blasphemer will murder numerous saints through wars and executions in his efforts to rid the whole earth of godly people. He will also rebel against any established tradition, institution, or custom, and he will demand worship of his position and worldly accomplishments.

Verse 26- 'But the court shall be seated, and they shall take away his dominion, to consume and destroy it forever.

The "little horn" figure will seemingly control every facet of life because of the transcendent power he will possess. However, judgment is inevitable. The pronoun "they" in this verse seems to refer to the trinity of God, specifically the Father, Son, and Holy Spirit—the court of the perfect Judge in Whom rests the sole authority to bestow and withdraw worldly dominion according to His sovereignty. God will ultimately consume the little horn's power and destroy him. God's verdict will then stand final. Furthermore, this sequence of events will demonstrate to the world that the One Who creates and decides all things is not the little horn but is, in fact, the supreme and all-powerful God of creation.

Verse 27- Then the kingdom and dominion, and the greatness of the kingdoms under the whole heaven, shall be given to the people, the saints of the Most High. His kingdom is an everlasting kingdom, and all dominions shall serve and obey Him.'

God offers assurance that the awesome dominion of the kingdom of Heaven will be granted to His saints. After judging the little horn, God will present the earth to His faithful followers, and all creation will dwell under the perfect authority of Christ Jesus, the King of kings and Lord of lords.

Again, this kingdom bestowed upon the Son of Man is an ever-lasting dominion. As other verses confirm, Christ's reign over the earth will mark the end of time, as the world now exists, and will pre-cede the final judgment of mankind, which begins the new earth and the new heaven prepared by God as the eternal dwelling of all believers. *"Now I saw a new heaven and a new earth, for the first heaven and the first earth had passed away." (Revelation 21.1a) "And there shall be no more curse, but the throne of God and of the Lamb shall be in it, and His servants shall serve Him." (Revelation 22.3)*

Verse 28- "This is the end of the account. As for me, Daniel, my thoughts greatly troubled me, and my countenance changed; but I kept the matter in my heart."

Daniel concluded his account by conveying all that needed to be said on the matter. As he considered these things laid before him in the vision, Daniel's outward appearance changed because he felt burdened by knowing such momentous events. Daniel literally saw the devastation that awaited mankind. Nevertheless, he "kept the matters in his heart." He did not tell anyone about his vision or its interpretation.

Notes/Applications

Daniel had a panoramic view of the end of the world. He wit-nessed the turmoil that would befall mankind, but He also saw the glorious outcome. Fortunately, the persecution of God's people will only last for a time, and then every ruler and dominion will bow to the Most High. God's saints will finally unite with Him to abide for-ever in His heavenly kingdom.

God's kingdom has not ended in the past, nor will it begin some-time in the future. Just as God is infinite, His kingdom always has been and always will be. *"Your kingdom is an everlasting kingdom, and Your dominion endures throughout all generations." (Psalm 145.13)* God

Almighty ordains the beginning and ending of earthly rulers, so ultimately, all of creation will bow to the authority of its Creator. *"²⁷All the ends of the world shall remember and turn to the LORD, and all the families of the nations shall worship before You. ²⁸For the kingdom is the LORD's, and He rules over the nations."* (Psalm 22.27–28) As Absolute Ruler, God rules justly, so nothing, including persecution, that He allows to happen to His creation is without significance. *"Your throne, O God, is forever and ever; a scepter of righteousness is the scepter of Your kingdom."* (Psalm 45.6)

As a result of understanding Daniel's vision, we may grow uncomfortable in realizing the peril that may come upon us because we are children of God. However, we should also rest confidently in the knowledge that we worship the true, victorious God, who is the Most High. *"The LORD has established His throne in heaven, and His kingdom rules over all."* (Psalm 103.19)

Chapter Eight

Daniel 8.1–7

At the conclusion of chapter seven, Daniel changed his writings from Aramaic to Hebrew, his native language. This is an interesting note, considering the remainder of the chapters in the book of Daniel deal more specifically with his people, the nation of Israel.

Verse 1- In the third year of the reign of King Belshazzar a vision appeared to me—to me, Daniel—after the one that appeared to me the first time.

Belshazzar, as we studied in chapter five, ruled over the city of Babylon for about fourteen years under the authority granted to him by Nabonidus, the king of the Babylonian Empire. This chapter presents a prophecy that further describes the rise of the Medo-Persian and Greco-Macedonian Empires, which eventually succeeded the Babylonian Empire. Daniel recorded this as his second vision, which occurred around 552–551 BC in the third year of Belshazzar's reign, two years after the vision recorded in chapter seven.

Verse 2- I saw in the vision, and it so happened while I was look-ing, that I was in Shushan, the citadel, which is in the province of Elam; and I saw in the vision that I was by the River Ulai.

Daniel's vision revealed that the capital city would be moved from Babylon to Shushan, one of the Babylonian Empire's major cit-ies after the rise of the Medo-Persian Empire. Daniel saw himself in the palace at Shushan when he received this vision. This city was located in the province of Elam by the River Ulai. The dream appears to be prophetic in nature; therefore, we may conclude that Daniel was probably unfamiliar with the palace mentioned in this verse.[1]

Verse 3- Then I lifted my eyes and saw, and there, standing beside the river, was a ram which had two horns, and the two horns were high; but one was higher than the other, and the higher one came up last.

Daniel looked up and beheld a ram by the river. Two horns were perched upon the ram's head, and the second horn eventually grew to be taller than the first, thereby defying normal expectations.

Verse 4- I saw the ram pushing westward, northward, and south-ward, so that no animal could withstand him; nor was there any that could deliver from his hand, but he did according to his will and became great.

The ram moved away from his position by the River Ulai in west-ward, northward, and southward directions, trampling every other beast in his path. No animals could successfully oppose the ram's campaign or hinder his capacity to subjugate any territory that he desired.

Later verses more specifically discuss the interpretation of this vision. However, for the purpose of clarifying details that appear in this verse and not within the subsequent interpretation, it is impor-tant to preface the vision's interpretation and mention that this ram symbolizes the Medo-Persian Empire. *"The ram which you saw, having the two horns—they are the kings of Media and Persia." (Revelation 8.20)*

This segment of Daniel's vision historically corresponds with the military excursions of Cyrus, King of Persia (represented by the larger of the two horns), whose conquered territories extended "westward" into Babylon, Syria, and Asia; "northward" into Albania, Armenia, and Iberia; and "southward" into Arabia, Ethiopia, and Egypt.[2] Therefore, the animals mentioned in this verse evidently represent the territories conquered by King Cyrus.

Verse 5- And as I was considering, suddenly a male goat came from the west, across the surface of the whole earth, without touching the ground; and the goat had a notable horn between his eyes.

Daniel reflected upon his vision to this point. As he pondered, something else unfolded in the vision. A male goat with a sizable horn between its eyes approached from the west. In describing the great speed and power with which the goat advanced, Daniel noted that the goat did not touch the ground.

Verse 6- Then he came to the ram that had two horns, which I had seen standing beside the river, and ran at him with furious power.

Charging with fierce power, the goat swiftly overtook the ram. The ram, probably unaware and defenseless while preoccupied at its drinking spot, grew complacent in its authoritative power.

Verse 7- And I saw him confronting the ram; he was moved with rage against him, attacked the ram, and broke his two horns. There was no power in the ram to withstand him, but he cast him down to the ground and trampled him; and there was no one that could deliver the ram from his hand.

The raging male goat quickly attacked the ram and broke its horns. Since a ram's protection depends upon the strength of its horns, their absence rendered this ram defenseless. The goat then tossed the ram to the ground and crushed it. As this verse indicates, no person or group of persons could aid or rescue the ram because of the goat's overpowering strength and speed.

Notes/Applications

Comparable to the goat in this passage, Satan seeks to kill and to destroy us, both physically and spiritually, and he preys upon the areas in which we are most vulnerable. *"Be sober, be vigilant; because your adversary the devil walks about like a roaring lion, seeking whom he may devour." (1 Peter 5.8)*

What do we rely upon as our primary defense weapon against his attacks? If we rely upon our own strength to overcome him, we will certainly meet defeat. Therefore, we must daily arm ourselves with prayer and Bible study to prepare for the spiritual battles before us:

> [13]*Therefore take up the whole armor of God, that you may be able to withstand in the evil day, and having done all, to stand.* [14]*Stand therefore, having girded your waist with truth, having put on the breastplate of righteousness,* [15]*and having shod your feet with the preparation of the gospel of peace;* [16]*above all, taking the shield of faith with which you will be able to quench all the fiery darts of the wicked one.* [17]*And take the helmet of salvation, and the sword of the Spirit, which is the word of God;* [18]*praying always with all prayer and supplication in the Spirit, being watchful to this end with all perseverance and supplication for all the saints. (Ephesians 6.13–18)*

We must recognize that we are involved in spiritual warfare and that Satan desires to ruin our Christian influence upon others. However, we do not have to fight this battle alone. We can firmly stand knowing we may suffer external injury, but nothing can rob the victory from us. *"But thanks be to God, who gives us the victory through our Lord Jesus Christ." (1 Corinthians 15.57)* Are we prepared daily for the battle before us? Through our Lord Jesus Christ, the source of our strength, we are more than conquerors. *"[7]The LORD is my strength and my shield; my heart trusted in Him, and I am helped; therefore my heart greatly rejoices, and with my song I will praise Him. [8]The LORD is their strength, and He is the saving refuge of His anointed." (Psalm 28.7–8)*

Daniel 8.8–14

Verse 8- Therefore the male goat grew very great; but when he became strong, the large horn was broken, and in place of it four notable ones came up toward the four winds of heaven.

The goat attained military power. Its horn was destroyed, but four more replaced it. The description of these horns rising "toward the four winds of heaven" probably refers to the four main directions of the earth, describing a territory that exceeded the ram's victories, whose conquests stretched only "westward, northward, and south-ward." Apparently, the four horns arose after the large horn expanded the prosperity of the male goat.

Verse 9- And out of one of them came a little horn which grew exceedingly great toward the south, toward the east, and toward the Glorious Land.

The horn mentioned in this verse is not described as little to sug-gest insignificance. Rather, this description simply compares its power to that of the "large horn" that preceded it. Even so, this little horn proved to have a vast dominion that reached toward the south and east and, more relevantly, into the "Glorious Land," the land of Israel, which God had prepared for the habitation of His people.

As in chapter seven, this verse speaks of the rise of a "little horn" among the other horns. However, this little horn does not represent the same figure as the little horn mentioned in the previous chapter. How do we know this to be true? Notice that this horn arose from among four horns, not ten. Furthermore, we can ascertain that the prophecies of this vision and Daniel's first vision refer to different time periods. Both little horns, however, have proven and will prove to be extremely hostile toward the children of God.

Verse 10- And it grew up to the host of heaven; and it cast down some of the host and some of the stars to the ground, and trampled them.

This little horn achieved greatness. The word host in this verse comes from the Hebrew word *tsaba*, which means "a mass of persons, especially organized for war."[3] With this in mind, this verse most likely depicts the brutal persecution that this little horn would inflict upon the Jews, God's people, called "the host of heaven." It does not stand to reason that this *host* signifies angels, as some expositors have suggested, for the interpretation of this prophecy, which is given in later verses, discusses an actual, physical series of events versus a spiritual one, except in the sense of the spiritual refinement that takes place as a result of persecution.[4]

Verse 11- He even exalted himself as high as the Prince of the host; and by him the daily sacrifices were taken away, and the place of His sanctuary was cast down.

The little horn would magnify himself as God, would seize control over the holy temple in Jerusalem, and would then forbid the daily sacrifices that took place there. By these actions, he would prohibit the Jews from practicing the religious ordinances that distinguished them from the heathen, and he would also cleverly coerce their allegiance to him.

Verse 12- Because of transgression, an army was given over to the horn to oppose the daily sacrifices; and he cast truth down to the ground. He did all this and prospered.

The truth was cast down and ungodliness prevailed as the little horn was permitted to continue his horrible acts against God's people. Furthermore, he was given "an army" to enforce these policies that forbade the Jews from worshipping in the temple, and instead, he mandated its desecration. Considering the list of atrocities committed by this little horn, perhaps most disturbing is the last statement: "He did all this *and prospered.*" What a horrifying thought were it not for the providential hand of God over all things!

Verse 13- Then I heard a holy one speaking; and another holy one said to that certain one who was speaking, "How long will the vision be, concerning the daily sacrifices and the transgression of desolation, the giving of both the sanctuary and the host to be trampled under foot?"

In Daniel's vision, apparently several others, referred to as *holy ones,* witnessed the events taking place. The phrase *holy ones* does not necessarily identify these beings as angels, though this seems to be the most likely case. Daniel heard one of these beings question how long the dreadful reign of the little horn would last. In other words, this holy one wanted to know the duration of the temple's desecration and the persecution of the Jews by the little horn.

Verse 14- And he said to me, "For two thousand three hundred days; then the sanctuary shall be cleansed."

The holy one rendered an answer—2300 days. Though some scholars have interpreted the 2300 days in this verse as 2300 years, meaning a week of years rather than a week of days *(see commentary on Daniel 9.24),* the accurate translation of the time period indicated in this verse is a twenty-four hour day.[5] This conclusion is supported by the fulfillment of this prophecy in verse twenty-six of this chapter, which renders these days as "evening and mornings." Therefore, the "transgression of desolation" described in verse thirteen would last for 2300 days or 6.3 years.

Notes/Applications

In Daniel's second vision, the evil ruler prohibited people from worshipping God Almighty. It is difficult to understand why God would allow the desolation of His temple and the persecution of His servants to occur.

Why does a good God allow bad things to happen to "good" people? This is a natural, timeless question that has universally stumped every person at one time or another. However, there is a fallacy in this question. This question is unanswerable because our finite, imperfect minds can never fully understand all of God's ways. *"'You asked, "Who is this who hides counsel without knowledge?" Therefore I have uttered what I did not understand, things too wonderful for me, which I did not know.'"* *(Job 42.3)* Rather than focusing on the "why," we must focus on the "Who." It is important to understand, as fully as possible, Who God is, which begins by recognizing that God is both sovereign and good.

The sovereignty of God refers to His supremacy. God is the Potter, the Creator, and we are the clay, the creation that he lovingly molds. Whether we accept or reject God's supremacy does not alter His position as the Most High. God is sovereign, so He does not need a reason for doing anything that He chooses to do because all of His actions are, by His very nature, perfect.

Almighty God, in His goodness, coupled with His great love for us and His great hatred for sin, allows and even causes affliction to happen, even to His very own if that will further mold them into His image. Many situations that appear to be dreadful are actually God's hand working in our spiritual, physical, and emotional best interest. In his book, *The Attributes of God,* A.W. Tozer, author and twentieth century theologian, simply yet accurately describes our Lord's goodness in simple, human terms:

> *When I say that God is good, that God has a kind heart, I mean that He has a heart infinitely kind and that there is no boundary to it...God is not only infinitely good, He is perfectly good. God is never partway anything...If you don't feel that way about it, it's unbelief that makes you feel otherwise; it's preoccupation with this world. If you would believe God you would know this to be true.* [6]

Since we can never fully comprehend or define the perfect sovereignty or goodness of Almighty God, our Christian growth comes in learning to praise the Lord simply because of Who He is and to trust in His constant goodness. *"But now, O LORD, You are our Father; we are the clay, and You our potter; and all we are the work of Your hand."* (Isaiah 64.8) Has unbelief clouded our focus upon and acceptance of God's sovereign control and perfect goodness? Are we willing to accept both triumphs and trials as blessings from God?

Daniel 8.15–22

Verse 15- Then it happened, when I, Daniel, had seen the vision and was seeking the meaning, that suddenly there stood before me one having the appearance of a man.

By man's standards, Daniel's abilities qualified him as an expert dream and vision interpreter. However, Daniel sought his answers from all-knowing God. When Daniel searched, God responded by sending a messenger. It was not a man but, as stated in the verse, "the *appearance* of a man." Through this being, God revealed to Daniel the interpretation of this prophetic vision, just as Daniel had previously made known the interpretation of others' visions and dreams.

Verse 16- And I heard a man's voice between the banks of the Ulai, who called, and said, "Gabriel, make this man understand the vision."

A voice called to this man and identified him as Gabriel, whose name means "man of God."[7] Other biblical accounts describe later episodes when Gabriel was again sent to Daniel to interpret the prophecy of the seventy weeks *(Daniel 9)*, to Jerusalem to announce the birth of John the Baptist to Zacharias *(Luke 1.19)*, and also to Nazareth to announce to the Virgin Mary that she would give birth to the Messiah *(Luke 1.26)*.

However, in this verse, Daniel was by the River Ulai when he heard a man's voice sounding from between the banks of the river. This was not the voice of the one described in the previous verse as having the "appearance of a man." The voice instructed Gabriel to tell Daniel the interpretation of the vision in its entirety, so the voice apparently came from the very mouth of God, He Who has command over all of the angels.[8]

Verse 17- So he came near where I stood, and when he came I was afraid and fell on my face; but he said to me, "Understand, son of man, that the vision refers to the time of the end."

Gabriel then moved closer to Daniel, and as he did, Daniel fell prostrate in fear before him. The angel preempted a detailed interpretation of the vision by explaining that it concerned the "time of the end." How this phrase is interpreted depends upon how the vision as a whole is interpreted. A few expositors contend that this refers to the end of the world and the time of the final antichrist.[9] Most scholars, however, agree that the "end" here refers to the promised completion of the 2300 days, explained in verse fourteen, that conclude the "transgression of desolation" and to which this entire vision relates.[10] The latter interpretation is more easily defendable, as further explained in verse nineteen.

Verse 18- Now, as he was speaking with me, I was in a deep sleep with my face to the ground; but he touched me, and stood me upright.

While Daniel laid face down on the ground, he fell into a deep sleep. He did not slumber due to boredom but from physical and emotional exhaustion. Then, Gabriel touched Daniel, lifted him upright, and restored his consciousness.

Verse 19- And he said, "Look, I am making known to you what shall happen in the latter time of the indignation; for at the appointed time the end shall be.

Gabriel announced that he would proclaim the meaning of the vision, and surely, Daniel yearned to understand the mystery. Perhaps, he realized the urgency and magnitude of this vision. Gabriel assured Daniel that there was indeed an "appointed time [for] the end" of the persecution inflicted upon the Jews by the little horn.

Verse 20- "The ram which you saw, having the two horns—they are the kings of Media and Persia.

Gabriel first explained the symbolic meaning of the ram and its two horns. Darius ruled as the king of Media, and Cyrus ruled as the king of Persia. Though rising to prominence shortly after the Median dominion and ultimately ruling concurrently with it, Cyrus the Persian, would prove to be the greater of the two powers. Therefore, in Daniel's vision, the larger horn that came up after the smaller horn symbolizes Cyrus. The ram in the vision represents the union of these two kingdoms into the Medo-Persian Empire, which was depicted as the silver portion of the image in Nebuchadnezzar's first dream *(Daniel 2.39)* and the bear-like beast in Daniel's first vision *(Daniel 7.5)*.

Verse 21- "And the male goat is the kingdom of Greece. The large horn that is between its eyes is the first king.

The male goat represents the Greco-Macedonian Empire, and the horn between its eyes symbolizes the first king of that empire. This king and kingdom correspond with the bronze portion of the image in Nebuchadnezzar's first dream *(Daniel 2.39)* and with the four-winged, four-headed leopard in Daniel's first recorded vision *(Daniel 7.6)*. Most scholars conclude that the large horn on this goat represents Alexander the Great, a very distinguished world leader that ascended to power and devised swift military conquests.[11]

Verse 22- "As for the broken horn and the four that stood up in its place, four kingdoms shall arise out of that nation, but not with its power.

The breaking of the horn describes the downfall of Alexander, who died in 323 BC at only thirty-three years of age at the height of his power and conquest.[12]

Gabriel foretold the events surrounding the division of Alexander's kingdom into four parts. Where there had once been a single king leading a single kingdom, there would now be four kings and four separate kingdoms. Historically, these four horns represent the following kings and kingdoms that succeeded Alexander:[13]
- Ptolemy (Egypt in the south)
- Seleucus (Syria in the east)
- Cassander (Macedonia in the northwest)
- Lysimachus (Asia Minor in the northeast)

None of these kings ever received the notoriety for conquering as many nations as Alexander the Great, and none of their kingdoms ever prospered as Alexander's kingdom did.

Notes/Applications

Josephus, the renowned first century historian, discusses in his book, *Antiquities of the Jews,* Alexander the Great's reaction to the prophecies written in the book of Daniel. According to Josephus, Alexander sent orders to Jaddua, the high priest in Jerusalem, offering the priest his allegiance as well as supplies for the Persian armies. Jaddua, however, refused Alexander's aid because, as a priest, his loyalty belonged to the Persian king. Infuriated, Alexander then decided to march into Jerusalem himself. Despite the Jews' surmounting fear as Alexander and his army approached the city, the high priests of Jerusalem dressed in their priestly robes and garments, threw open the city gates, and prepared to meet Alexander the Great face to face, as God, through a dream, had directed Jaddua to do.

When Alexander arrived in Jerusalem, however, he refused to allow any harm to come upon the people because he also had a dream in which he had seen these priests dressed identically to what they now wore. As a result, Alexander offered sacrifices to Almighty God, granted the Jews the right to enjoy the laws of their forefathers, and left their city unharmed.[14] Because Jaddua the priest acted in faith by responding according to God's leading, even when these actions seemed contrary to human logic, God divinely intervened.

Do we desire God's divine intervention to transform our circumstances? Do we long to experience God in a unique way, unexplainable by human logic? When we respond to pressing situations in the manner that the Holy Spirit leads us, God will intervene. He generally responds to our cries by changing the situation, our perspective of it, or both. However, when we plan our own escape route according to our own way and timing, we will become entangled in a web of undesirable consequences.

Most of us have allowed our circumstances to defeat us, and as a result, we do not think that we are daily experiencing God. However, God miraculously proves Himself every day, but to see God working in our lives, we must stop dwelling upon the circumstances and redirect our attention upon the One who commands the circumstances. *"But my eyes are upon You, O GOD the Lord; in You I take refuge; do not leave my soul destitute." (Psalm 141.8)*

Daniel 8.23–27

Verse 23- "And in the latter time of their kingdom, when the trans-gressors have reached their fullness, a king shall arise, having fierce features, who understands sinister schemes.

Some expositors explain the phrase "when the transgressors have reached their fullness" as a reference to the apostate Jews who had forsaken their faith and embraced the manners of the heathen during the reign of Alexander and his four successors.[15] After these four generals ruled for some time, a new king emerged—a vicious, greedy king who stubbornly disregarded Almighty God. Aside from his imposing demeanor, this king possessed great power with which he carried out his "sinister schemes."

As we have already studied, the goat in this chapter symbolizes the Greco-Macedonian Empire, whose kingdom, though in the future at the time Daniel had this vision, has long since ceased. Therefore, this little horn does not symbolize the end-times antichrist figure that is also depicted as a little horn in the previous chapter. The little horn in this chapter most likely represents Antiochus IV, also called Antiochus Epiphanes, the notoriously wicked king of the Seleucus dynasty in Syria.[16]

Antiochus Epiphanes was the son of Antiochus III the Great, ruler over Syria from 176 BC to 164 BC. The younger Antiochus proved to be brutally tyrannical, one of the most bloodthirsty enemies of the Jewish Nation. He called himself Antiochus the Illustrious, though others considered him to be a madman. In his youth, his father surrendered him as a hostage to the Romans, but he was eventually recaptured by his brother, Seleucus IV, who reigned as leader at the time and who sent his own son as Antiochus' replacement. Later that same year, Seleucus IV was murdered, so Antiochus Epiphanes seized the throne. When his sister Cleopatra, queen of Egypt, died, Antiochus laid claim to Palestine and battled against Egypt, and it was during this war against the Egyptians that he perpetrated unspeakable cruelties against the Jews, as prophesied in later verses.[17]

Verse 24- His power shall be mighty, but not by his own power; he shall destroy fearfully, and shall prosper and thrive; he shall destroy the mighty, and also the holy people.

Satan controlled this king. Antiochus singled-out and destroyed those who posed a threat to his plans. In other words, he did not kill simply for the sake of killing. He had an agenda. He targeted specific people: "the mighty," who were the politically motivated; "the holy people," who were the spiritually motivated; and any other people groups that opposed him. God allowed this man of unspeakable wickedness to prosper in his endeavors until His sovereign will was accomplished in this empire.

Verse 25- "Through his cunning he shall cause deceit to prosper under his rule; and he shall exalt himself in his heart. He shall destroy many in their prosperity. He shall even rise against the Prince of princes; but he shall be broken without human means.

Deception flourished under this man's administration. He exalted himself in his own prideful heart. This man rebelled against the high priest in God's holy temple, against God's chosen people, and even against the "Prince of princes," God Almighty Himself.[18]

Many of those that Antiochus killed were slain "in their prosperity," meaning they lived under a false pretense of peace, which seems to typify a ploy of the spirit of antichrist both in this leader and in the end-times figure. We see an example of this deception when Antiochus acquired Syria from his nephew under the pretense of uniting their forces to fortify a defense against their common enemies.[19]

As foretold in this verse, Antiochus' death was obviously dictated by an act of God. Antiochus marched into Persia and robbed the temple at Elymais and was finally driven away by a tumultuous resistance. He then received news of the defeat of his armies against the Jews and of the restoration of their temple services. The emotional quandary in which he found himself quickly took its toll on his physical health, and he died shortly thereafter, which prompted the belief that the cause of his death was directly related to Antiochus' unmerciful atrocities against the Jews and to his blatant irreverence for Almighty God.[20]

According to Josephus, the Jewish temple was then cleansed, and the sacrifice ritual was reinstated on the twenty-fifth day of the ninth month in the one hundred forty-eighth year of Seleucus.[21] Therefore, the calculation of the duration of Antiochus IV's desecration of the temple until it was restored and proper sacrifices reconvened was exactly 2300 days, which corresponds with the prophesy in verse fourteen. This also confirms that this little horn personified Antiochus and not the future antichrist figure discussed in Revelation and other scriptures, though strong similarities clearly exist between the two types of antichrist.

Verse 26- "And the vision of the evenings and mornings which was told is true; therefore seal up the vision, for it refers to many days in the future."

Gabriel concluded by stating that this vision was prophetic, true, and unalterable. It was also specific about the duration of these events lasting 2300 days. Now that the vision and its interpretation were unveiled, Gabriel told Daniel to "seal up" or conceal this message since the events of the prophecy were still many years away.

Verse 27- And I, Daniel, fainted and was sick for days; afterward I arose and went about the king's business. I was astonished by the vision, but no one understood it.

Evidently, Daniel retained some official capacity in the Babylonian court after the death of Nebuchadnezzar. Daniel was so intensely disturbed by the ramifications of this vision that he fell ill for several days. Nevertheless, after a short while, he regained his strength and returned to his routine. The vision, however, remained emblazoned in his mind and in his thoughts. Apparently, others noticed Daniel's bewilderment, but since he was told to conceal the vision, he was forbidden to share the matter with anyone. The phrase "no one understood it" likely refers to other people's inability to comprehend why Daniel behaved so strangely, yet several scholars argue that this phrase relates to others' inability to make sense of the vision itself.[22] However, the rendering of the latter meaning seems improbable since believing that such is the case requires us to conclude that Daniel did not conceal the matter as he had been instructed, which does not appear to be consistent with what we have already learned about Daniel's unimpeachable character.

Notes/Applications

At the completion of this vision, Gabriel, God's messenger, told Daniel two things. First, Gabriel emphasized that the vision was true and unalterable, and second, he admonished Daniel to seal the vision along with Daniel's other writings until a later time. The idea that the vision was unalterable reaffirms that God does not merely react to mankind. His pre-designed master plan will be accomplished without any deviation, regardless of the seemingly reckless actions of His creation. However, God's instruction for Daniel to seal up the message required action on Daniel's part and proved that God employs His creation in accomplishing His will. Although Daniel lacked detailed understanding of the vision's interpretation, he still obediently followed the angel's instructions.

What excuse do we have for disobeying the voice of our God? We either have not learned how to discern His voice, or we have chosen to disobey it. We contend that if God would only send His message to us via an angel, as He did with Daniel, we, too, would obey Him. However, God reveals His instructions to us in a myriad of ways. God speaks to us through His Holy Word, yet we neglect to study it. God speaks to us through others, such as godly ministers and teachers, yet we ignore their counsel. *"Therefore you shall obey the voice of the LORD your God, and observe His commandments and His statutes which I command you today.'"* (Deuteronomy 27.10)

God expects our obedience even though He rarely divulges comprehension of His plan. Nevertheless, our lack of full understanding does not nullify our responsibility to obey. God speaks, but we must begin to listen and to obey:

> [11]*Then He said, 'Go out, and stand on the mountain before the LORD.' And behold, the LORD passed by, and a great and strong wind tore into the mountains and broke the rocks in pieces before the LORD, but the LORD was not in the wind; and after the wind an earthquake, but the LORD was not in the earthquake;* [12]*and after the earthquake a fire, but the LORD was not in the fire; and after the fire a still small voice. (1 Kings 19.11–12)*

Are we intimately familiar with the manner in which God speaks to us? Do we easily recognize His voice? Do we readily obey God despite uncertainty concerning His plan?

Chapter Nine

Daniel 9.1–7

Verses 1, 2- *[1]In the first year of Darius the son of Ahasuerus, of the lineage of the Medes, who was made king over the realm of the Chaldeans—[2]in the first year of his reign I, Daniel, understood by the books the number of the years specified by the word of the LORD through Jeremiah the prophet, that He would accomplish seventy years in the desolations of Jerusalem.*

During the sixty-eighth year of the Jewish captivity, approximately 538 BC, Darius, the son of Ahasuerus the Mede, was appointed as ruler of Babylon by Cyrus the Persian.[1] Darius presided over the "realm of Chaldeans" or the immediate region of Babylonia, which included the captive Israelites.

In the first year of Darius' reign, Daniel, who had familiarized himself with the writings of his contemporaries, concluded through the prophecies of Jeremiah that the Jewish people were to remain captives for seventy years. The Jews had disobeyed God's laws given to them through the prophet Moses concerning reverence for God's Sabbath. *"[11]'And this whole land shall be a desolation and an astonishment, and these nations shall serve the king of Babylon seventy years. [12]Then it will come to pass, when seventy years are completed, that I will punish the king of Babylon and that nation, the land of the Chaldeans, for their iniquity,' says the LORD; 'and I will make it a perpetual desolation.'" (Jeremiah 25.11–12)* God required the Hebrew nation to observe a time of rest for the land every seven years:

[3]'Six years you shall sow your field, and six years you shall prune your vineyard, and gather its fruit; [4]but in the seventh year there shall be a sabbath of solemn rest for the land, a sabbath to the LORD. You shall neither sow your field nor prune your vineyard. [5]What grows of its own accord of your harvest you shall not reap, nor gather the grapes of your untended vine, for it is a year of rest for the land.' (Leviticus 25.3–5)

If this were not observed, God would still ensure the observation of His Sabbath by sending His people into captivity, thereby allowing, by His intervention, the land to rest. *"[33]'I will scatter you among the nations and draw out a sword after you; your land shall be desolate and your cities waste. [34]Then the land shall enjoy its sabbaths as long as it lies desolate and you are in your enemies' land; then the land shall rest and enjoy its sabbaths. [35]As long as it lies desolate it shall rest—for the time it did not rest on your sabbaths when you dwelt in it.'" (Leviticus 26.33–34)*

However, the disobedient people did not observe the Sabbath for the land. Consequently, God's judgment fell upon them, and they were taken captive by the Babylonians:

[8]'Therefore thus says the LORD of hosts: "Because you have not heard My words, [9]behold, I will send and take all the families of the north," says the LORD, "and Nebuchadnezzar the king of Babylon, My servant, and will bring them against this land, against its inhabitants, and against these nations all around, and will utterly destroy them, and make them an astonishment, a hissing, and perpetual desolations. [10]Moreover I will take from them the voice of mirth and the voice of gladness, the voice of the bridegroom and the voice of the bride, the sound of the millstones and the light of the lamp. [11]And this whole land shall be a desolation and an astonishment, and

*these nations shall serve the king of Babylon seventy years.'" (Jere-
miah 25.8–11)*

**Verse 3- Then I set my face toward the Lord God to make request
by prayer and supplications, with fasting, sackcloth, and ashes.**

Daniel committed himself to interceding on behalf of his nation.
He turned his face "toward the Lord God," perhaps as he knelt at his
window facing Jerusalem. Daniel fervently sought the Lord without
false pretense or wrongful motivation. He wore sackcloth, which was
usually made of dark and generally shapeless goat's hair.[2] Daniel was
a man of high political stature who generally wore royal robes, so this
gesture demonstrated his deep sorrow and repentance for his own
sins and for those of his people. It outwardly expressed his inward
earnestness and utter humility before Holy God.

**Verse 4- And I prayed to the LORD my God, and made confession,
and said, "O Lord, great and awesome God, who keeps His covenant and mercy with those who love Him, and with those who keep
His commandments,**

As preparation to meet God, Daniel cast aside all of his worldly
concerns. Although Daniel's daily, personal relationship with God
was unencumbered, he took extra measures for an intimate and
uninterrupted communion with the Heavenly Father. After preparing
himself to approach God, Daniel prayed fervently.

Daniel first confessed his own iniquities. Before he asked God for
anything, he praised God for Who He is—the "great and awesome
God"—and then for what He does—"keeps His covenant."

DIG DEEPER: *MERCY*

Daniel acknowledged the Lord as One Who is merciful toward those who love Him and keep His commandments. Mercy is compassionate leniency that is demonstrated toward some undeserving person. Although no one deserves the love and compassion of a holy and perfect God, the Lord abundantly bestows His mercies upon His children. *(Ephesians 2.4–5; 1 Peter 1.3; Psalm 25.6–10; Psalm 89)*

Verse 5- "we have sinned and committed iniquity, we have done wickedly and rebelled, even by departing from Your precepts and Your judgments.

In Daniel's confession, he admitted first and foremost that *we* have sinned, thereby including himself among the transgressors. Despite his close relationship with God, he still counted himself as a sinner in need of forgiveness. Daniel said, "We have done wickedly and rebelled," acknowledging that they, the Israelites, had turned away from God's principles.

Verse 6- "Neither have we heeded Your servants the prophets, who spoke in Your name to our kings and our princes, to our fathers and all the people of the land.

Daniel confessed further acts of disobedience. He admitted that the Israelites, God's chosen people, had not listened to God's servants, the prophets. The Lord spoke directly to His people through these men and had forewarned their kings, princes, fathers, and elders of His judgment. However, the Israelites stubbornly disregarded and rejected the things that they did not want to hear.

Verse 7- "O Lord, righteousness belongs to You, but to us shame of face, as it is this day—to the men of Judah, to the inhabitants of Jerusalem and all Israel, those near and those far off in all the countries to which You have driven them, because of the unfaithfulness which they have committed against You.

Daniel attributed righteousness to God alone. He contended that his people deserved their fateful captivity in a foreign land and the destruction of their homeland as judgment for their disobedience. They had all sinned and were guilty of willful disobedience, which was compounded by their unrepentant attitude.

Notes/Applications

Daniel fervently sought the Lord through prayer and fasting. He did not do this selfishly based upon his own desires, but after realizing the spiritual transgressions of his Israelite brethren, he petitioned God on the entire nation's behalf.

Fasting is a voluntary abstinence from food for one or more meals. Scriptural fasting, however, does not merely refrain from eating but replaces physical food with spiritual food, such as prayer and Bible study. Therefore, this abstinence from physical food must be a conscious, strategic effort made by a Christian for spiritual reasons. Physically, fasting cleanses an individual's blood, thereby allowing one's mind and body to function more healthily. Spiritually, fasting focuses one's attention upon God's will for his life.

The discipline of fasting is not a magic genie bottle that we, as Christians, rub in order to get our wishes fulfilled, for in God's eyes, an acceptable fast does not seek fulfillment of selfish desires:

> *3b'In fact, in the day of your fast you find pleasure, and exploit all your laborers. 4Indeed you fast for strife and debate, and to strike with the fist of wickedness. You will not fast as you do this day, to make your voice heard on high. 5Is it a fast that I have chosen, a day for a man to afflict his soul? Is it to bow down his head like a bulrush, and to spread out sackcloth and ashes? Would you call this a fast, and an acceptable day to the LORD?' (Isaiah 58.3b–5)*

The main purpose of an acceptable fast is to tune out the world and to tune into the voice of God. However, we may also fast in order to repent of our sins, to humble ourselves, to worship God, to intercede for others, to grieve a loss, to obtain power and deliverance, to seek God's guidance, and to petition for our needs. *"6'Is this not the fast*

that I have chosen: to loose the bonds of wickedness, to undo the heavy bur-
dens, to let the oppressed go free, and that you break every yoke? [7]Is it not to
share your bread with the hungry, and that you bring to your house the poor
who are cast out; when you see the naked, that you cover him, and not hide
yourself from your own flesh?'" (Isaiah 58.6–7)

A fast should be an intimate time between the individual
believer and Almighty God. Therefore, it should be conducted as pri-
vately as possible. We should not broadcast to everyone when we are
fasting. In truth, we are to do our best to conceal the fact that we are
fasting:

> [16]*'Moreover, when you fast, do not be like the hypocrites, with a sad*
> *countenance. For they disfigure their faces that they may appear to*
> *men to be fasting. Assuredly, I say to you, they have their reward.*
> [17]*But you, when you fast, anoint your head and wash your face, [18]so*
> *that you do not appear to men to be fasting, but to your Father who*
> *is in the secret place; and your Father who sees in secret will reward*
> *you openly.' (Matthew 6.16–18)*

God rewards those who seek Him for the right reasons. In
response to our fasting, God may choose to change our circumstances or to change us in the midst of them. Either way, He will
move miraculously in our lives and in the lives of those around us.

Daniel 9.8–14

Verse 8- "O Lord, to us belongs shame of face, to our kings, our princes, and our fathers, because we have sinned against You.

Daniel acted as a spokesman for the Israelites. He placed the blame for the spiritual condition of the Israelite nation upon his shoulders and upon the shoulders of his people. God does not move away from man; man moves away from God. Without exception, man is always at fault.

Daniel first repented on behalf of the kings because they were the leaders. Many times, as we have already studied, the kings' actions by way of decree or otherwise led the people either toward God or away from Him. Next, Daniel interceded for the princes and those in authority under the king, and he then included the sins of the elders and fathers of the land. Finally, the rest of the people received blame because not a single person, Daniel included, was without fault to some degree.

Verse 9- "To the Lord our God belong mercy and forgiveness, though we have rebelled against Him.

Daniel acknowledged that God's mercy and forgiveness are never depleted despite mankind's disobedience. He again included himself among the transgressors when he said, *"We* have rebelled against Him." Although the Jews rebelled, God was willing to forgive them if they sought His forgiveness.

Verse 10- "We have not obeyed the voice of the LORD our God, to walk in His laws, which He set before us by His servants the prophets.

The Jews disobeyed the voice of the Lord by not obeying His laws and by disregarding the forewarnings of the prophets, who were a direct mouthpiece of God. By his mention of these specific things, Daniel was admitting not to the passive disobedience of ignorance but to willful disobedience. God had given His laws directly to His people through their fellow man, and God had warned of judgment directly through their fellow man.

Verse 11- "Yes, all Israel has transgressed Your law, and has departed so as not to obey Your voice; therefore the curse and the oath written in the Law of Moses the servant of God have been poured out on us, because we have sinned against Him.

In addition to disobeying the Law given to Moses, the Israelites also turned away from God by attempting to leave Him out of their lives altogether:

> 'Alas, sinful nation, a people laden with iniquity, a brood of evildo-
> ers, children who are corrupters! They have forsaken the LORD, they
> have provoked to anger the Holy One of Israel, they have turned
> away backward.' (Isaiah 1.4) ⁵'Why has this people slidden back,
> Jerusalem, in a perpetual backsliding? They hold fast to deceit, they
> refuse to return. ⁶I listened and heard, but they do not speak aright.
> No man repented of his wickedness, saying, "What have I done?"
> Everyone turned to his own course, as the horse rushes into the bat-
> tle.' (Jeremiah 8.5–6)

They gave God no consideration whatsoever. They had departed from God's ways so far that they could no longer discern His voice or recognize His prophets. Therefore, the curse that had been poured out upon them was the seventy years of desolation or captivity as prophesized in the Law of Moses.

Verse 12- "And He has confirmed His words, which He spoke against us and against our judges who judged us, by bringing upon us a great disaster; for under the whole heaven such has never been done as what has been done to Jerusalem.

God kept His promise. "He spoke against" Israel and judged it with a curse of captivity. One of their transgressions, as already mentioned, was in not allowing the land to rest every seventh year. There were many ways the Jews turned their back on God, but this particular reason was singled out. Furthermore, Daniel said that no other nation had ever endured the hardships that were placed upon Israel because it, as a nation, had been given so much from God.

There are definite consequences for those who disobey God's laws and commandments. When God speaks against us, He judges us for our disobedience. His laws and standards are not subject to situational ethics or to individual interpretation. They are absolute and final.

Verse 13- "As it is written in the Law of Moses, all this disaster has come upon us; yet we have not made our prayer before the LORD our God, that we might turn from our iniquities and understand Your truth.

In the Law of Moses, God had outlined the physical and spiritual principles by which His people were to abide in order to live healthy and holy lives. The Israelites were, therefore, without excuse. Because they departed from God's ways and then refused to acknowledge their sinful condition, God disciplined them by allowing curses to befall them. Still, they did not repent. The Israelites, like a wayward child who willfully refuses to correct his behavior, rebelled more vehemently than before. The people had become so hard-hearted that they would not even pray to God their Father. If they had earnestly prayed and sought God's face, their sin would have been revealed to them, and they could have turned from their destructive and disobedient ways. However, Israel wallowed in her rebellion and, as a result, wandered further and further from God. God finally judged His people by ousting them from their homeland and transporting them to Babylon as captives.

Verse 14- "Therefore the LORD has kept the disaster in mind, and brought it upon us; for the LORD our God is righteous in all the works which He does, though we have not obeyed His voice.

God watched with great disappointment the evil disobedience of His people. Did God now hate the Israelites? No. God's disappointment and His displeasure are not synonymous with hate. In fact,

God's deep love for His people motivated His severe judgment of them.

Daniel admitted that the Israelites deserved the consequences they received since they had disobeyed God, thereby rejecting His love. Daniel further deemed this judgment from the Lord as both justifiable and "righteous." God is immovable. He is the same yesterday, today, and forever. It is mankind that refuses to listen to His voice and consequently strays from His guidance.

Notes/Applications

When Daniel prayed, he first confessed the sins of his people before he petitioned for God's mercy. Confession, acknowledgement of sin, should be a crucial ingredient in every believer's prayer life. However, true confession is not just saying apologetic words. The words must express a genuine remorse that is accompanied by an abandonment of sin.

To obtain everlasting life, we must embrace the naked truth about ourselves: We sin, and therefore, we are sinners in need of Christ's redemptive work on Calvary to bridge the gap between us, an imperfect people, and God, true perfection. *"9If we confess our sins, He is faithful and just to forgive us our sins and to cleanse us from all unrighteousness. 10If we say that we have not sinned, we make Him a liar, and His word is not in us." (1 John 1.9–10)* We must then accept, based upon a genuine conviction, Who Jesus Christ is, what He did, and what He promises to do. There is no doubt that confession is the first step to repentance, a turning from sin, and true repentance promotes transformation and restoration with Holy God:

> *10For godly sorrow produces repentance leading to salvation, not to be regretted; but the sorrow of the world produces death. 11For observe this very thing, that you sorrowed in a godly manner: what diligence it produced in you, what clearing of yourselves, what indignation, what fear, what vehement desire, what zeal, what vindication! In all things you proved yourselves to be clear in this matter.*
> *(2 Corinthians 7.10–11)*

Once we have entered into this relationship with God, through the threshold of His beloved Son the Lord Jesus Christ, we should commit ourselves to the spiritual discipline of regularly confessing our sins. This post-conversion confession does not resave us. The God Who draws us to salvation also keeps us. However, what perpetual confession does accomplish is a close fellowship with our Redeemer. It shows that we do not make excuses for our sinful actions but seek to walk closer with God. *"He who covers his sins will not prosper, but whoever confesses and forsakes them will have mercy."* *(Proverbs 28.13)* *"For You, Lord, are good, and ready to forgive, and abundant in mercy to all those who call upon You."* *(Psalm 86.5)*

Daniel 9.15–23

Verse 15- "And now, O Lord our God, who brought Your people out of the land of Egypt with a mighty hand, and made Yourself a name, as it is this day—we have sinned, we have done wickedly!

Daniel referred to the time of Moses and acknowledged that God was the One Who brought His children out of slavery in Egypt. No credit was given to Moses. Moses was the instrument that God used to accomplish His purposes. Daniel said that God had created a name for Himself when He delivered the Israelites out from under the bondage of Egypt. Daniel lauded God for His greatness and also admitted how sinful the Israelite people had become.

Daniel 16- "O Lord, according to all Your righteousness, I pray, let Your anger and Your fury be turned away from Your city Jerusalem, Your holy mountain; because for our sins, and for the iniquities of our fathers, Jerusalem and Your people are a reproach to all those around us.

Daniel made his request for forgiveness after confessing the Israelite nation's reproach against God and admitting that the Israelites deserved the punishment that they received. Daniel recognized that the Lord judged the Israelites according to His perfect and unchanging goodness, as evidenced in his remark "according to all Your righteousness." They had suffered the consequences of their sins, and according to the prophecies of Jeremiah, the period of judgment was almost over *(verse 2)*.

Daniel asked God to turn away His anger and fury from Jerusalem, the holy mountain, which is commonly interpreted as a reference to Mount Moriah.[3] Daniel asked God to turn away His fury from the Israelites and from the city of Jerusalem, so they could once again inherit the land where God had intended for them to rebuild His temple, and so they would no longer be the object of mockery and scorn to neighboring nations. Eighteenth century scholar John Gill depicts Daniel's petition as a heart's cry—a pouring out of this prophet's plea for God's mercy upon the Israelites and the city of Jerusalem. Gill states, "The prophet earnestly entreats, that the marks of divine displeasure, which were upon it, might be removed; that the punishments or judgments inflicted, as the effects of the anger and wrath of God, might cease, and the city be rebuilt, and restored to its former glory."[4] Simply stated, Daniel prayed that God would send His presence to dwell once again within the city of Jerusalem and within its temple.

Verse 17- *"Now therefore, our God, hear the prayer of Your servant, and his supplications, and for the Lord's sake cause Your face to shine on Your sanctuary, which is desolate.*

Throughout this prayer, Daniel used the plural pronoun *we* in order to address God on behalf of the nation of Israel. However, in this verse, he asked God to hear his prayers. Daniel referred to himself not as an enlightened teacher, great interpreter of visions, eloquent statesman, or faithful man of God. Though he was all of these things, Daniel shed each of his earthly titles and humbly called himself a servant of God. He asked God to shine His glory once again upon the temple in Jerusalem and to dwell in the Holy of Holies.

Verse 18- *"O my God, incline Your ear and hear; open Your eyes and see our desolations, and the city which is called by Your name; for we do not present our supplications before You because of our righteous deeds, but because of Your great mercies.*

Daniel desired to sense God's presence in a genuine, intimate way. He implored the Lord to hear his petition. He wanted the Lord to see the desolation they were in as a nation and as a city because of their transgressions. God, of course, knew all of this, for He is sovereign over all things that happen to all nations. However, Daniel appealed in such a way that did not petition God based upon the Israelites' righteousness but upon God's mercy.

Verse 19- "O Lord, hear! O Lord, forgive! O Lord, listen and act! Do not delay for Your own sake, my God, for Your city and Your people are called by Your name."

Daniel appealed to God to listen, to forgive, but also to act without hesitation. He asked God not to defer allowing His chosen people to reoccupy their land, and God, in His time, eventually reunited His people with their land. In 538 BC, King Cyrus the Persian, shortly after conquering the Babylonian Empire, passed a decree releasing the Jews from their captivity to begin the rebuilding of the temple in Jerusalem.[5]

Verses 20, 21- ²⁰Now while I was speaking, praying, and confessing my sin and the sin of my people Israel, and presenting my supplication before the LORD my God for the holy mountain of my God, ²¹yes, while I was speaking in prayer, the man Gabriel, whom I had seen in the vision at the beginning, being caused to fly swiftly, reached me about the time of the evening offering.

Daniel was in a spirit of prayer and in a position for prayer. He focused his physical, emotion, mental, and spiritual energy upon this time before God's throne. As Daniel earnestly sought the Lord in confession and supplication, the angel Gabriel appeared. Daniel recognized Gabriel as the same messenger who had interpreted his first vision. *(Daniel 8.16)* Gabriel arrived around the time of the evening offering, which was generally the ninth hour of the day or about three o'clock in the afternoon.[6]

Verse 22- And he informed me, and talked with me, and said, "O Daniel, I have now come forth to give you skill to understand.

Gabriel explained that his mission was to give Daniel the insight to comprehend this vision.

Verse 23- "At the beginning of your supplications the command went out, and I have come to tell you, for you are greatly beloved; therefore consider the matter, and understand the vision:

According to this explanation, God had commissioned Gabriel to help Daniel understand the vision as soon as Daniel first began praying. God knows what we need before we ask, but He still wants us to ask. *"'Therefore do not be like them. For your Father knows the things you have need of before you ask Him.'" (Matthew 6.8)* Daniel was also told that he was greatly loved by God, and then he was instructed to meditate upon the matter and to understand the vision.

Notes/Applications

Daniel deeply loved his fellow Israelites. How do we know this? Because Daniel prayerfully interceded on their behalf. He faithfully and passionately prayed for the spiritual, physical, and emotional healing of his people.

People all around us are collapsing under the weight of their sin and sorrow. If we think that we can do nothing to help them, we underestimate the power of intercessory prayer. Recognizing that the Lord Jesus Christ lovingly intercedes on our behalf should motivate us to pray for the needs of other people. *"Therefore He is also able to save to the uttermost those who come to God through Him, since He always lives to make intercession for them." (Hebrews 7.25)* Christ's love can be demonstrated through us in no better way than to reach out to others by selflessly praying for them while knowing that we may receive no direct benefit from doing so.

A godly intercessor not only prays for friends and loved ones but also for the "unlikable," those who are difficult to love. This person may be a temperamental neighbor, a fallen pastor or teacher, a hardened criminal, or a corrupt politician. Only God can equip us with the love to reach out in compassion to these individuals, and many times, He does this through our prayers. By continually praying for them, God transforms our hearts and attitudes, so we can love the unlovable. *"⁴In return for my love they are my accusers, but I give myself to prayer. ⁵Thus they have rewarded me evil for good, and hatred for my love." (Psalm 109.4–5)*

To make intercessory prayer a part of our prayer life requires heightened awareness to the spiritual, physical, and emotional needs around us. It requires us to see people as God sees them and to love them as He loves us. It requires us to commit ourselves to being more outwardly focused in our prayers instead of totally self-absorbed. *"Praying always with all prayer and supplication in the Spirit, being watchful to this end with all perseverance and supplication for all the saints." (Ephesians 6.18)* With Christ as our example, how faithful are we in praying for the needs of others?

Daniel 9.24–27

Verse 24- "Seventy weeks are determined for your people and for your holy city, to finish the transgression, to make an end of sins, to make reconciliation for iniquity, to bring in everlasting righteousness, to seal up vision and prophecy, and to anoint the Most Holy.

The last four verses of this chapter have been called by some the most controversial passage in the entire Bible, and they have been the subject of great debate among biblical scholars throughout the ages.[7] Only two major views, however, agree on certain issues that seem to be basic interpretative truths within this text, and therefore, only these two views warrant reasonable consideration. Other views, which will not hereafter be referenced, shift arbitrarily between figurative and literal meanings in certain segments of the text in order to fit them within the confines of their otherwise improbable interpretations, and should not, therefore, be deemed reliable.[8] With careful determination to convey what seems to be the truest sense of the writer's intention through the study of related Scripture passages, various esteemed commentators, and a balanced dose of prudence and reason, we will examine this passage in light of these two viewpoints and draw conclusions that seem most dependable and consistent.

For the most part, these two views disagree on two major elements of the text: 1) the meaning of the phrases listed in verse twenty-four, and 2), the eschatological rendering of verse twenty-seven. The first position, labeled a "first advent" interpretation, considers the entire prophecy to be fulfilled in the birth, death, and resurrection of the Messiah, the Lord Jesus Christ. The second viewpoint, labeled a "second advent" position, actually combines the first advent viewpoint with an indefinite interruption of time between the sixty-ninth and seventieth week, thereby projecting the eventual fulfillment of this prophecy to end times, specifically to the last seven years before Christ Jesus' Second Coming. Whereas the "second advent" position has gained widespread acceptance over the last hundred years or so, its dependency upon a series of future events for the ultimate fulfillment of this prophecy seems unnecessary since it can be more easily demonstrated how the prophecy was fulfilled in its entirety upon the resurrection of Jesus Christ.

One crucial matter that both positions agree upon is the meaning of the word *week* as used in this verse, which is derived from the Hebrew word *shabuwa* and denotes a general grouping of seven.[9] It does not in any way constitute a week of days, as the word is commonly understood by its modern English definition. This is comparable to the word *dozen,* which only means a grouping of twelve and does not by itself identify that group as consisting of eggs, donuts, or any other specific item. This group of seven could, therefore, consist of either days or years, depending on the situation. Historically, reference to a week of years was as common to Jewish tradition as was a week of days:

> [27]'*Fulfill her week, and we will give you this one also for the service which you will serve with me still another seven years.' *[28]*Then Jacob did so and fulfilled her week. So he gave him his daughter Rachel as wife also. *[29]*And Laban gave his maid Bilhah to his daughter Rachel as a maid. *[30]*Then Jacob also went in to Rachel, and he also loved Rachel more than Leah. And he served with Laban still another seven years. (Genesis 29.27–28)*

With this in mind, Gabriel seems to be responding to Daniel's heartfelt prayer quoted in verses four through nineteen. Though there have been many variations in the specific interpretation of this verse, it is generally agreed that the phrases found herein all refer to the first advent of the Messiah. This verse, in a sense, is the synopsis of God's message and could serve as a conclusion just as adequately as it serves as a preface.[10]

Daniel sought to know the fate of his people, the Jews, and of their city, Jerusalem. God's response was probably not what Daniel expected to hear. The relationship that the Jews had both enjoyed and neglected as God's chosen people and as citizens of God's holy city would not be the everlasting covenant they thought it would be.

"If those ordinances depart from before Me, says the LORD, then the seed of Israel shall also cease from being a nation before Me forever." (Jeremiah 31.36) Daniel was informed that in four hundred and ninety years, this exclusive relationship would be finished. After that duration had ended, the Messiah would come to "finish the transgression, to make an end of sins, to make reconciliation for iniquity, to bring in everlasting righteousness, to seal up vision and prophecy, and to [be anointed as] the Most Holy." Christ's resurrection provided the atonement for the sins of the world. *"In Him we have redemption through His blood, the forgiveness of sins, according to the riches of His grace." (Ephesians 1.7)* Through His atonement, salvation would become obtainable to all who believe, both Jew and Gentile. *"That if you confess with your mouth the Lord Jesus and believe in your heart that God has raised Him from the dead, you will be saved." (Romans 10.9)* Furthermore, all "vision and prophecy" regarding the Messiah were fulfilled and vindicated with the advent of Christ Jesus, in Whom all prophecies, having been fulfilled, would cease or be "sealed up." *"Then He took the twelve aside and said to them, 'Behold, we are going up to Jerusalem, and all things that are written by the prophets concerning the Son of Man will be accomplished.'" (Luke 18.31)*

Verse 25- "Know therefore and understand, that from the going forth of the command to restore and build Jerusalem until Messiah the Prince, there shall be seven weeks and sixty-two weeks; the street shall be built again, and the wall, even in troublesome times.

God, through His messenger Gabriel, advised Daniel to ponder the significance of these events. The message is clear: the period of time that would elapse between the edict to rebuild Jerusalem until the time of the Messiah would be 483 years—seven weeks of years (49 years) plus sixty-two weeks of years (434 years). The difficulty, though, is in both determining which decree by which king is hereby intended and also which event (birth, baptism, or resurrection) of the Messiah is meant. Some commentators argue that the beginning of the seventy weeks was marked with Cyrus' issuing of the decree to rebuild the temple in Jerusalem (587 BC), but this seems improbable since the time span between this decree and the Messiah is too long except with the permission of creative calculating.[11] *(Ezra 1.1–2)* However, most scholars, regardless of their rendering of verse twenty-seven, agree that the beginning of this period more likely began with the decree issued by Artaxerxes I (Longimanus) during the seventh year of his reign in 457 BC.[12] *(Ezra 7.8–28)* Forty-nine years after this decree was issued, in 408 BC, the rebuilding of Jerusalem was completed.[13]

Using the aforementioned as the most defensible benchmark, a quick computation reveals that by adding sixty-nine weeks of years (483 years) to the issuing of this decree by Artaxerxes I in 457 BC we arrive at 27 AD (not 26, since there is no 0 AD), which is generally agreed to be about the time that Jesus, the Messiah, began his public ministry.[14]

Verse 26- "And after the sixty-two weeks Messiah shall be cut off, but not for Himself; and the people of the prince who is to come shall destroy the city and the sanctuary. The end of it shall be with a flood, and till the end of the war desolations are determined.

The purpose of the Messiah was clear. He did not come into the world "for Himself" but to fulfill the will of God for reconciling the sins of the world.

There is a bit of ambiguity surrounding the identity of the "prince who is to come." Many conclude that this is Satan, the prince of this world. Whereas Satan was certainly as persistent in his efforts against the people of God then as he is today, there is no reason to presume that this prophecy suddenly makes an abstract shift here from an earthly premise to a strictly spiritual one. These "people," more likely, were the Romans who, under the leadership of their prince, Titus Vespasian, would destroy the city and the sanctuary.[15] This segment of the prophecy—the *only* segment that is clearly separated from its surrounding events as "to come"—was ultimately fulfilled in 70 AD, when Jerusalem was destroyed by Titus. The "desolations" spoken of in this verse carry the same meaning as destruction, indicating that the end of Jerusalem both as a city and a nation would culminate in vast ruin of a great flood (most likely a figurative sense of the word denoting the intensity) and devastating wars.[16] Ultimately, the fulfillment of this prophecy is not in the actions of either the "people of the prince" or the "prince" himself but in the providential acts of God to complete His old covenant with the Jews and introduce the new covenant through the Messiah, as explained in the following verse.[17]

Verse 27- Then he shall confirm a covenant with many for one week; but in the middle of the week he shall bring an end to sacrifice and offering. And on the wing of abominations shall be one who makes desolate, even until the consummation, which is determined, is poured out on the desolate."

This verse is where many otherwise like-minded theologians part ways. Many presume that the person mentioned here suddenly refers to the end-times antichrist figure and, therefore, they separate the seventieth week of this prophecy to apply to the last years before the second advent of the Lord Jesus Christ.[18] However, an eschatological leap at this verse seems more out of preference than necessity and perhaps is better reserved for chapter eleven, where prophetic descriptions are more difficult to reconcile with specific historical events and persons. On the other hand, all matters discussed within this verse can easily be shown to have been fulfilled not in the end-times antichrist but in the person of Christ Jesus Himself.

Though the elements described herein sound like treacherous behavior in light of an antichrist interpretation, the very same elements seem much less threatening when viewed as Messianic prophecy. Indeed the things named in this verse are not cause for alarm but for celebration.

Jesus "confirmed a covenant with many" through his public ministry in which he performed miracles and preached of a new covenant.[19] *"But now He has obtained a more excellent ministry, inasmuch as He is also Mediator of a better covenant, which was established on better promises." (Hebrews 8.16) "For this is My covenant with them, when I take away their sins." (Romans 11.27)* In the middle of this seventieth week, a short three years into His ministry, the Lord brought an end to the old covenant of sacrifice and offering with His own sacrifice at Calvary:

⁹It was symbolic for the present time in which both gifts and sacrifices are offered which cannot make him who performed the service perfect in regard to the conscience, ¹⁰concerned only with foods and drinks, various washings, and fleshly ordinances imposed until the time of reformation. ¹¹But Christ came as High Priest of the good things to come, with the greater and more perfect tabernacle not made with hands, that is, not of this creation. ¹²Not with the blood of goats and calves, but with His own blood He entered the Most Holy Place once for all, having obtained eternal redemption. ¹³For if the blood of bulls and goats and the ashes of a heifer, sprinkling the unclean, sanctifies for the purifying of the flesh, ¹⁴how much more shall the blood of Christ, who through the eternal Spirit offered Himself without spot to God, cleanse your conscience from dead works to serve the living God? ¹⁵And for this reason He is the Mediator of the new covenant, by means of death, for the redemption of the transgressions under the first covenant, that those who are called may receive the promise of the eternal inheritance. (Hebrews 9.9–15)

With the resurrection of Christ, the offerings and sacrifices required under the Law became obsolete and unnecessary.[20] *"In that He says, 'A new covenant,' He has made the first obsolete. Now what is becoming obsolete and growing old is ready to vanish away." (Hebrews 8.13)* Furthermore, those Jews who failed to recognize the "one who [made] desolate" their acts of worship in the temple would soon be forced to stop their futile ceremonies by God's providential hand in the destruction of the temple by Titus. It seems gratuitous to presume this final verse refers to an end-times antichrist who will cause sacrifice and offering to cease in the temple since these ceremonial acts as well as the temple itself have already long since been eliminated, in both a spiritual sense and a physical one, at the time of Christ.

In effect, the Jews who failed to recognize Jesus as the Messiah had actually become the "desolate" who committed these very acts of "abominations" by their continued adherence to the old covenant and by their rejection of the new covenant of Christ Jesus. *"³For they being ignorant of God's righteousness, and seeking to establish their own righteousness, have not submitted to the righteousness of God. ⁴For Christ is the end of the law for righteousness to everyone who believes." (Romans 10.3–4)*

Notes/Applications

In these verses, God revealed a portion of His plan for extending grace upon Israel and the rest of mankind. He would sacrifice His Son. It is difficult to comprehend why God would send His Son to suffer the penalty for the world's sins. And why would God's Son, this Messiah, leave Heaven's splendor in order to die for such reprobate people? *"For you know the grace of our Lord Jesus Christ, that though He was rich, yet for your sakes He became poor, that you through His poverty might become rich." (2 Corinthians 8.9)*

Verse twenty-six in this passage states, "Messiah shall be cut off, but not for Himself." The Messiah did not come for Himself but for each one of us. *"But we see Jesus, who was made a little lower than the angels, for the suffering of death crowned with glory and honor, that He, by the grace of God, might taste death for everyone." (Hebrews 2.9)* God did not need to save us. He did not need our companionship or our obedience. Certainly, our worship and ministry please the Lord, but He did not need them or any part of us. God graciously extended salvation to us because He loved us and because it pleased Him to do so. When we consider the cost of grace, we grasp, in small part, the value of this undeserved gift.

By His grace, we have been saved. *"⁸For by grace you have been saved through faith, and that not of yourselves; it is the gift of God, ⁹not of works, lest anyone should boast. ¹⁰For we are His workmanship, created in Christ Jesus for good works, which God prepared beforehand that we should walk in them." (Ephesians 2.8–10)* By His grace, we live. *"Let us therefore come boldly to the throne of grace, that we may obtain mercy and find grace to help in time of need." (Hebrews 4.16)* And, by His grace, we will one day die and enter eternity where we will praise Him face to face: *"¹⁰But may the God of all grace, who called us to His eternal glory by Christ*

Jesus, after you have suffered a while, perfect, establish, strengthen, and settle you. [11]To Him be the glory and the dominion forever and ever." (1 Peter 5.10– 11)

> *Amazing grace! How sweet the sound, that saved a wretch like me!*
> *I once was lost, but now am found, was blind, but now I see.*
> *'Twas grace that taught my heart to fear, and grace my fears relieved;*
> *How precious did that grace appear the hour I first believed!*
> *Thro' many dangers, toils, and snares, I have already come;*
> *'Tis grace hath bro't me safe thus far, and grace will lead me home.*
> *The Lord has promised good to me, His Word my hope secures;*
> *He will my shield and portion be as long as life endures.*
> *Yea, when this flesh and heart shall fail, and mortal life shall cease,*
> *I shall possess, within the veil, a life of joy and peace.*
> *The earth shall soon dissolve like snow, the sun forbear to shine;*
> *But God, Who called me here below, shall be forever mine.*
> *When we've been there ten thousand years, bright shining as the sun,*
> *We've no less days to sing God's praise than when we'd first begun.[21]*

Chapter Ten

Daniel 10.1–7

Verse 1- In the third year of Cyrus king of Persia a message was revealed to Daniel, whose name was called Belteshazzar. The message was true, but the appointed time was long; and he understood the message, and had understanding of the vision.

Scholars have dated the year of this vision between 554 and 532 BC, depending on their delineation of King Cyrus' third year of reign. The strongest evidence suggests that this historical point of reference does not refer to Cyrus' initial rise to power over Persia (~558 BC) but to the expansion of his dominion over the entire Medo-Persian territory (~538 BC). As such, this vision probably occurred around 535–534 BC.[1] Although the events of the vision would not be fulfilled for many years, Daniel was told that they would surely come to pass. He was also given full understanding of the vision's meaning. The final two chapters of the Book of Daniel are the continuation and completion of the prophecy that begins in this chapter.

Verse 2- In those days I, Daniel, was mourning three full weeks.

Much speculation has been focused upon the reason for Daniel's mourning. Some attribute his grief to the timing of the vision during the feasts of Passover and Unleavened Bread.[2] These, however, were celebrations to the Lord and, as such, scarcely seem reason for mourning. Others contend that Daniel was still grieving over the vision of the seventy weeks, as recorded in the previous chapter.[3] This, too, seems an unlikely reason since that vision had occurred at least two years earlier *(Daniel 9.1–2)*. Most likely, Daniel was grieved by the complacency of his people. Several years had passed since Cyrus had signed the decree that freed the Israelites from their captivity in Babylon, thereby allowing them the liberty to return to their homeland to restore the city and temple. However, only a handful of the Israelites desired to leave the foreign land to which they had grown so accustomed.[4] Furthermore, according to chapters two and three of Ezra, Jerusalem and its temple were still in ruins at this time. When the Israelites were finally prepared to rebuild the temple, many of them, including the priestly tribe, had become corrupted from intermarriage with the Babylonians:

> *[1]When these things were done, the leaders came to me, saying, 'The people of Israel and the priests and the Levites have not separated themselves from the peoples of the lands, with respect to the abominations of the Canaanites, the Hittites, the Perizzites, the Jebusites, the Ammonites, the Moabites, the Egyptians, and the Amorites. [2]For they have taken some of their daughters as wives for themselves and their sons, so that the holy seed is mixed with the peoples of those lands. Indeed, the hand of the leaders and rulers has been foremost in this trespass.' (Ezra 9.1–2)*

Any one or more of these explanations serve as possible reasons for Daniel's bereavement. Whatever the cause may be, Daniel mourned for three weeks. Unlike the use of the word *weeks* in the previous chapter that referred to a grouping of seven years, *weeks* here signifies a grouping of seven days, as confirmed by verse thirteen, which calls these three weeks a literal twenty-one days.

Verse 3- I ate no pleasant food, no meat or wine came into my mouth, nor did I anoint myself at all, till three whole weeks were fulfilled.

Daniel mourned and fasted. He did not abstain from sustenance altogether; rather, he adhered to a strict discipline of foods that he deemed allowable. He ate no rich-tasting breads, meats, or wines, which was similar to the diet he maintained during the early years of his captivity. Simply stated, he deprived himself of any luxurious, highly seasoned foods that satisfied human desires. Neither did he tend to his hygiene. He did only the bare minimum required to survive. Daniel's physical deprivation mirrored his spiritual emptiness and searching. His plight was a private one of lamenting and fasting for three weeks over his sin and his people's sin against God.

Verses 4, 5- ⁴Now on the twenty-fourth day of the first month, as I was by the side of the great river, that is, the Tigris, ⁵I lifted my eyes and looked, and behold, a certain man clothed in linen, whose waist was girded with gold of Uphaz!

Daniel dated this last recorded vision by referencing the year of the king's reign and by specifying the date as the twenty-fourth day of Nisan, the first month of the Jewish year, which falls within our months of March and April.[5]

Daniel was along the shore of the great Tigris River, called *Hiddekel* in some translations, when he saw a man "clothed in linen, whose waist was girded with gold of Uphaz." *Uphaz* is commonly believed to be another name for the country of Ophir because of the similarity between the Hebrew spellings of the words.[6] This interpretation seems to be credible because the Bible refers to Ophir as a place renowned for its vast quantities of fine gold. *(1 Kings 9.28; Job 22.24; Isaiah 13.12)*

Verse 6- His body was like beryl, his face like the appearance of lightning, his eyes like torches of fire, his arms and feet like burnished bronze in color, and the sound of his words like the voice of a multitude.

The descriptions given in verses five and six warrant a conclusion that this glorious being was most likely an appearance of a pre-incarnate Christ, Whose majesty here can only be described by Daniel as an exquisite gemstone like beryl.[7] We can also presume that this was a Christophany because of similarities with other biblical depictions identified as Jesus Christ:

> [13]*And in the midst of the seven lampstands One like the Son of Man, clothed with a garment down to the feet and girded about the chest with a golden band. [14]His head and hair were white like wool, as white as snow, and His eyes like a flame of fire; [15]His feet were like fine brass, as if refined in a furnace, and His voice as the sound of many waters. (Revelation 1.13–15)*

Verse 7- And I, Daniel, alone saw the vision, for the men who were with me did not see the vision; but a great terror fell upon them, so that they fled to hide themselves.

Only Daniel witnessed this vision. The other men with Daniel were unable to view this appearance because they were stricken with fear and, therefore, retreated.

Notes/Applications

Most of us have never actually seen God with our eyes. Most of us have never felt Him literally take us by the hand or heard Him call our names. However, as believers, we have certainly experienced God through His presence, especially during moments when, like Daniel, we have desperately needed His peace and reassurance.

The presence of our Lord can be a place of quiet refreshment where He rejuvenates us for the day's journey. *"'Repent therefore and be converted, that your sins may be blotted out, so that times of refreshing may come from the presence of the Lord.'" (Acts 3.19)* Moments spent in His presence steadies us for the day by fixing His will upon our hearts, but when we neglect spending time in God's presence on a daily basis, the winds of chaos quickly blow us down.

As a testimony to the heavenly peace found only in the presence of God, hymnist Cleland Boyd McAfee penned the following lyrics after his two nieces died from diphtheria:

There is a place of quiet rest near to the heart of God.
A place where sin cannot molest, near to the heart of God.

There is a place of comfort sweet near to the heart of God.
A place where we our Savior meet, near to the heart of God.

There is a place of full release near to the heart of God.
A place where all is joy and peace, near to the heart of God.

Refrain:
O Jesus, blest Redeemer, sent from the heart of God,
Hold us who wait before Thee near to the heart of God.[8]

Do we need the comfort and reassurance found in the Lord's presence? Have we entered today into that place near to the heart of God? May we come before Him and be assured that He will meet us in the quietness of this moment. *"Draw near to God and He will draw near to you." (James 4.8a)*

Daniel 10.8–14

Verse 8- Therefore I was left alone when I saw this great vision, and no strength remained in me; for my vigor was turned to frailty in me, and I retained no strength.

Daniel reemphasized that he was alone during this vision since the others had gone to hide themselves. He was already weakened from three weeks of fasting, and what little energy might have remained in him was completely drained by this staggering vision. The overwhelming experience of standing in the presence of God affected his entire appearance.

Verse 9- Yet I heard the sound of his words; and while I heard the sound of his words I was in a deep sleep on my face, with my face to the ground.

Daniel collapsed as though dead as a result of being so completely overwhelmed by the vision; all of his faculties yielded to a state of temporary paralysis.[9] Despite this helpless condition, Daniel was still able to hear the words that were being spoken to him.

Daniel's response is similar to John's reaction to the appearance of the Son of Man in the book of The Revelation. *"And when I saw Him, I fell at His feet as dead." (Revelation 1.17a)* In comparing the passage in Revelation chapter one and this passage in Daniel chapter ten, we see many parallels in both the vision of the Christophany and in the response of these two witnesses. However, there is one notable difference between these prophets' experiences. When the Christophany appeared to Daniel at a time long before the birth of Christ, He lacked something that was present with Him when He later appeared to the Apostle John long after Christ's ascension—the keys of death and Hell! *"'I am He who lives, and was dead, and behold, I am alive forevermore. Amen. And I have the keys of Hades and of Death.'" (Revelation 1.18)* What a wonderful assurance that Jesus has conquered death and hell and that He lives forevermore at the right hand of the Father as the glorified, risen Christ!

Verse 10- Suddenly, a hand touched me, which made me tremble on my knees and on the palms of my hands.

While Daniel was in this weakened condition, a hand reached down, touched him, and placed him onto his hands and knees.

Verse 11- And he said to me, "O Daniel, man greatly beloved, understand the words that I speak to you, and stand upright, for I have now been sent to you." While he was speaking this word to me, I stood trembling.

Daniel assumed an upright position, though he still shuddered with fear, and found himself in the presence of a being different than the first.[10] Although the introduction of another being is not clearly described, we may conclude by the surrounding evidence that Daniel was visited by two separate beings. The description in verses five and six of the first being depicts an unmistakable and glorious appearance that is distinctive to the Son of God when compared to His similar appearances recorded in the Bible. Therefore, such a magnificent description within those verses likely characterizes a Being greater than an angel. Furthermore, the one who now stood before Daniel seems, by his own words, to be simply a messenger "sent to you [Daniel]," which would indicate that this being was an angel of God. In verse thirteen, it will be explained how his efforts in response to Daniel's prayers were hampered by the "prince of the kingdom of Persia." Nothing can ever impede the inclinations of the Lord, and it should be concluded, therefore, that these were two separate and unique beings that appeared to Daniel.[11]

The angel addressed Daniel as "a man greatly beloved" of God. What a privilege it must have been to be called the beloved of God! As evidenced throughout his life, Daniel had truly cultivated a deep fellowship with God and commitment to prayer. He did not waiver in his convictions but firmly stood upon the principles and promises of God.

Verse 12- Then he said to me, "Do not fear, Daniel, for from the first day that you set your heart to understand, and to humble yourself before your God, your words were heard; and I have come because of your words.

The messenger arrived at the appointed time to comfort and reassure Daniel. Daniel was told not to fear because his voice had been heard in Heaven from the first moment he uttered his heartfelt prayer. The angel explained that he had been sent immediately in response to Daniel's prayers, but there had been a delay, as explained in the following verse.

Verse 13- "But the prince of the kingdom of Persia withstood me twenty-one days; and behold, Michael, one of the chief princes, came to help me, for I had been left alone there with the kings of Persia.

The angel contended that "the prince of the kingdom of Persia withstood me [him] twenty-one days" until the archangel Michael came to his assistance. This prince should not be misinterpreted to mean either Cyrus, the king of Persia, or his son, Cambyses. Rather, this is a prince of a spiritual realm, a principle agent among the vast forces of Satan.[12] This verse implies that God immediately sent the angel when Daniel first prayed, but then this angel was thwarted in spiritual battle along the way. This was the reason given for the delay when responding to Daniel's prayer. Nevertheless, this delay does not diminish the total sovereignty of Almighty God over all matters.

With all the significant visions, wonderful miracles, and valuable lessons packed within the book of Daniel, this verse in conjunction with others in this chapter offers us an amazing insight that is often understated or overlooked altogether. In a manner not found any-where else in the Bible, we are given a firsthand account of the spiritual warfare that takes place all around us yet remains unseen by the human eye. *"For we do not wrestle against flesh and blood, but against principalities, against powers, against the rulers of the darkness of this age, against spiritual hosts of wickedness in the heavenly places." (Ephesians 6.12)*

Verse 14- "Now I have come to make you understand what will happen to your people in the latter days, for the vision refers to many days yet to come."

The angel told Daniel that he could be stalled no longer from coming to make Daniel understand the future of the Israelites. Through the message given to him, Daniel was given spiritual insight of a prophetic nature because he had not sought God in a token, ritualistic way. He humbled, deprived, and prepared himself to talk to and to hear from Almighty God, and as we see in these verses, the Lord graciously answered Daniel's prayers.

Notes/Applications

According to the angel, the Lord answered Daniel's prayers from the very moment that Daniel completely surrendered himself to God. For our prayers to be effectual, we must be certain that we have not erected roadblocks that hinder our communication with God. *"The LORD is far from the wicked, but He hears the prayer of the righteous." (Proverbs 15.29)*

Sin obstructs our communication with God. When we clutter our minds and hearts with sin, our relationship with God will be strained due to our hardened hearts, and Holy God will not honor the prayers of those who live in disobedience to His commands. *"If I regard iniquity in my heart, the Lord will not hear." (Psalm 66.18) "One who turns away his ear from hearing the law, even his prayer is an abomination." (Proverbs 28.9)* Our busy schedules, family obligations, and other worldly preoccupations can also detour us away from prayer because they drain our time and energy. Ironically, when these daily pressures become unbearable, we often neglect what should be our first priority. Therefore, we must learn to differentiate between what seems to be most urgent with what is most important—time spent in communion with God. *"'For the LORD searches all hearts and understands all the intent of the thoughts. If you seek Him, He will be found by you; but if you forsake Him, He will cast you off forever.'" (1 Chronicles 28.9b)*

The roadblocks to an effectual prayer life can be easily removed if we will set our hearts to loving and obeying God. When Daniel sought Him, God was easily found. God promises that if we whole-heartedly seek Him, we, too, will find Him. *"But from there you will seek the LORD your God, and you will find Him if you seek Him with all your heart and with all your soul.'" (Deuteronomy 4.29)* What roadblocks are hindering our intimacy with God? Have we focused our whole attention on seeking intimate conversation with God?

Daniel 10.15–21

Verse 15- When he had spoken such words to me, I turned my face toward the ground and became speechless.

Daniel, while utterly dumbfounded and unable to speak, again put his face to the ground. This being had come as a direct messenger of God, and he spoke truth. Daniel, perhaps beginning to understand the monumental importance of this angel's visit, was incapable of uttering even a single word.

Verse 16- And suddenly, one having the likeness of the sons of men touched my lips; then I opened my mouth and spoke, saying to him who stood before me, "My lord, because of the vision my sorrows have overwhelmed me, and I have retained no strength.

This was likely the same being that had touched Daniel in verse ten and had been conversing with him since then. The first words Daniel uttered were, "My lord." We know from earlier verses that Daniel was not addressing the Lord God but was respectfully addressing this messenger. Daniel admitted that he was overwhelmed by all he saw, that he was deeply grieved by these things, and that he was utterly weakened as a result.

Verse 17- "For how can this servant of my lord talk with you, my lord? As for me, no strength remains in me now, nor is any breath left in me."

Daniel did not feel strong enough to speak with the angel that he again addressed as lord. As previously stated, he was physically weakened from his fasting and emotionally drained from his mourning.

Verse 18- Then again, the one having the likeness of a man touched me and strengthened me.

When the angel again touched Daniel, his strength was instantaneously restored to him by the power of God through one simple touch from this messenger.

Verse 19- And he said, "O man greatly beloved, fear not! Peace be to you; be strong, yes, be strong!" So when he spoke to me I was strengthened, and said, "Let my lord speak, for you have strengthened me."

The messenger restated that Daniel was a man greatly loved by God, so Daniel was to combat his anxieties by resting in the assurance of God's love. To fully grasp what was occurring, Daniel had to release all of his fears and be willing to trust. The angel then proclaimed, "Peace be to you," and when the angel spoke these things, Daniel immediately regained his strength. Daniel then encouraged the angel to deliver the message he had been sent to convey.

Verse 20- Then he said, "Do you know why I have come to you? And now I must return to fight with the prince of Persia; and when I have gone forth, indeed the prince of Greece will come.

It seems the angel answered Daniel's petition to know the message with a rhetorical question, almost as if to settle any uncertainty concerning Daniel's ability to grasp the magnitude of his current situation. Then the angel said that he had to return to fight with the prince of Persia, and when that empire had run its preordained course, the Grecian Empire would attain power, and the angel would then have to battle with the controlling demons of that empire.[13] By the angel's words, we again sense the on-going spiritual warfare between good and evil. Satan and his angels are a powerful force that only God can conquer. Satan constantly tries to interfere with God's plan for creation and, more specifically, with those who seek the will of God, but he is only able to do that which is allowed by Sovereign God. Therefore, this warfare is not a war, at least as most people generally understand the term, because Almighty God has already won the victory.

Verse 21- "But I will tell you what is noted in the Scripture of Truth. (No one upholds me against these, except Michael your prince.

The messenger told Daniel that he would reveal those things that are true. Then, the messenger claimed that no other angel except Michael, the watchman over the nation of Israel, could help him in this battle against Satan's forces and their relentless hostility toward the Jews.[14] *"At that time Michael shall stand up, the great prince who stands watch over the sons of your people." (Daniel 12.1a)*

Notes/Applications

Daniel was physically exhausted from fasting and fervently praying. Despite Daniel's infirmity, God strengthened him, thereby empowering the prophet to withstand this test of his faith.

We are fragile pots, ceramic vessels. We appear to be strong enough to withstand any trial or temptation, but all of us have experienced or will experience a breaking point. When unexpected events turn tragic, we quickly find that we are not resilient and that we need more sustenance than we can muster. At that hour, when our spirit is utterly broken, God picks up the rubble of our lives and binds the pieces together by His miraculous power. In our weakness, God is made stronger because we realize, more then ever before, how much we need Him. *"And He said to me, 'My grace is sufficient for you, for My strength is made perfect in weakness.' Therefore most gladly I will rather boast in my infirmities, that the power of Christ may rest upon me. [10] Therefore I take pleasure in infirmities, in reproaches, in needs, in persecutions, in distresses, for Christ's sake. For when I am weak, then I am strong." (2 Corinthians 12.9–10)*

Times of weakness empty us and cleanse us of our pride, so we can be used for God's purposes. We become consecrated vessels, ready to be filled with His power and to pour forth a living testimony to other people who also need Him. *"Therefore if anyone cleanses himself from the latter, he will be a vessel for honor, sanctified and useful for the Master, prepared for every good work." (2 Timothy 2.21)* Have we experienced our breaking point before the Lord? What has God accomplished both in us and through us as a result of our brokenness?

Chapter Eleven

Daniel 11.1–8

Verse 1- "Also in the first year of Darius the Mede, I, even I, stood up to confirm and strengthen him.)

The angel, not Daniel as some expositors have speculated, continued speaking as evidenced in the obvious flow and continuation of this text from the previous chapter. As the angel had promised, he would now reveal to Daniel the fate of the nation of Israel in future times. *"Now I have come to make you understand what will happen to your people in the latter days, for the vision refers to many days yet to come." (Daniel 10.14)* Apparently, the Lord had also sent this angel to strengthen Darius the Mede, which suggests that God had used the king as an instrument within His divine plan.

Verse 2- "And now I will tell you the truth: Behold, three more kings will arise in Persia, and the fourth shall be far richer than them all; by his strength, through his riches, he shall stir up all against the realm of Greece.

Through this messenger, God first revealed to Daniel the truth about what would become of the Medo-Persian Empire. The angel explained that three kings would follow Darius the Mede and that a fourth king would be far richer than the previous kings. This passage arouses debate over the identity of these four kings, who ruled concurrently with Cyrus the Persian. The second king is likely Cambyses, sometimes referred to as Artaxerxes, who was the son and successor of Cyrus the Persian.[1] Because Cambyses perceived the strengthening of the Jews as a threat to his authority, he overturned his father's earlier decree and forbade the continuation of the rebuilding of Jerusalem for several years.[2] A mere six years into his reign, Cambyses died, and for seven months thereafter the ruler over the empire was Gaumata, who is often called Pseudo-Smerdis because he deceitfully obtained the throne by claiming to be Smerdis, son of Cyrus.[3] Afterwards, Darius I (not Darius the Mede, but the son of Hystaspes) became king.[4] The fourth king mentioned in this verse refers to Xerxes, also named Ahasuerus, who rose to power after the death of his father in 486 BC and inherited enormous wealth.[5] After amassing the largest army ever assembled to that point in history, Xerxes devoted himself to the conquest of Greece to avenge his father's death, which marked the beginning of the fall of the Persian Empire. In addition, historical records reveal that there were several other kings of the Persian Empire, but only these four are mentioned in this vision since the above-noted kings all had some influence over the affairs of the Jewish people, the restoration of their temple, or the rebuilding of Jerusalem.[6]

Verse 3- *"Then a mighty king shall arise, who shall rule with great dominion, and do according to his will.*

Since the kingdom of Persia was in a state of decline, this verse refers to the ruler of the kingdom that would follow, which was the Greco-Macedonian Empire. A powerful king would obtain great dominion and rule as he pleased. This king proved to be Alexander the Great, who became a world leader at a very young age. He withstood the battle against an experienced Persian army, defeated them, and thereby brought Greece onto the scene as the third great world empire.[7]

Verse 4- "And when he has arisen, his kingdom shall be broken up and divided toward the four winds of heaven, but not among his posterity nor according to his dominion with which he ruled; for his kingdom shall be uprooted, even for others besides these.

Once Alexander the Great reached the pinnacle of his power, his kingdom was separated into four kingdoms according to the four basic directions of the earth—north, east, south, and west. The division of this kingdom and the dissolution of its ruling authority weakened its dominion. By the sovereignty of God Almighty, the death of Alexander the Great allowed less powerful rulers to share authority in his place. These emerged as four generals that individually ruled over the four divided nations, and this sharing of authority contributed to the decline of the Greco-Macedonian Empire.[8] Alexander lost his power and his empire's dominance because, as evident in verse three, he did all things according to his own will.

Verse 5- "Also the king of the South shall become strong, as well as one of his princes; and he shall gain power over him and have dominion. His dominion shall be a great dominion.

Ptolemy I (Soter), a strong leader who claimed the title "King of Egypt," developed the southern kingdom into a great nation of commerce. The phrase "one of his princes" does not refer to the king of the South but to Alexander, whose kingdom was divided among four generals, one of which was this "prince." This leader was Seleucus I (Nicator), who became the king of the North over the region of Syria and who ultimately gained dominion over the king of the South.[9]

Verse 6- "And at the end of some years they shall join forces, for the daughter of the king of the South shall go to the king of the North to make an agreement; but she shall not retain the power of her authority, and neither he nor his authority shall stand; but she

shall be given up, with those who brought her, and with him who begot her, and with him who strengthened her in those times.

After a number of years, there was a marriage between royal families of the kingdom of the South and the kingdom of the North. As was often the case, the union was strictly political. In an attempt to establish peace, such royal marriages were sometimes arranged so that warring kingdoms could settle their differences and unite their power.[10]

Berenice, the daughter of Ptolemy II (Philadelphus), was given to be married to the king of the North, Antiochus II (Theos), who had illegally divorced his wife, Laodice, and disinherited their son in order to marry Berenice.[11] As we will see, this scheme would fail on all fronts, primarily because Berenice would not remain queen for very long. In addition, the phrase "those who brought her" likely refers to all the conspirators who played a role in the promotion and implementation of the plan. "Him who begot her [Berenice]" seems to signify a parental reference, although this may not be the intention since, according to some historical sources, Berenice's father, Ptolemy II, was already dead by this point. Therefore, this phrase could more accurately be conveyed as "him who was begotten *by* her," referring to the child born to Berenice and Antiochus II.[12] Indeed, this prophecy seems to be more clearly fulfilled in their son, upon whose head, by virtue of this marriage, the crown would have ultimately fallen were it not for the intervention of Laodice, Antiochus' first wife. Though she would eventually reconcile with Antiochus, Laodice contracted the murders of both Berenice and her infant son in Antioch, thereby assuring that they would not retain any authority. The crown would then be passed down to Laodice's own son, Seleucus II (Callinicus).[13] Furthermore, after reuniting with Antiochus, Laodice allegedly poisoned Antiochus to death, thereby eliminating any risk of future betrayal by "him who strengthened her [Berenice]" and any threat of surrendering her son's royal inheritance.[14] Consequently, both kingdoms were weakened instead of strengthened by the union of Berenice and Antiochus.

Verse 7- "But from a branch of her roots one shall arise in his place, who shall come with an army, enter the fortress of the king of the North, and deal with them and prevail.

The phrase "her roots" refers to Berenice's father, Ptolemy II, upon whose death Ptolemy III (Euergetes) ascended the throne as king of Egypt, the king of the South. Ptolemy III, accompanied by an enormous army, marched into the kingdom of the North to avenge the murder of his sister, Berenice. He fought the Seleucids and prevailed, killing Laodice in the process.[15] As a result, the king of the South dominated the king of the North.

Verse 8- "And he shall also carry their gods captive to Egypt, with their princes and their precious articles of silver and gold; and he shall continue more years than the king of the North.

Ptolemy III confiscated the idols of the northern kingdom and carried these precious golden and silver vessels back into Egypt. These vessels came out of the temples of the gods and the palaces of the kings.[16] His armies also captured sons of the northern king, referred to here as princes, and according to this verse, the kingdom of the South lasted longer than the kingdom of the North.

Notes/Applications

When one kingdom crumbled under the weight of its own greed and pride, another kingdom eventually conquered it. Both the northern and southern kingdoms governed themselves according to man's shifting standards rather than by God's steadfast principles.

People live their lives, their own "kingdoms," in a number of ways. Our world embraces this collage of alternative lifestyles, and it spouts that we are all headed to the same place, just arriving by different roadmaps. However, as believers, we know that the Lord Jesus Christ is the only pathway to eternity in Heaven and that all other roads lead to eternity in Hell. *"13'Enter by the narrow gate; for wide is the gate and broad is the way that leads to destruction, and there are many who go in by it. ¹⁴Because narrow is the gate and difficult is the way which leads to life, and there are few who find it.'" (Matthew 7.13–14)*

Life's broad road, convenient and widely traveled, appears to be paved with pleasure and freedom, whereas the narrow road appears to be cluttered with potholes of rules. The broad road entices the multitudes because it accommodates every manifestation of individual expression, but eventually, this one-lane fast track destines its traveler to self-destruction and separation from God. The narrow road leads to truly abundant life and freedom in Christ, a life that is not free from tribulation but is free from the penalty of sin. However, this road is less traveled. Although it is the highway to eternal life, few tread this path because they seek immediate gratification of their desires.

What path have we been traveling? The broad with the many or the narrow with the chosen few? *"²⁶Ponder the path of your feet, and let all your ways be established. ²⁷Do not turn to the right or the left; remove your foot from evil." (Proverbs 4.26–27)* If we have been living the kingdom of our lives according to our own sense of direction, we must change our course and enter God's kingdom through His Gatekeeper, the Lord Jesus Christ.

Daniel 11.9–16

Verse 9- *"Also the king of the North shall come to the kingdom of the king of the South, but shall return to his own land.*

Historical records contend that many years after the invasion of the Seleucid Kingdom by Ptolemy III, Laodice's son, Seleucus II (Callinicus), attempted an invasion of Egypt. However, this campaign of revenge failed, and the Seleucid armies were forced to retreat back to their own kingdom in defeat.[17]

Verse 10- *"However his sons shall stir up strife, and assemble a multitude of great forces; and one shall certainly come and overwhelm and pass through; then he shall return to his fortress and stir up strife.*

Years later, the descendents of the king of the North again revolted against the king of the South, Ptolemy IV (Philopater). Soon, a great leader arose from among the kingdom of the North. This was Antiochus III, also known as Antiochus the Great, who assembled vast and powerful armies to rise against the southern kingdom.[18]

Verse 11- *"And the king of the South shall be moved with rage, and go out and fight with him, with the king of the North, who shall muster a great multitude; but the multitude shall be given into the hand of his enemy.*

The king of the South, Ptolemy IV, became enraged with the threat of the northern kingdom's campaign against his armies. Therefore, Ptolemy gathered his armies to wage war against Antiochus III, who had amassed an army even larger than that of his foe. Nevertheless, by the providential hand of God, Ptolemy was victorious and Antiochus was "given into the hand of his enemy."[19]

Verse 12- *"When he has taken away the multitude, his heart will be lifted up; and he will cast down tens of thousands, but he will not prevail.*

After defeating the great armies of Antiochus III the Great, Ptolemy IV was filled with pride and inflated confidence. Despite this extraordinary military victory, in which it is reported that his armies slaughtered seventeen thousand of Antiochus' soldiers, Ptolemy was content to reclaim the territories he had lost in earlier battles and to make peace with Antiochus.[20] Ultimately, his failure to take full advantage of the spoils of his triumph would backfire.

Verse 13- "For the king of the North will return and muster a multitude greater than the former, and shall certainly come at the end of some years with a great army and much equipment.

Antiochus the Great, king of the North, though defeated, had escaped from the hands of Ptolemy IV and had returned to the northern kingdom to recover his losses. Through various military and political strategies, including the formation of an alliance with Philip V of Macedon, Antiochus the Great assembled a multitude that was much larger than his previous army. He spent many years and much money preparing for his second attack against the South.[21]

Verse 14- "Now in those times many shall rise up against the king of the South. Also, violent men of your people shall exalt themselves in fulfillment of the vision, but they shall fall.

The king of the North was not the only enemy that opposed the king of the South. By virtue of its geographical location, Israel had many natural enemies. The country was constantly being trampled and pillaged by the armies of the North and the South during their wars with each other. The order to rebuild Jerusalem and the temple had been given, but Israel still experienced obvious difficulties in fulfilling the tasks because of her warring neighbors.

Apparently, several Jewish renegades who ignored the laws of God participated in the spoils and plunder of their warring neighbors and contributed to the destruction of the southern kingdom. Nevertheless, as this verse indicates, those Israelites that forsook their roles as God's chosen people would neither progress nor profit from their actions but would suffer the consequences for their disobedience, as will be further described in the details of the verses to follow.[22]

Verse 15- "So the king of the North shall come and build a siege mound, and take a fortified city; and the forces of the South shall not withstand him. Even his choice troops shall have no strength to resist.

The king of the North, Antiochus the Great, eventually overpowered the king of the South. With relative ease, Antiochus' armies brought even the most fortified cities of his enemy—seemingly the best-defended and most-protected cities—under the subjection of his authority.[23] As Antiochus' armies marched, they again had to go through Israel, and the resulting effects will be explained in the verse to follow.

The greatest efforts of the Egyptian armies could not withstand the invasion headed by Antiochus. The Egyptians simply had no strength against this crushing Seleucid army. God granted strength at the appointed time and withdrew strength when it was time to fall. As was true for these empires, all earthly powers rise and fall according to God's plan and God's timing.[24]

Verse 16- "But he who comes against him shall do according to his own will, and no one shall stand against him. He shall stand in the Glorious Land with destruction in his power.

Because of the certain destruction that awaited any who opposed Antiochus III, the Jews pledged their support to him and the Seleucid forces. Antiochus was afforded all of the provisions that Israel could make available and was warmly received into Jerusalem, "the Glorious Land."[25]

Notes/Applications

Amazingly, king after king conquered the richest lands and people, yet these kings were still never satisfied. They warred with one another for more wealth, more land, and more power. This reveals mankind's true nature. The more we get, the more we want until the pursuit of worldly desires consumes us. *"¹⁵Do not love the world or the things in the world. If anyone loves the world, the love of the Father is not in him. ¹⁶For all that is in the world—the lust of the flesh, the lust of the eyes, and the pride of life—is not of the Father but is of the world." (1 John 2.15–16)* As was the case for these kingdoms, any nation, community, church, home, or life built on greed eventually collapses.

A spirit of greed recklessly pursues its prize to the point of ignoring the spiritual, emotional, and physical needs of others. *"'Yes, they are greedy dogs which never have enough. And they are shepherds who cannot understand; they all look to their own way, every one for his own gain, from his own territory.'" (Isaiah 56.11)* This sin, like all other sin, arouses a lustful desire that can never be satisfied no matter how much money, pleasure, success, or material goods are obtained. Like a dog that chases its own tail, a greedy person lives a vicious cycle of endless searching. The spiritual aspect of this problem is that the sin of greed usually progresses into other sinful appetites since this lust cannot be quenched. *"For the love of money is a root of all kinds of evil, for which some have strayed from the faith in their greediness, and pierced themselves through with many sorrows." (1 Timothy 6.10)*

Have we succumbed to the sin of greed in our pursuit for more? Here are a few steps that we can take to find contentment in every area of our lives:

1. Recognize that nothing satisfies us except a relationship with our Lord and Savior Jesus Christ. *"¹³Jesus answered and said to her, 'Whoever drinks of this water will thirst again, ¹⁴but whoever drinks of the water that I shall give him will never thirst. But the water that I shall give him will become in him a fountain of water springing up into everlasting life.'" (John 4.13–14)*

2. Confess our pursuit of worldly things as greed. *"²⁴If I have made gold my hope, or said to fine gold, 'You are my confidence'; ²⁵if I have rejoiced because my wealth was great, and because my hand had gained much; ²⁶if I have observed the sun when it shines, or the moon moving in brightness, ²⁷so that my heart as been secretly enticed, and my mouth has*

kissed my hand; [28]this also would be an iniquity deserving of judgment, for I would have denied God who is above." (Job 31.24–28)

3. Recognize that the things of this world are temporal, and commit to pursuing everlasting treasures. *"[19]'Do not lay up for yourselves treasures on earth, where moth and rust destroy and where thieves break in and steal; [20]but lay up for yourselves treasures in heaven, where neither moth nor rust destroys and where thieves do not break in and steal. [21]For where your treasure is, there your heart will be also.'" (Matthew 6.19–21)*

4. Remember that all we have, including our very lives, belongs to Almighty God, so recognize everything as a blessing from Him rather than as a product of our own doing. *"The rich man's wealth is his strong city, and like a high wall in his own esteem." (Proverbs 18.11) "[17]Surely, in vain the net is spread in the sight of any bird; [18]But they lie in wait for their own blood, they lurk secretly for their own lives. [19]So are the ways of everyone who is greedy for gain; it takes away the life of its owners." (Proverbs 1.17–19)*

Daniel 11.17–24

Verse 17- "He shall also set his face to enter with the strength of his whole kingdom, and upright ones with him; thus shall he do. And he shall give him the daughter of women to destroy it; but she shall not stand with him, or be for him.

Antiochus III, who sought to enter his conquered territories with all the might of his entire kingdom, was also accompanied by *upright* people, likely referring to the previously mentioned Jews who had forsaken their spiritual inheritance to pursue the carnal, material pleasures obtainable by swearing their allegiance to Antiochus.

Antiochus the Great, in a familiar scheme to gain the favor of the Egyptians without employing military force, offered his daughter Cleopatra to Ptolemy V, the king of the South, in order to promote an alliance with him and, accordingly, to secure some degree of influence in the affairs of Egypt. His daughter, however, would eventually grow sympathetic toward the Egyptian cause. Since Cleopatra did not remain loyal to her father, the whole scheme ultimately failed.[26]

Verses 18, 19- "[18]*After this he shall turn his face to the coastlands, and shall take many. But a ruler shall bring the reproach against them to an end; and with the reproach removed, he shall turn back on him.* [19]*Then he shall turn his face toward the fortress of his own land; but he shall stumble and fall, and not be found.*

Antiochus III steered his armies toward the islands of the Mediterranean Sea. Although he enjoyed some initial success in these endeavors, he was ultimately turned back and forced to retreat from Greece, where the Romans had joined forces with those who opposed the Seleucid campaign. The Roman army, led by "a ruler" named Lucius Cornelius Scipio, pursued Antiochus' larger army back to Asia Minor and defeated him at the Battle of Magnesia.[27]

Verse 20- "There shall arise in his place one who imposes taxes on the glorious kingdom; but within a few days he shall be destroyed, but not in anger or in battle.

Another ruler then arose within the kingdom of the North, Seleucus IV (Philopater), who was the son of Antiochus the Great. Seleucus IV extorted from the people and robbed them with heavy taxation.[28] He, like others before him, also stole from the temple in Jerusalem. Seleucus IV died having reigned over the kingdom of the North for only a short period of time.

Verse 21- "And in his place shall arise a vile person, to whom they will not give the honor of royalty; but he shall come in peaceably, and seize the kingdom by intrigue.

When Seleucus IV died, the crown should have been passed to his son, the rightful successor, Demetrius I (Soter), who was held captive in Rome at that time. However, Seleucus IV had a younger brother, Antiochus IV (Epiphanes), who instead gained the power of authority over the kingdom of the North through scheming and deceit.[29] Antiochus IV, wanting to appear as though he were acting out of duty and obligation, ascended the throne in Demetrius' absence, vowing to relinquish authority as soon as the rightful heir to the throne was freed from his captivity. Yet, once his leadership was established, Antiochus secretly planned to gain the favor of the people through flattery and force. He had no intention of surrendering his power once he obtained it.[30]

Verse 22- "With the force of a flood they shall be swept away from before him and be broken, and also the prince of the covenant.

After he had gained the kingdom, Antiochus Epiphanes earned a reputation for being very bloodthirsty, especially against any who opposed his authority or any whose destruction would benefit him. Armies that tried to invade his territories were completely overthrown.[31]

Interpretations vary regarding this reference to the "prince of the covenant." Some identify this as the High Priest Onias III, also called

Menelaus, who had been sent to Syria to be executed by Antiochus in an attempt to silence his efforts of organizing a revolt among the Jews.[32] Most likely, though, this simply refers to Ptolemy VII (Philometer), the son of Cleopatra (Antiochus' sister), with whom Antiochus had formed a treaty.[33]

Verses 23, 24- "[23]And after the league is made with him he shall act deceitfully, for he shall come up and become strong with a small number of people. [24]He shall enter peaceably, even into the richest places of the province; and he shall do what his fathers have not done, nor his forefathers: he shall disperse among them the plunder, spoil, and riches; and he shall devise his plans against the strongholds, but only for a time.

Antiochus betrayed those with whom he had formed an alliance. He designed treaties and contracts to accomplish his own purposes, and when it suited him, he broke them. This verse likely refers specifically to the treaty he had formed with his nephew, Ptolemy VII, as described in the previous verse.

Once he had gained the trust of his nephew, Antiochus was able to "enter peaceably" even into the "richest places of the province," since Ptolemy, feeling secure and confident with his uncle's intentions because of the treaty, offered no resistance. Consequently, Antiochus was able to gain control over these territories despite his relatively small armies.[34] Such deceitful schemes were strategies possibly never considered and certainly never employed by his forefathers, who sought to conquer their adversaries through warfare. Furthermore, once he had obtained these regions, Antiochus distributed the wealth of his plunder among his lowly followers as a form of welfare for the purpose of gaining their favor.[35] Because of the early success he achieved from such ploys, he formulated plans to gain control over even larger strongholds of his opponent. Such conspiracies, however, were short-lived, and so were the successes he enjoyed from them.

Notes/Applications

Antiochus the Great was ultimately overcome in much the same way as he had conquered others. Similarly, every man's evil eventually revisits him. *"But if you do not do so, then take note, you have sinned against the LORD; and be sure your sin will find you out."* (Numbers 32.23) *"Do not be deceived, God is not mocked; for whatever a man sows, that he will also reap."* (Galatians 6.7)

It is difficult to watch as the evil in our world continually escalates while evildoers prosper. We may wonder why a murderer is paroled before completing his sentence or why a doctor who performs abortions gains wealth. Where is the justice, especially for the victims of these crimes? Where is God in all of this?

Although life's scales often seem drastically unfair, God still reigns over it all, so evil runs its course only for the duration that Almighty God has preordained—no more and no less. What now appears to be prosperity for the evildoer is only temporal gain; in God's time, He will avenge all evilness. *"Beloved, do not avenge yourselves, but rather give place to wrath; for it is written, 'Vengeance is Mine, I will repay,' says the Lord."* (Romans 12.19)

Instead of becoming disheartened by what appears to be injustice, we can rejoice in knowing that our God is perfect and that His ways and timing are also perfect. Though we cannot understand the ways of God, we can rest assured that God's perfect justice will ultimately prevail. *"¹Do not fret because of evildoers, nor be envious of the workers of iniquity. ²For they shall soon be cut down like the grass, and wither as the green herb. ³Trust in the LORD, and do good; dwell in the land, and feed on His faithfulness. ⁹For evildoers shall be cut off; but those who wait on the LORD, they shall inherit the earth."* (Psalm 37.1–3, 9)

Daniel 11.25–31

Verse 25- "He shall stir up his power and his courage against the king of the South with a great army. And the king of the South shall be stirred up to battle with a very great and mighty army; but he shall not stand, for they shall devise plans against him.

By the time Antiochus Epiphanes was prepared to abandon all treaties with Egypt and to confront the king of the South in unrestrained warfare, he had assembled a great army and increased his former strength tremendously. His nephew, Ptolemy VII (Philometer), was prepared for the battle with a great army of his own. Nevertheless, the king of the South was soundly defeated, although not by the hand of an overpowering opposition but by having fallen too far into the traps of his uncle's deception before realizing that he was being played as a fool.[36]

Verse 26- "Yes, those who eat of the portion of his delicacies shall destroy him; his army shall be swept away, and many shall fall down slain.

The people who Ptolemy VII once trusted eventually betrayed him. Though Ptolemy had armies comparable in size and strength to those of Antiochus Epiphanes, his kingdom crumbled from within, and many of his soldiers were slaughtered.

Verse 27- "Both these kings' hearts shall be bent on evil, and they shall speak lies at the same table; but it shall not prosper, for the end will still be at the appointed time.

These battles resulted in both parties gathering "at the same table," apparently a negotiation table, around which treaties were made and sure to be broken. Since both parties operated in the same ruthless and deceptive manner—the uncle being a treacherous conniver from the start and his nephew no longer willing to play the naive fool—neither one was able to gain clear advantage over the other.[37]

The angel that related all of these things to Daniel inserted a reminder of God's sovereignty over all matters so that Daniel would not forget in the midst of such suspenseful discourse that mankind's conniving and warring are relevant only in its own eyes. Nothing in the world, regardless of how momentous it may seem, can or will ever come to pass until its "appointed time," which is solely determined by Almighty God and is not in the least influenced by the words, thoughts, intentions, or actions of mankind.

Verse 28- "While returning to his land with great riches, his heart shall be moved against the holy covenant; so he shall do damage and return to his own land.

The prophecies revealed to this point by the angel, though occurring at a future time from when he revealed such things to Daniel, seem to be merely background for the events that follow hereafter. In a sense, the foundation was being laid for Daniel to understand the persecution of his people that would result from these events.

Antiochus IV returned to his own land with many riches but not as a triumphant victor as he had anticipated. As a result, Antiochus Epiphanes took his fury out on Israel, perpetrating unspeakable atrocities "against the holy covenant." Only after he had killed 80,000 Jews and had taken another 40,000 captive did he finally return to his northern homeland.[38]

Verse 29- "At the appointed time he shall return and go toward the south; but it shall not be like the former or the latter.

When the time was right according to the Lord's providence, Antiochus IV again sought to march toward Egypt in battle. This campaign, however, differed from his others. This time, Antiochus advanced his armies toward the southern territories, but it would ultimately result in his doom.

Verse 30- "For ships from Cyprus shall come against him; therefore he shall be grieved, and return in rage against the holy cove-

nant, and do damage. So he shall return and show regard for those who forsake the holy covenant.

Upon learning of Antiochus' plans to attack again, Ptolemy VII (Philometer) entreated the assistance of Rome, who sent ambassadors such as Gaius Popilius Laenas in ships from Cyrus to meet with Antiochus Epiphanes and to demand his immediate retreat from Egypt or else suffer the consequences.[39] Antiochus realized he had no realistic alternative, so he relented and withdrew. With his pride crushed but his armies still intact, he once again decided to vent his frustration and rage by lashing out against Israel. He sent orders through one of his commanders, Apollonius, to randomly slay the Jews and to carry out the atrocities described in the verses that follow.

As indicated in the last part of this verse, the Jews who had renounced their Jewish heritage and readily complied with all that Antiochus demanded were likely the ones that enabled the king's successful execution of his campaigns against Israel. Therefore, their betrayal assisted Antiochus in his repeated attacks against Israel, so these apostate Jews, if not openly rewarded for such, at the very least escaped the slaughter and turmoil to which the faithful Jews were subjected.[40]

Verse 31- "And forces shall be mustered by him, and they shall defile the sanctuary fortress; then they shall take away the daily sacrifices, and place there the abomination of desolation.

We begin to see some of the horrible desecration for which Antiochus was responsible. According to the Law of Moses, the only people allowed in the temple were the priests of the tribe of Levi and the different families within that tribe that had been appointed to areas of service. More importantly, only the high priest was allowed to enter the Holy of Holies and only once a year. However, by order of Antiochus Epiphanes, non-Jews entered the temple, even into the Holy of Holies, and polluted it with their mere presence. Moreover, they destroyed the temple by disallowing proper ceremonial sacrifices to take place and by making sacrilegious offerings that utterly desecrated the temple.[41]

Once again, God only allowed this utter defilement to take place for its appointed time and to fulfill His purposes. The enemies of God will always hate God and His people. However, this hatred is useless and cannot be acted out against the children of God unless God has preordained it.

Notes/Applications

Some people speak colorful lies and identify themselves as individuals of good, moral fiber when their hearts actually stir with mischievous intent. Although it is easy to be fooled by colorful rhetoric, we must cling to what is true. A change of heart always initiates a change of action. Therefore, time will ultimately reveal if a person's life points to the throne of God or to the throne of self.

Take a moment and remember what life was like before salvation. Each of us wandered hopelessly, bumping into worldly trend after worldly trend. In our quest for Truth, we blindly and readily settled for worldly doctrines that pronounced our inherent goodness. Our total existence revolved around serving our selfish motives. Gripped by guilt and failure, we were physically alive but spiritually dead in our sins.

Our new life greatly contrasts that old man. We confess our inability to obtain salvation apart from God's grace. Everything from our lifestyle to our temperament focuses on glorifying Christ, the abundant Life-giver. We now build our lives upon His solid-as-a-rock, eternal truth, and we live to love and serve the One who loved and served us to His very death on the cross. Therefore, the change that took place at our spiritual birth is more than a "changing of the guards" or "putting on a new face." It transformed us from within. God literally recreated us from a sinner to a saint. *"⁸But now you yourselves are to put off all these: anger, wrath, malice, blasphemy, filthy language out of your mouth. ⁹Do not lie to one another, since you have put off the old man with his deeds, ¹⁰and have put on the new man who is renewed in knowledge according to the image of Him who created him." (Colossians 3.8–10)*

As new creatures in Christ, no difference should exist between what we say and how we act. If there is not an obvious distinction between who we once were and who we now are, we need to examine ourselves to confirm whether or not we have truly died to the old self and live as a new creation in Christ. *"²²That you put off, concerning your former conduct, the old man which grows corrupt according to the deceitful lusts, ²³and be renewed in the spirit of your mind, ²⁴and that you put on the new man which was created according to God, in true righteousness and holiness." (Ephesians 4.22–24)* What evidence in our lives shows that we are new creatures in Christ?

Daniel 11.32–38

Verse 32- "Those who do wickedly against the covenant he shall corrupt with flattery; but the people who know their God shall be strong, and carry out great exploits.

The Israelites who did not stand firmly upon God's truth were manipulated by the king's flatteries, so they allied themselves with the king in breaking the covenant and in tyranny against their Jewish brethren. However, the Israelites who possessed a personal relationship with God were able to withstand the deceptions of the king. They remained faithful to the Lord despite their circumstances and would, therefore, accomplish great things in God's eyes.

Verse 33- "And those of the people who understand shall instruct many; yet for many days they shall fall by sword and flame, by captivity and plundering.

Those Jews who recognized the spiritual trials that besieged them tried to encourage others to uphold their faith in God and not to be lured by the enemy's empty promises. They remained firm and strong, and they persuaded many others to remain likewise. As a result, many of these faithful ones suffered extreme persecution for their faith. They were subjected to the pillage of others, taken from their homes and families against their will, and in many cases, killed by sword and by fire:

> *36Still others had trial of mockings and scourgings, yes, and of chains and imprisonment. 37They were stoned, they were sawn in two, were tempted, were slain with the sword. They wandered about in sheepskins and goatskins, being destitute, afflicted, tormented— 38of whom the world was not worthy. They wandered in deserts and mountains, in dens and caves of the earth. (Hebrews 11.36–38)*

Verse 34- "Now when they fall, they shall be aided with a little help; but many shall join with them by intrigue.

The faithful Jews received some degree of help in both their physical and spiritual battles against Antiochus IV. This is likely a reference to the early assistance the Jews received from Mattathias and his comparatively small number of Maccabean troops.[42] Despite this assistance, many additional Jews ultimately abandoned the faith of their fathers when the struggle became too great. They joined forces with Antiochus' armies.

Verse 35- "And some of those of understanding shall fall, to refine them, purify them, and make them white, until the time of the end; because it is still for the appointed time.

During this time of great suffering, some of those who were not deceived, "those of understanding," also fell. However, this "falling" was not in the same sense as the apostate Jews who abandoned their faith and heritage. This use of "fall" is of a physical sense, indicating the suffering and persecution that befell these faithful Jews. Some of them were subjected to the full impact of Antiochus' schemes and were martyrs for their faith. Even so, this suffering occurred to glorify God and to "make them white," indicating the righteousness and holiness that they would gain by their deaths. *"He who overcomes shall be clothed in white garments." (Revelation 3.5a)*

Once again, the angel assured Daniel that all this persecution that would befall his people was appointed by the Lord within His sovereign plan and would only last for as long as God ordained it.

Verse 36- "Then the king shall do according to his own will: he shall exalt and magnify himself above every god, shall speak blasphemies against the God of gods, and shall prosper till the wrath has been accomplished; for what has been determined shall be done.

A mask of ambiguity clouds the intention of the remaining verses of this chapter, and as a result, this text has been the object of greatly varied interpretations throughout the ages. One thing is agreed upon almost unanimously: the remainder of this vision no longer refers to

Antiochus Epiphanes since he did not "prosper till the wrath has been accomplished," and the events mentioned hereafter do not consistently conform to historical events of his time. Since some but not all of the following descriptions can be fully reconciled in the person of Antiochus Epiphanes, other conclusions must be drawn. Some early commentators, such as Gill and Calvin, pose convincing arguments that the remaining verses do not depict a specific king so much as an entire kingdom prototype, namely the Roman Empire that would follow the fall of the Greco-Macedonian Empire.[43] Though such an argument serves as a definite possibility, the lack of precise matches between the textual prophecies and historical evidence leaves room for doubt and, consequently, room for speculation.[44] Most traditional interpretations contend the verses beginning here and concluding near the end of chapter twelve point not at any specific historical king but to the end times global leader known as the antichrist.[45] Whether or not a particular historical figure(s) is hereafter intended, the text describes characteristics and selfish actions that surely parallel with the ultimate embodiment of this antichrist figure. The commentary that follows, therefore, will approach these verses from this interpretation, although not with any intention of dismissing the validity of other reasonable interpretations.

Certainly, the character spoken of in this verse alludes to antichrist, also described as the "beast," which, as explained in the book of The Revelation, will exalt himself above every god. *"3Let no one deceive you by any means; for that Day will not come unless the falling away comes first, and the man of sin is revealed, the son of perdition, 4who opposes and exalts himself above all that is called God or that is worshiped, so that he sits as God in the temple of God, showing himself that he is God." (2 Thessalonians 2.3–4)* He will speak horrible blasphemy against God, yet he will prosper only until God's appointed time for him is accomplished.

Verse 37- "He shall regard neither the God of his fathers nor the desire of women, nor regard any god; for he shall exalt himself above them all.

More details of the true character of this figure are disclosed. He will not regard Almighty God as the Creator, Maker, or Sustainer of life. Because of the phrasing "God of his fathers" used in this verse, some commentators believe that the end-times antichrist will emerge from the Jewish race.[46] In a sense, this seems plausible since a false messiah of the Jews certainly could not be expected to arise from among Gentiles.

As with much of the remaining text, the phrase "desire of women" has been broadly interpreted. Possibly, it simply denotes this "king's" reluctance to share his glory, position, or power with anyone; he will not allow himself or his decisions to be influenced by anyone or anything else.

In addition, he will totally reject all other gods by ultimately forbidding the worship of anyone or anything other than himself; therefore, he will magnify himself above all men and all gods. *"All who dwell on the earth will worship him, whose names have not been written in the Book of Life of the Lamb slain from the foundation of the world." (Revelation 13.8)*

Verse 38- *"But in their place he shall honor a god of fortresses; and a god which his fathers did not know he shall honor with gold and silver, with precious stones and pleasant things.*

The antichrist will favor himself as a god more powerful than any other god. He will deceive many by his propaganda and, when necessary, by force because he will see himself and his influence as an impenetrable fortress. Once he is established in a position of global influence, he will demand mankind to worship him alone. His forefathers, meaning all those who will have existed before his emergence to power, will not recognize him as a god because they will have known nothing of his existence as such until his deity is self-proclaimed. As the ultimate act of self-glorification and blasphemy, he will worship and adorn himself with every symbol of wealth this world has to offer.

Notes/Applications

Verse thirty-five of this section states that God's people endured persecution for their faith "to refine them, purify them, and make them white." Our finite minds can never fully comprehend all aspects of God's preordained plan for His creation, so we may struggle with understanding the purpose of persecution in our lives. Simply stated, God's purging prepares us for ministry by shifting our focus away from earthly preoccupations and onto the Heavenly Father, so the purification of our faith equips us to accomplish all that God calls us to do.

No one enjoys the purification process. It is painfully costly because it usually requires that we lose something dear to us: our way, our dreams, or our loved ones. However, in losing, we gain. The waters of persecution erode our pride and remind us of God's wonderful, sustaining power to carry us through anything. Also, our obedience and faithfulness during a crisis will point others to Christ, so our trials will help us to better understand another's pain and to relate to him in his time of need. In His time, God will replenish what the waters of persecution sweep away from us. *"And the LORD restored Job's losses when he prayed for his friends. Indeed the LORD gave Job twice as much as he had before."* *(Job 42.10)* Despite the rising tides, He will preserve our souls and restore our joy.

God has not left us shipwrecked. As promised in His Word, the purification process is a part of His plan for us, and it only lasts "for the appointed time." Almighty God directs the flow of the purification waters, and He will not allow us to drown in them.

Daniel 11.39–45

Verse 39- "Thus he shall act against the strongest fortresses with a foreign god, which he shall acknowledge, and advance its glory; and he shall cause them to rule over many, and divide the land for gain.

The antichrist will overcome the strongest governments of the world. This "foreign god" refers to his self-exalted status as god *(verse 36)*; he is not foreign to himself, obviously, but to those who have never regarded him as a god.[47] The rulers that bow to him will be given some measure of authority and a portion of land to govern on the antichrist's behalf. These are likely the ten leaders depicted as the ten toes of the clay and iron image in Nebuchadnezzar's dream, and they serve as the antichrist's confederacy. Even though the antichrist will place himself in the temple as a god, he will never be God nor be omnipresent as only God is. Therefore, the antichrist will need these ten rulers to control their respective regions of the world for him so that he can ultimately obtain absolute control over the world's most powerful nations.

Verse 40- "At the time of the end the king of the South shall attack him; and the king of the North shall come against him like a whirlwind, with chariots, horsemen, and with many ships; and he shall enter the countries, overwhelm them, and pass through.

This verse further supports interpretations which conclude that this figure is not Antiochus but is the ultimate prophetic fulfillment of the antichrist in the last days, for once Antiochus retreated from Egypt after meeting with the ships from Cyprus, history reveals that he never again mounted a campaign against Egypt or any of its territories.[48]

In this verse, it is uncertain whether the king of the South will come against the king of the North in an attempt to overthrow him or if he will come against the "king" mentioned in verses thirty-six through thirty-nine with the assistance of the king of the North. The latter depiction seems more suitable in this context. The geographic location of these kings and their kingdoms are likely given in relation to their position to the antichrist, who at this point will be ruling from his headquarters, which from all biblical indications will be in Jerusalem. *"And they will tread the holy city underfoot for forty-two months." (Revelation 11.2b)* Though these kings come at him like a great wind with all their available forces, they will be overthrown.

Verse 41- "He shall also enter the Glorious Land, and many countries shall be overthrown; but these shall escape from his hand: Edom, Moab, and the prominent people of Ammon.

When the antichrist enters into Israel, there will be much worldwide destruction. Many countries will be toppled in the process. A few, however, will escape his hand. These countries are Edom, Moab, and Ammon, which are all located in the area that is now known as Jordan. The reason this territory escapes destruction is uncertain. Perhaps, it will remain neutral in the conflict or will ally itself with the antichrist, thereby avoiding the consequences of his wrath.[49]

Verse 42- "He shall stretch out his hand against the countries, and the land of Egypt shall not escape.

We are told that Egypt is one of the lands that will be overthrown. The ruling hand of the antichrist will stretch around the world, for his influence and power will have a global impact.

Verse 43- "He shall have power over the treasures of gold and silver, and over all the precious things of Egypt; also the Libyans and Ethiopians shall follow at his heels.

This future "king" will ultimately control the economies of the world, specifically the fiscal structures of Egypt, Libya, and Ethiopia. Libya borders Egypt on the west, and Ethiopia is separated from Egypt by Sudan to the southeast. These countries will be at his "heels," which means that they will be fully under his authority, though it is uncertain whether this submission will be offered willingly or by coercion.

Verse 44- "But news from the east and the north shall trouble him; therefore he shall go out with great fury to destroy and annihilate many.

Dissension will arise from the east and from the north. Therefore, the antichrist will go forth in a rage with great strength to destroy them. These kings will want to overthrow the antichrist because of his widespread oppression. These two leaders along with the leader from the South mentioned in verse forty possibly comprise the three leaders that will be subdued or overthrown by the antichrist, as previously described by Daniel. *"'I was considering the horns, and there was another horn, a little one, coming up among them, before whom three of the first horns were plucked out by the roots.'" (Daniel 7.8)*

Verse 45- "And he shall plant the tents of his palace between the seas and the glorious holy mountain; yet he shall come to his end, and no one will help him.

We are told that the antichrist will build the tabernacles of his palace between "the seas," which most likely refers to the Mediterranean Sea and the Dead Sea, and the "glorious holy mountain," which is Jerusalem.[50] This will function as his temporary royal quarters. The antichrist will place himself in the center of the world to rule over it all.

Notes/Applications

What a blessing it is that we are foretold how the end of the world will occur and what the result will be! Many terrible things will befall the earth during the last days. Therefore, regardless of the doctrinal view concerning Christ's Second Coming that one embraces, each of us must be prepared. *"'Therefore you also be ready, for the Son of Man is coming at an hour you do not expect.'" (Matthew 24.44)*

Part of being prepared includes understanding what the Word of God has to say about the end times. Scripture admonishes us to study and know the truth lest we be deceived or confused by any perversion of truth. *"For false christs and false prophets will rise and show great signs and wonders to deceive, if possible, even the elect.'" (Matthew 24.24) "'Beware of false prophets, who come to you in sheep's clothing, but inwardly they are ravenous wolves.'" (Matthew 7.15)*

This will be a difficult time for all of creation, but praise the Lord for the assurance that He has already won the victory! *"For this lawlessness is already at work secretly, and it will remain secret until the one who is holding it back steps out of the way. Then the man of lawlessness will be revealed, whom the Lord Jesus will consume with the breath of his mouth and destroy by the splendor of his coming. " (2 Thessalonians 2.7–8)*

Chapter Twelve

Daniel 12.1–7

Verse 1- "At that time Michael shall stand up, the great prince who stands watch over the sons of your people; and there shall be a time of trouble, such as never was since there was a nation, even to that time. And at that time your people shall be delivered, every one who is found written in the book.

This chapter continues the previous chapter's prophecy of the end times, wherein the angel had been explaining to Daniel the fate of his people, the Israelites. At that time, during the last days, the archangel Michael, the protector of God's people, will stand guard over them especially during this time of tribulation worse than any nation has ever known.[1] *"'For then there will be great tribulation, such as has not been since the beginning of the world until this time, no, nor ever shall be.'" (Matthew 24.21)*

Whereas the angel related the fate of the Jewish people in end times, he also conveyed the message of hope that exists for all mankind, both Jew and Gentile. Whether or not Daniel realized this unique intricacy is unclear. The angel appears to refer to the collective, eternal record called the Book of Life, in which the names of all people determined to be reconciled to God are revealed:

> *¹⁰And he carried me away in the Spirit to a great and high mountain, and showed me the great city, the holy Jerusalem, descending out of heaven from God, ¹¹ having the glory of God. Her light was like a most precious stone, like a jasper stone, clear as crystal. ²⁷But there shall by no means enter it anything that defiles, or causes an abomination or a lie, but only those who are written in the Lamb's Book of Life. (Revelation 21.10–11, 27)*

In describing the atrocious end times affliction that will befall Daniel's people, and ultimately all who have their eternal inheritance guaranteed in Heaven, the angel also delivered a message of hope: many, specifically those whose names are found "written in the book," will be "delivered." Details of this delivery, however, are unclear—whether by rapture or by perseverance amidst turmoil or by ultimate delivery of physical death unto eternal life. However, to understand the reason for such ambiguity, one must remember to whom this message was originally intended—Daniel. The angel assured Daniel that, though his people would experience intense hardships in both the near and distant future, God would never abandon His faithful followers. We, as believers with the benefit of New Testament revelation, understand that this prophecy has far-reaching significance not limited to only Jewish believers.

Verse 2- And many of those who sleep in the dust of the earth shall awake, some to everlasting life, some to shame and everlasting contempt.

Daniel was not told that all of his people would inherit the kingdom of Heaven, though he was assured that indeed many would. Rather, the angel then spoke about a resurrection whereby the dust of the ground would give up the dead, and all of Daniel's people would be judged either unto eternal life in Heaven or unto eternal condemnation. Through the use of other scripture, Christians understand this judgment to be true for all mankind. Those who have died knowing Christ as their personal Lord and Redeemer, will finally meet Him face to face in all of His glory and will be united with Him for eternity:

> *[13]But I do not want you to be ignorant, brethren, concerning those who have fallen asleep, lest you sorrow as others who have no hope. [14]For if we believe that Jesus died and rose again, even so God will bring with Him those who sleep in Jesus. [15]For this we say to you by the word of the Lord, that we who are alive and remain until the coming of the Lord will by no means precede those who are asleep. [16]For the Lord Himself will descend from heaven with a shout, with the voice of an archangel, and with the trumpet of God. And the dead in Christ will rise first. (1 Thessalonians 4.13–16)*

Those who did not receive Christ's gift of salvation or, in other words, those whose names are not found written in the Book of Life, will be raised to "shame and everlasting contempt" and will be sentenced to the lake of fire, which is the second death spoken of in Revelation:

> *[12]And I saw the dead, small and great, standing before God, and books were opened. And another book was opened, which is the Book of Life. And the dead were judged according to their works, by the things which were written in the books. [13]The sea gave up the dead who were in it, and Death and Hades delivered up the dead who were in them. And they were judged, each one according to his works. [14]Then Death and Hades were cast into the lake of fire. This is the second death. [15]And anyone not found written in the Book of Life was cast into the lake of fire. (Revelation 20.12–15)*

Though this resurrection does not pertain exclusively to Jews, Daniel's people are surely included within it. Although the angel offered Daniel no further clarification regarding the ultimate fulfillment of this plan, the angel did explain that not all Jews would inherit righteousness simply because they were Jews but only those, as described in verse one, whose names are "found written in the book."[2] There will be a distinct separation made at the time of the resurrection—some to everlasting life, the rest to everlasting contempt.

Verse 3- Those who are wise shall shine like the brightness of the firmament, and those who turn many to righteousness like the stars forever and ever.

The wise, those who possess the truth of Christ Jesus, will shine forever in God's Heaven "like the brightness of the firmament." God created the heavens, called the firmament, to embody light for the world. *"God set them in the firmament of the heavens to give light on the earth." (Genesis 1.17)* Therefore, these individuals who by their witness turn other men's hearts toward God will be a light to a lost world. They will be rewarded, and the legacy of their testimony will eternally glorify God. *"19Brethren, if anyone among you wanders from the truth, and someone turns him back, 20let him know that he who turns a sinner from the error of his way will save a soul from death and cover a multitude of sins." (James 5.19–20)*

Verse 4- "But you, Daniel, shut up the words, and seal the book until the time of the end; many shall run to and fro, and knowledge shall increase."

God told Daniel to record all these things but, thereafter, to shut the words and seal them "until the time of the end," which refers to a period long after Daniel's lifetime. *"Now I have come to make you understand what will happen to your people in the latter days, for the vision refers to many days yet to come." (Daniel 10.14)*

Based upon this verse, many theologians contend that knowledge and world travel will increase during the end times.[3] However, that interpretation seems inept within this context and does not appear to be the true intention of the phrase "shall run to and fro." Rather, the expression likely suggests the lengths that people will go in "the time of the end" to search for knowledge and understanding of the mayhem and turmoil occurring to them and around them.[4]

Verse 5- Then I, Daniel, looked; and there stood two others, one on this riverbank and the other on that riverbank.

The two figures described in this verse appear to be angels since they are described as "others," likely as compared to the angel that had been relaying the vision to this point. Daniel observed one of these angels standing on each side of the river, apparently the Tigris River, the same river Daniel was standing beside at the onset of the vision. *"Now on the twenty-fourth day of the first month, as I was by the side of the great river, that is, the Tigris."(Daniel 10.4)* The appearance of these beings seems to launch us into the conclusion of this vision.[5]

Verse 6- And one said to the man clothed in linen, who was above the waters of the river, "How long shall the fulfillment of these wonders be?"

One of these angels spoke to a person who stood upon the waters of the river between the two angels. Some interpreters are vague as to the identity of this "man clothed in linen," leaving it open to speculation that this being was Gabriel, the angel that translated the prophecy to Daniel.[6] It seems more plausible to identify this person as the same preincarnate Christ Who appeared to Daniel before the beginning of this vision.[7] *"5I lifted my eyes and looked, and behold, a certain man clothed in linen, whose waist was girded with gold of Uphaz! 6His body was like beryl, his face like the appearance of lightning, his eyes like torches of fire, his arms and feet like burnished bronze in color, and the sound of his words like the voice of a multitude." (Daniel 10.5–6)* An angel asked the One clothed in linen how long it would be until these prophecies were fulfilled.

Verse 7- Then I heard the man clothed in linen, who was above the waters of the river, when he held up his right hand and his left hand to heaven, and swore by Him who lives forever, that it shall be for a time, times, and half a time; and when the power of the holy people has been completely shattered, all these things shall be finished.

In the vision, the Lord stood upon the waters and lifted both of His hands to Heaven, giving glory to God the Father by which there is no higher authority to swear the truth. *"⁵The angel whom I saw standing on the sea and on the land raised up his hand to heaven ⁶and swore by Him who lives forever and ever, who created heaven and the things that are in it, the earth and the things that are in it, and the sea and the things that are in it, that there should be delay no longer." (Revelation 10.5–6)* Christ then answered the angel for the purpose of ensuring Daniel's understanding of the vision, and He proclaimed that the period of tribulation would be "a time, times, and half a time." Many biblical scholars contend, based upon a common interpretation, that each appearance of the word *time* in this context signifies one year, and this interpretation corroborates all other scriptural accounts that the period of great tribulation will be three and a half years:⁸

> *And they will tread the holy city underfoot for forty-two months. (Revelation 11.2b) Then the woman fled into the wilderness, where she has a place prepared by God, that they should feed her there one thousand two hundred and sixty days. (Revelation 12.6) And he was given a mouth speaking great things and blasphemies, and he was given authority to continue for forty-two months. (Revelation 13.5)*

When the shattering (destruction) of the power (unity) of the holy people (the Israelites) is completed and they are finally forced to reconsider their rejection of the redemptive message of the Lord Jesus Christ, then the end will come.

Notes/Applications

Studying these scriptures is like looking in a mirror and seeing reflections of our fast-paced world. As the Holy Spirit reveals the meaning of these passages to us, we realize that we are living in the last days to which these verses refer, and we, therefore, desperately need to evaluate our spiritual condition.

By virtue of great technological achievements, we quickly approach an age where hearts are hardened against God's message. Mankind worships itself and believes that salvation lies in human accomplishment. Seemingly, the extent of what we can achieve is only limited by our imaginations. We frequently travel to the moon and to distant planets. Advances in medicine help us to live longer, healthier lives. Computers effortlessly spout reams of data, and intercontinental communication is instantaneous. However, with all of man's modern inventions, not one of them has been able to soothe a wounded heart. Not one has been able to prevent death altogether, and not one can deliver us from the inevitable judgment that awaits each of us at the end of time. *"And as it is appointed for men to die once, but after this the judgment." (Hebrews 9.27)*

All of man's technological advances may enable him to attain virtually any level of temporary comfort at the touch of a button, but no amount of human knowledge will ever surpass that of the all-knowing Creator, and no technological alternative will ever secure an eternal life in the presence of God. Nothing can ever secure an eternal hope except a vibrant relationship with a loving, personal, faithful Savior and Redeemer. *"'Talk no more so very proudly; let no arrogance come from your mouth, for the LORD is the God of knowledge; and by Him actions are weighed.'" (1 Samuel 2.3) "Jesus said to him, 'I am the way, the truth, and the life. No one comes to the Father except through Me.'" (John 14.6)*

Daniel 12.8–13

Verse 8- Although I heard, I did not understand. Then I said, "My lord, what shall be the end of these things?"

Daniel admitted that he did not understand the meaning of the things he had heard, so he addressed the Lord directly and asked for further explanation.

Verse 9- And he said, "Go your way, Daniel, for the words are closed up and sealed till the time of the end.

This prophecy conveyed events that would occur long after Daniel's lifetime. The meaning of the prophecy would become more apparent as its time of fulfillment drew near, and its relevance would become more evident for those to whom it would pertain. Until then, its meaning would be somewhat mysterious and vague, and therefore, Daniel was to go on his way and not to concern himself with the meaning of the vision.[9]

Verse 10- "Many shall be purified, made white, and refined, but the wicked shall do wickedly; and none of the wicked shall understand, but the wise shall understand.

A warning is given in this verse that somewhat resembles the one given to the apostle John at the conclusion of the Revelation. *"'He who is unjust, let him be unjust still; he who is filthy, let him be filthy still; he who is righteous, let him be righteous still; he who is holy, let him be holy still.'" (Revelation 22.11)* In both instances, the "wicked," the unrighteous condemned to separation from God, will not behave differently than what is generally expected of them—to "do wickedly."[10]

On the other hand, the numerous hardships of the last days will result in the purification of true believers. The more that something such as gold is purified, the more refined its strength and quality become. Those individuals who assume the role of a Christian will be purged out from true believers, and these true believers will mature spiritually as their faith is deepened through their suffering.

They will understand that the purpose of their suffering is ultimately for the glorification of God, whereas the wicked or unjust will have no biblical foundation to recognize these events as sovereign acts of Almighty God.

It would seem unwise to suggest that God will pour out increased discernment in the last days regarding the Word of God. Knowledge is not hidden within the Scriptures in the form of encrypted codes that only an enlightened few are able to decipher. One needs only to note the many varied interpretations that have been derived from this book because of such "decoding" as proof that confusion and doubt were not what God had intended. *"For it is written: 'I will destroy the wisdom of the wise, and bring to nothing the understanding of the prudent.'" (1 Corinthians 1.19)*

In light of this, it seems most sensible to express simplicity in the interpretation of this passage. The wicked will continue as they always have—finding perplexity and ignorance in the Word of God and proclaiming lies and blasphemies against the things of God. But the "wise," those whose faith is founded in the true God of Creation, will recognize the events that take place around them for what they truly are according to their understanding of God's Holy Word.

Verse 11- *"And from the time that the daily sacrifice is taken away, and the abomination of desolation is set up, there shall be one thousand two hundred and ninety days.*

Though there are varied theories regarding the content of these final three verses, clear explanation of their interpretations cannot be offered without employing a considerable measure of speculation. The first topic that is subject to debatable interpretation is the 1290 days mentioned in this verse. Of course, an explanation for this number of days is dependent upon the definition of the parameters that are given: "from the time that the daily sacrifice is taken away, and the abomination of desolation is set up."

The traditional interpretation of this verse is that these days correlate with the end times period of great tribulation, which has already been determined to be three and a half years according to thirty-day months or 1260 days *(verse 7)*. The number we are given in this verse, though, consists of an additional thirty days that cannot be completely reconciled. Some expositors suggest that the three-and-a-half-year period given in other biblical references is a generalization and that the number given in this verse is the actual, specific number of days that the tribulation will entail.[11] However, this is contradicted by what we read in other Scripture verses. *"2But leave out the court which is outside the temple, and do not measure it, for it has been given to the Gentiles. And they will tread the holy city underfoot for forty-two months. 3And I will give power to my two witnesses, and they will prophesy one thousand two hundred and sixty days, clothed in sackcloth." (Revelation 11.2–3)* Others explain the extra thirty days as the span of God's judgment that will follow the tribulation.[12] Though interesting, this, too, is unsubstantiated speculation. Still, other scholars contend that the events mentioned in this verse refer to the first advent of the Messiah (see commentary on Daniel 9.24–27).[13] Whereas this point is compellingly defended, the duration of 1290 days that follow the resurrection of Christ do not appear to be substantiated by any specific historical event that would appear to fulfill this prophecy, and therefore, this seems an unlikely solution to this issue.

The resolution of these 1290 days is an uncertainty. Perhaps, as we are told in the previous verse, we will one day understand the significance of the number as the time draws near for this prophecy to be fulfilled. Until then, Christians can at least be comforted in knowing that all things that happen, no matter how horrible they may seem, will only last for an exact duration that God has predetermined.

Verse 12- "Blessed is he who waits, and comes to the one thousand three hundred and thirty-five days.

Once again, we are given a number that is not definable by anything we are told elsewhere in Scripture. Once again, we are offered a collage of explanations and calculations by a variety of scholars who favor theories that best suit their own interpretations. Yet once again, we are confronted with an ambiguous puzzle that cannot be resolved except for what is reachable through mere guesswork. Some speculate that these additional seventy-five days that exceed or extend beyond the 1260 days of tribulation will be used to set up the millennial government or to celebrate the reunion of Christ with His saints.[14] In reality, only God truly knows the perfect plan and reasoning of His divine timeline, and to present any theory as fact would be to read more into the verse than what is disclosed.

What we can presume with reasonable certainty is that this verse specifically and exclusively addresses Christians, those who will suffer the persecution already mentioned but also those who, in some unspecified manner, will be "blessed" by the Lord God Almighty, presumably for their perseverance during these trials.

Verse 13- But you, go your way till the end; for you shall rest, and will arise to your inheritance at the end of the days."

Daniel was again admonished to cast any anxieties about these prophecies from his mind and to return to his normal life. Daniel was about ninety years old by this time, and God likely granted him peace and rest in his remaining years of life without giving him any additional revelations, which would seemingly have been included with the other accounts in this book. However, it can also be surmised with reasonable confidence that the "rest" God bestowed upon Daniel also described the peaceful tranquility that Daniel would experience *after* his physical life had ended and would experience until the end of this world's days, not just *his* days. This faithful servant will then "arise to [his] inheritance" at that time with the other saints of God who possess the righteousness of Christ. *"[7]I have fought the good fight, I have finished the race, I have kept the faith. [8]Finally, there is laid up for me the crown of righteousness, which the Lord, the righteous Judge, will give to me on that Day, and not to me only but also to all who have loved His appearing." (2 Timothy 4.7–8)*

Notes/Applications

Over the course of his lifetime, Daniel had observed the perils of his people under the wiles of Babylonian captivity, and Daniel himself had endured severe discrimination for his Jewish ethnicity and for his unwavering belief in the supremacy of Almighty God.

The Lord revealed to this faithful servant the progression of the world's final days leading to the magnification of Jesus Christ as King of kings and Lord of lords. However, these last days would be overshadowed by peril unlike any the world had or has ever experienced. Daniel, no doubt, shuddered as he pondered the reality of continued persecution of his people, but God's messenger assured him that there would be an appointed end to these sufferings. Some would be delivered from this time, some delivered out of it, and some delivered through it, but ultimately, all whose names are written in the Book of Life would receive their deliverance through the gift of eternal life.

As we scan Christian history, our attention is captured by several occurrences in which God's people have been miraculously delivered from dire circumstances. However, countless believers have not been delivered from similar circumstances and have died for their faith. Why is there so much variation in the outcome? Does God favor some over others? The only distinction between believers is God's sovereignty. The Lord's purpose for some and plan for others varies in course but not in result, which is the magnification of God. All Christians are called to be martyrs, to die to self and ultimately to the world and its system, yet the experiences of this call are as diverse as the sands that line the seas.

A martyr is someone "who chooses to suffer death rather than denounce religious principles." Although further definitions of this term reduce its meaning to "one who endures great suffering," its purest definition couples the initial meaning of "being a witness" with "great sacrifice."[15] Contrary to rampant easy-believism philosophies that pervade much of modern Christian teaching, true Christianity *demands* martyrdom. We must die to our natural, selfish desires on a daily basis, never willing to renounce our faith in the Lord Jesus Christ our Savior even if at the cost of our own lives:

> [24]*'For whoever desires to save his life will lose it, but whoever loses his life for My sake will save it. [25]For what profit is it to a man if he gains the whole world, and is himself destroyed or lost? [26]For whoever is ashamed of Me and My words, of him the Son of Man will be ashamed when He comes in His own glory, and in His Father's, and of the holy angels.' (Luke 9.24–26) 'He who loves his life will lose it, and he who hates his life in this world will keep it for eternal life.' (John 12.25)*

Daniel's faith was preserved and deepened through his sufferings as a servant of Almighty God. God charges us, as His saints, with the same challenge that He laid before this Old Testament saint, who was willing to die to self and to man and who by his unwavering commitment ultimately proclaimed, "In God I trust." Are we prepared to encounter persecution for our faith in Christ? Are we willing to be martyrs for Truth? Do we count our sufferings as opportunities to glorify God?

> [3]*Blessed be the God and Father of our Lord Jesus Christ, who according to His abundant mercy has begotten us again to a living hope through the resurrection of Jesus Christ from the dead, [4]to an inheritance incorruptible and undefiled and that does not fade away, reserved in heaven for you, [5]who are kept by the power of God through faith for salvation ready to be revealed in the last time. [6]In this you greatly rejoice, though now for a little while, if need be, you have been grieved by various trials, [7]that the genuineness of your faith, being much more precious than gold that perishes, though it is tested by fire, may be found to praise, honor, and glory at the revelation of Jesus Christ, [8]whom having not seen you love. Though now you do not see Him, yet believing, you rejoice with joy inexpressible and full of glory, [9]receiving the end of your faith—the salvation of your souls. (1 Peter 1.3–9)*

Text Notes

All scriptural references, unless otherwise noted, are quoted from **The Holy Bible, New King James Version,** ©1982 by Thomas Nelson, Inc. Used by permission.

INTRODUCTION
1. *The New Encyclopaedia Britannica,* 15th ed., s.v. "Babylonia."
2. *The Complete Works of Flavius Josephus,* trans. William Whiston (Grand Rapids: Kregel Publications, 1960), 225.
3. J.B. Jackson, *A Dictionary of Scripture Proper Names* (Neptune, NJ: Loizeaux Brothers, 1909), 25.

CHAPTER ONE
1. J.B. Jackson, *A Dictionary of Scripture Proper Names* (Neptune, NJ: Loizeaux Brothers, 1909), 50.
2. Charles F. Pfeiffer and Everett F. Harrison, *The Wycliffe Bible Commentary* (Chicago: Moody Press, 1962), 773.
3. Jackson, *Proper Names,* 25, 38, 66, 13, 55.
4. Jackson, *Proper Names,* 16, 83, 65, 1.
5. James Strong, *Strong's Exhaustive Concordance of the Bible* (Iowa Falls: World Bible Publishers, 1986), 336.

CHAPTER TWO
1. James Strong, *Strong's Exhaustive Concordance of the Bible* (Iowa Falls: World Bible Publishers, 1986), 1302.
2. Strong, *Exhaustive Concordance,* 866, 112.
3. J.B. Jackson, *A Dictionary of Scripture Proper Names* (Neptune, NJ: Loizeaux Brothers, 1909), 10.
4. Alan Redpath, *Victorious Christian Living: Studies in the Book of Joshua* (Grand Rapids: Fleming H. Revel Co., 1993)
5. *American Heritage Dictionary,* 3rd ed., s.v. "knowledge" and "wisdom."
6. *American Heritage Dictionary,* 3rd ed., s.v. "specific gravity."
7. *VanNostrand's Scientific Encyclopedia,* ed. Douglas M. Considine (New York: VanNostrand Reinhold, 1989), 2653–2656, 1352, 2586, 764, 1599, 648.
8. Robert Jamieson, Andrew R. Fausset, and David Brown, *New Commentary on the Whole Bible: Old Testament Volume,* ed. J.D. Douglas (Wheaton, IL: Tyndale House Publishers, 1990), 1171.
9. Strong, *Exhaustive Concordance,* 919.
10. Charles F. Pfeiffer and Everett F. Harrison, *The Wycliffe Bible Commentary* (Chicago: Moody Press, 1962), 780.
11. John Gill, *Exposition of the Old and New Testaments,* vol. 6 (1810; reprint, Paris, AR: The Baptist Standard Bearer, 1989), 284.
12. Pfeiffer and Harrison, *Wycliffe Bible Commentary,* 781.

CHAPTER THREE
1. John Gill, *Exposition of the Old and New Testaments,* vol. 6 (1810; reprint, Paris, AR: The Baptist Standard Bearer, 1989), 288.
2. J.D. Douglas, ed., *New Bible Dictionary,* 2nd ed. (Wheaton, IL: Tyndale House Publishers, 1962), 1075.
3. *New Geneva Study Bible,* ed. R.C. Sproul (Nashville: Thomas Nelson Publishers, 1995), 1335.
4. Gill, *Exposition of the Old and New Testaments,* 288.
5. Robert Jamieson, Andrew R. Fausset, and David Brown, *New Commentary on the Whole Bible: Old Testament Volume,* ed. J.D. Douglas (Wheaton, IL: Tyndale House Publishers, 1990), 1172.

6. James Strong, *Strong's Exhaustive Concordance of the Bible* (Iowa Falls: World Bible Publishers, 1986), 1101.
7. *New Geneva Study Bible,* 1335.
8. J. Vernon McGee, *Thru the Bible,* vol. 3 (Nashville: Thomas Nelson Publishers, 1982), 545.
9. Jamieson, Fausset and Brown, *New Commentary on the Whole Bible,* 1173.
10. Gill, *Exposition of the Old and New Testaments,* 291.
11. Strong, *Exhaustive Concordance,* 1095.

CHAPTER FOUR
1. John Calvin, "Commentaries on the Book of the Prophet Daniel," vol. 1, in vol. 12 of *Calvin's Commentaries,* trans. Thomas Myers (1843; reprint, Grand Rapids: Baker Books, 1999), 245.
2. Calvin, "Commentaries on the Book of the Prophet Daniel," vol. 1, *Calvin's Commentaries,* vol. 12, 244.
3. John Gill, *Exposition of the Old and New Testaments,* vol. 6 (1810; reprint, Paris, AR: The Baptist Standard Bearer, 1989), 297.
4. James Strong, *Strong's Exhaustive Concordance of the Bible* (Iowa Falls: World Bible Publishers, 1986), 1431.
5. Strong, *Exhaustive Concordance,* 1490, 656.
6. Matthew Henry, *Matthew Henry's Commentary on the Whole Bible* (Hendrickson Publishers, 1991), 1439.
7. J. Vernon McGee, *Thru the Bible,* vol. 3 (Nashville: Thomas Nelson Publishers, 1982), 556.

CHAPTER FIVE
1. John Calvin, "Commentaries on the Book of the Prophet Daniel," vol. 1, in vol. 12 of *Calvin's Commentaries,* trans. Thomas Myers (1843; reprint, Grand Rapids: Baker Books, 1999), 305-306.
2. Charles F. Pfeiffer and Everett F. Harrison, *The Wycliffe Bible Commentary* (Chicago: Moody Press, 1962), 785.
3. Pfeiffer and Harrison, *Wycliffe Bible Commentary,* 785.

4. *The Complete Works of Flavius Josephus,* trans. William Whiston (Grand Rapids: Kregel Publications, 1960), 225.
5. Calvin, "Commentaries on the Book of the Prophet Daniel," vol. 1, *Calvin's Commentaries,* vol. 12, 311.
6. Robert Jamieson, Andrew R. Fausset, and David Brown, *New Commentary on the Whole Bible: Old Testament Volume,* ed. J.D. Douglas (Wheaton, IL: Tyndale House Publishers, 1990), 1178.
7. Jamieson, Fausset and Brown, *New Commentary on the Whole Bible,* 1179.
8. Calvin, "Commentaries on the Book of the Prophet Daniel," vol. 1, *Calvin's Commentaries,* vol. 12, 320.
9. Jamieson, Fausset and Brown, *New Commentary on the Whole Bible,* 1178.
10. James Strong, *Strong's Exhaustive Concordance of the Bible* (Iowa Falls: World Bible Publishers, 1986), 296.
11. Jamieson, Fausset and Brown, *New Commentary on the Whole Bible,* 1179.
12. Calvin, "Commentaries on the Book of the Prophet Daniel," vol. 1, *Calvin's Commentaries,* vol. 12, 328.
13. Pfeiffer and Harrison, *Wycliffe Bible Commentary,* 786.
14. John Gill, *Exposition of the Old and New Testaments,* vol. 6 (1810; reprint, Paris, AR: The Baptist Standard Bearer, 1989), 310.
15. *Josephus,* 225.

CHAPTER SIX
1. John Calvin, "Commentaries on the Book of the Prophet Daniel," vol. 1, in vol. 12 of *Calvin's Commentaries,* trans. Thomas Myers (1843; reprint, Grand Rapids: Baker Books, 1999), 347–348.
2. J.D. Douglas, ed., *New Bible Dictionary,* 2nd ed. (Wheaton, IL: Tyndale House Publishers, 1962), 1075.
3. John Gill, *Exposition of the Old and New Testaments,* vol. 6 (1810; reprint, Paris, AR: The Baptist Standard Bearer, 1989), 312.
4. Warren W. Wiersbe, *Wiersbe's Expository Outline on the Old Testament* (Colorado Springs: Victor Books, 1993) 569–570.

5. Gill, *Exposition of the Old and New Testaments*, 313.
6. Corrie ten Boom, *Not I, But Christ* (Nashville: Thomas Nelson Publishers, 1984), 94.
7. James M. Freeman, *The New Manners and Customs of the Bible*, ed. Harold J. Chadwick (North Brunswick, NJ: Bridge-Logos Publishers, 1998), 386.
8. Freeman, *The New Manners and Customs of the Bible*, 386.
9. Freeman, *The New Manners and Customs of the Bible*, 79.

CHAPTER SEVEN
1. John Gill, *Exposition of the Old and New Testaments*, vol. 6 (1810; reprint, Paris, AR: The Baptist Standard Bearer, 1989), 318.
2. Matthew Henry, *Matthew Henry's Commentary on the Whole Bible* (Hendrickson Publishers, 1991), 1446.
3. James Strong, *Strong's Exhaustive Concordance of the Bible* (Iowa Falls: World Bible Publishers, 1986), 1200.
4. Gill, *Exposition of the Old and New Testaments*, 319.
5. John Calvin, "Commentaries on the Book of the Prophet Daniel," vol. 2, in vol. 13 of *Calvin's Commentaries,* trans. Thomas Myers (1843; reprint, Grand Rapids: Baker Books, 1999), 16.
6. Walter Chalmers Smith, "Immortal, Invisible" [ca. 1867] in Baptist Hymnal (Nashville: Convention Press, 1975), 32. Public Domain.
7. *New Geneva Study Bible,* ed. R.C. Sproul (Nashville: Thomas Nelson Publishers, 1995), 1343.
8. Robert Jamieson, Andrew R. Fausset, and David Brown, *New Commentary on the Whole Bible: Old Testament Volume*, ed. J.D. Douglas (Wheaton, IL: Tyndale House Publishers, 1990), 1184.

CHAPTER EIGHT
1. Charles F. Pfeiffer and Everett F. Harrison, *The Wycliffe Bible Commentary* (Chicago: Moody Press, 1962), 791.
2. John Gill, *Exposition of the Old and New Testaments*, vol. 6 (1810; reprint, Paris, AR: The Baptist Standard Bearer, 1989), 330.

3. James Strong, *Strong's Exhaustive Concordance of the Bible* (Iowa Falls: World Bible Publishers, 1986), 661.

4. John Calvin, "Commentaries on the Book of the Prophet Daniel," vol. 2, in vol. 13 of *Calvin's Commentaries,* trans. Thomas Myers (1843; reprint, Grand Rapids: Baker Books, 1999), 97–98.

5. Gill, *Exposition of the Old and New Testaments,* 334.

6. A.W. Tozer, *The Attributes of God* (Camp Hill, PA: Christian Publications, Inc., 1997), 43–45.

7. J.B. Jackson, *A Dictionary of Scripture Proper Names* (Neptune, NJ: Loizeaux Brothers, 1909), 32.

8. Gill, *Exposition of the Old and New Testaments,* 335.

9. William MacDonald, *Believer's Bible Commentary,* ed. Art Farstad (Nashville: Thomas Nelson Publishers, 1995), 1084.

10. Robert Jamieson, Andrew R. Fausset, and David Brown, *New Commentary on the Whole Bible: Old Testament Volume,* ed. J.D. Douglas (Wheaton, IL: Tyndale House Publishers, 1990), 1189.

11. Calvin, "Commentaries on the Book of the Prophet Daniel," vol. 1, *Calvin's Commentaries,* vol. 12, 122.

12. Calvin, "Commentaries on the Book of the Prophet Daniel," vol. 1, *Calvin's Commentaries,* vol. 12, 122.

13. "Antiquities of the Jews," in *The Complete Works of Flavius Josephus,* trans. William Whiston (Grand Rapids: Kregel Publications, 1960), 245.

14. *Josephus,* 244.

15. Gill, *Exposition of the Old and New Testaments,* 336.

16. Jamieson, Fausset and Brown, *New Commentary on the Whole Bible,* 1189.

17. Josephus, 251-258; *New Geneva Study Bible,* ed. R.C. Sproul (Nashville: Thomas Nelson Publishers, 1995), 1153–1154.

18. Calvin, "Commentaries on the Book of the Prophet Daniel," vol. 1, *Calvin's Commentaries,* vol. 12, 128.

19. Gill, *Exposition of the Old and New Testaments,* 337.

20. *Josephus,* 262.

21. *Josephus,* 260.

22. Gill, *Exposition of the Old and New Testaments*, 337.

CHAPTER NINE
1. Kenneth L. Barker and John R. Kohlenberger III, ed., *Zondervan NIV Bible Commentary*, Vol. 1: Old Testament (Grand Rapids: Zondervan Publishing House, 1994), 1386.
2. W. E. Vine, *Vine's Expository Dictionary of Old and Testament Words* (Nashville: Thomas Nelson Publishers, 1997), 120.
3. John Gill, *Exposition of the Old and New Testaments*, vol. 6 (1810; reprint, Paris, AR: The Baptist Standard Bearer, 1989), 342.
4. Gill, *Exposition of the Old and New Testaments*, 342.
5. "Antiquities of the Jews," in *The Complete Works of Flavius Josephus*, trans. William Whiston (Grand Rapids: Kregel Publications, 1960), 228.
6. Robert Jamieson, Andrew R. Fausset, and David Brown, *New Commentary on the Whole Bible: Old Testament Volume*, ed. J.D. Douglas (Wheaton, IL: Tyndale House Publishers, 1990), 1192.
7. Stephen R. Miller, *The New American Commentary*, ed. E. Ray Clendenen (Nashville: Broadman and Holman Publishers, 1994), 252.
8. Miller, *The New American Commentary*, 252–257.
9. James Strong, *Strong's Exhaustive Concordance of the Bible* (Iowa Falls: World Bible Publishers, 1986), 1499; Barker and Kohlenberger, Zondervan NIV Bible Commentary, 1388.
10. Miller, *The New American Commentary*, 259.
11. Jamieson, Fausset and Brown, *New Commentary on the Whole Bible*, 1193.
12. Pfeiffer and Harrison, *Wycliffe Bible Commentary*, 794; Barker and Kohlenberger, *Zondervan NIV Bible Commentary*, 1389; Gill, *Exposition of the Old and New Testaments*, 345.
13. Barker and Kohlenberger, *Zondervan NIV Bible Commentary*, 1389; *New Geneva Study Bible*, ed. R.C. Sproul (Nashville: Thomas Nelson Publishers, 1995), 1351.

14. Barker and Kohlenberger, *Zondervan NIV Bible Commentary*, 1389.
15. Gill, *Exposition of the Old and New Testaments*, 346.
16. Miller, *The New American Commentary*, 268.
17. R.C. Sproul, *The Last Days According to Jesus* (Grand Rapids: Baker Books, 1998), 38-41.
18. J.Vernon McGee, *Thru the Bible*, vol. 3 (Nashville: Thomas Nelson Publishers, 1982), 588–589; Barker and Kohlenberger, *Zondervan NIV Bible Commentary*, 1389–1390; Jamieson, Fausset and Brown, *New Commentary on the Whole Bible*, 1193.
19. *New Geneva Study Bible*, 1350.
20. John Calvin, "Commentaries on the Book of the Prophet Daniel," vol. 2, in vol. 13 of *Calvin's Commentaries*, trans. Thomas Myers (1843; reprint, Grand Rapids: Baker Books, 1999), 226–227.
21. John Newton, "Amazing Grace" [ca. 1779] in *Baptist Hymnal* (Nashville: Convention Press, 1975), 165. Public Domain.

CHAPTER TEN

1. Robert Jamieson, Andrew R. Fausset, and David Brown, *New Commentary on the Whole Bible: Old Testament Volume*, ed. J.D. Douglas (Wheaton, IL: Tyndale House Publishers, 1990), 1194.
2. Jamieson, Fausset and Brown, *New Commentary on the Whole Bible*, 1194–1195.
3. John Gill, *Exposition of the Old and New Testaments*, vol. 6 (1810; reprint, Paris, AR: The Baptist Standard Bearer, 1989), 348.
4. J.Vernon McGee, *Thru the Bible*, vol. 3 (Nashville: Thomas Nelson Publishers, 1982), 590.
5. J.D. Douglas, ed., *New Bible Dictionary*, 2nd ed. (Wheaton, IL: Tyndale House Publishers, 1962), 159.
6. Gill, *Exposition of the Old and New Testaments*, 349.
7. Charles F. Pfeiffer and Everett F. Harrison, *The Wycliffe Bible Commentary* (Chicago: Moody Press, 1962), 796.

8. Cleland B. McAfee, "Near to the Heart of God" [ca. 1901] in *Baptist Hymnal* (Nashville: Convention Press, 1975), 354. Public Domain.

9. John Calvin, "Commentaries on the Book of the Prophet Daniel," vol. 2, in vol. 13 of *Calvin's Commentaries*, trans. Thomas Myers (1843; reprint, Grand Rapids: Baker Books, 1999), 246.

10. Gill, *Exposition of the Old and New Testaments*, 351.

11. Matthew Henry, *Matthew Henry's Commentary on the Whole Bible* (Hendrickson Publishers, 1991), 1455.

12. *New Geneva Study Bible*, ed. R.C. Sproul (Nashville: Thomas Nelson Publishers, 1995), 1351.

13. Gill, *Exposition of the Old and New Testaments*, 353.

14. Jamieson, Fausset and Brown, *New Commentary on the Whole Bible*, 1196.

CHAPTER ELEVEN

1. Matthew Henry, *Matthew Henry's Commentary on the Whole Bible* (Hendrickson Publishers, 1991), 1457.

2. "Antiquities of the Jews," in *The Complete Works of Flavius Josephus,* trans. William Whiston (Grand Rapids: Kregel Publications, 1960), 229.

3. Kenneth L. Barker and John R. Kohlenberger III, ed., *Zondervan NIV Bible Commentary,* Vol. 1: Old Testament (Grand Rapids: Zondervan Publishing House, 1994), 1392–1393.

4. Barker and Kohlenberger, *Zondervan NIV Bible Commentary,* 1393.

5. Robert Jamieson, Andrew R. Fausset, and David Brown, *New Commentary on the Whole Bible: Old Testament Volume*, ed. J.D. Douglas (Wheaton, IL: Tyndale House Publishers, 1990), 1196.

6. John Gill, *Exposition of the Old and New Testaments*, vol. 6 (1810; reprint, Paris, AR: The Baptist Standard Bearer, 1989), 354.

7. Stephen R. Miller, *The New American Commentary,* ed. E. Ray Clendenen (Nashville: Broadman and Holman Publishers, 1994), 291.

8. Gill, *Exposition of the Old and New Testaments*, 355.

9. Miller, *The New American Commentary*, 293.

10. Jamieson, Fausset and Brown, *New Commentary on the Whole Bible*, 1196.

11. John Calvin, "Commentaries on the Book of the Prophet Daniel," vol. 2, in vol. 13 of *Calvin's Commentaries*, trans. Thomas Myers (1843; reprint, Grand Rapids: Baker Books, 1999), 246.

12. Gill, *Exposition of the Old and New Testaments*, 356.

13. Jamieson, Fausset and Brown, *New Commentary on the Whole Bible*, 1196–1197.

14. Calvin, "Commentaries on the Book of the Prophet Daniel," vol. 2, *Calvin's Commentaries*, vol. 13, 281–282.

15. Jamieson, Fausset and Brown, *New Commentary on the Whole Bible*, 1197.

16. Gill, *Exposition of the Old and New Testaments*, 357.

17. *New Geneva Study Bible*, ed. R.C. Sproul (Nashville: Thomas Nelson Publishers, 1995), 1352.

18. Jamieson, Fausset and Brown, *New Commentary on the Whole Bible*, 1197.

19. Calvin, "Commentaries on the Book of the Prophet Daniel," vol. 2, *Calvin's Commentaries*, vol. 13, 287–290.

20. Miller, *The New American Commentary*, 295; Gill, *Exposition of the Old and New Testaments*, 358.

21. Jamieson, Fausset and Brown, *New Commentary on the Whole Bible*, 1197.

22. Gill, *Exposition of the Old and New Testaments*, 358.

23. Jamieson, Fausset and Brown, *New Commentary on the Whole Bible*, 1197.

24. Henry, *Matthew Henry's Commentary*, 1457.

25. *Josephus*, 251–252.

26. Calvin, "Commentaries on the Book of the Prophet Daniel," vol. 2, *Calvin's Commentaries*, vol. 13, 296.

27. Miller, *The New American Commentary*, 296.

28. William MacDonald, *Believer's Bible Commentary,* ed. Art Farstad (Nashville: Thomas Nelson Publishers, 1995), 1089.
29. Miller, *The New American Commentary,* 298–299.
30. Henry, *Matthew Henry's Commentary,* 1458.
31. Henry, *Matthew Henry's Commentary,* 1458.
32. Gill, *Exposition of the Old and New Testaments,* 361.
33. Calvin, "Commentaries on the Book of the Prophet Daniel," vol. 2, *Calvin's Commentaries,* vol. 13, 306–307; Jamieson, Fausset and Brown, *New Commentary on the Whole Bible,* 1198.
34. Calvin, "Commentaries on the Book of the Prophet Daniel," vol. 2, *Calvin's Commentaries,* vol. 13, 308.
35. Gill, *Exposition of the Old and New Testaments,* 362.
36. Calvin, "Commentaries on the Book of the Prophet Daniel," vol. 2, *Calvin's Commentaries,* vol. 13, 311.
37. Jamieson, Fausset and Brown, *New Commentary on the Whole Bible,* 1199.
38. Jamieson, Fausset and Brown, *New Commentary on the Whole Bible,* 1199.
39. Gill, *Exposition of the Old and New Testaments,* 363–364.
40. Miller, *The New American Commentary,* 301.
41. *Josephus,* 257.
42. Barker and Kohlenberger, *Zondervan NIV Bible Commentary,* 1400.
43. Calvin, "Commentaries on the Book of the Prophet Daniel," vol. 2, *Calvin's Commentaries,* vol. 13, 338–393.
44. Charles F. Pfeiffer and Everett F. Harrison, *The Wycliffe Bible Commentary* (Chicago: Moody Press, 1962), 797.
45. Miller, *The New American Commentary,* 305.
46. Pfeiffer and Harrison, *Wycliffe Bible Commentary,* 797.
47. Miller, *The New American Commentary,* 308.
48. *Josephus,* 258–262.
49. Miller, *The New American Commentary,* 311.
50. Jamieson, Fausset and Brown, *New Commentary on the Whole Bible,* 1201.

CHAPTER TWELVE

1. Kenneth L. Barker and John R. Kohlenberger III, ed., *Zondervan NIV Bible Commentary*, Vol. 1: Old Testament (Grand Rapids: Zondervan Publishing House, 1994), 1403.
2. John Calvin, "Commentaries on the Book of the Prophet Daniel," vol. 2, in vol. 13 of *Calvin's Commentaries*, trans. Thomas Myers (1843; reprint, Grand Rapids: Baker Books, 1999), 375.
3. William MacDonald, *Believer's Bible Commentary*, ed. Art Farstad (Nashville: Thomas Nelson Publishers, 1995), 1091.
4. Stephen R. Miller, *The New American Commentary*, ed. E. Ray Clendenen (Nashville: Broadman and Holman Publishers, 1994), 321.
5. Robert Jamieson, Andrew R. Fausset, and David Brown, *New Commentary on the Whole Bible: Old Testament Volume*, ed. J.D. Douglas (Wheaton, IL: Tyndale House Publishers, 1990), 1202.
6. Barker and Kohlenberger, *Zondervan NIV Bible Commentary*, 1404.
7. John Gill, *Exposition of the Old and New Testaments*, vol. 6 (1810; reprint, Paris, AR: The Baptist Standard Bearer, 1989), 372.
8. Miller, *The New American Commentary*, 323.
9. Gill, *Exposition of the Old and New Testaments*, 373.
10. Henry, *Matthew Henry's Commentary*, 1462.
11. Miller, *The New American Commentary*, 325.
12. Miller, *The New American Commentary*, 325.
13. Calvin, "Commentaries on the Book of the Prophet Daniel," vol. 2, *Calvin's Commentaries*, vol. 13, 393.
14. Miller, *The New American Commentary*, 326.
15. Strong, *Exhaustive Concordance*, 889.